D0113799

a **room** for learning

a room for learning

The Making of a School in Vermont

TAL BIRDSEY

ST. MARTIN'S PRESS   NEW YORK

www.stmartins.com

Grateful acknowledgment is given for permission to reprint the following:

Robert Frost: lines from "The Gift Outright" from *The Poetry of Robert Frost*, edited by Connery Lathem. Copyright 1969 by Henry Holt and Company. Copyright 1942 by Robert Frost, copyright 1970 by Lesley Frost Ballantine. Reprinted by arrangement with Henry Holt and Company, LLC.

W. B. Yeats: lines from "The Circus Animals' Desertion" and "Lapis Lazuli." Reprinted with the permission of Scribner, a Division of Simon and Schuster, Inc., from *The Collected Poems of W. B. Yeats*. Revised Second Edition edited by Richard J. Finneran. Copyright 1940 by Georgia Yeats; copyright renewed © 1968 by Bertha Georgie Yeats, Michael Butler Yeats, and Anne Yeats.

Seamus Heaney: lines from "Station Island" and "Personal Helicon" from *Opened Ground: Selected Poems 1966–1996* by Seamus Heaney. Copyright © 1998 by Seamus Heaney. Reprinted by permission of Farrar, Straus and Giroux, LLC.

Elie Wiesel: Excerpt from *Night* by Elie Wiesel, translated by Marion Wiesel. Translation copyright © 2006 by Marion Wiesel. Reprinted by permission of Hill and Wang, a division of Farrar, Straus and Giroux, LLC.

Wallace Stevens: lines from "Extracts from Addresses to the Academy of Fine Ideas" and "Prologues to What Is Possible" from *The Collected Poems of Wallace Stevens* by Wallace Stevens. Copyright 1954 by Wallace Stevens and renewed in 1982 by Holly Stevens. Used by permission of Alfred A. Knopf, a division of Random House, Inc.

Rumi: lines from *The Essential Rumi*, translated by Coleman Barks. Copyright © 1996 by Coleman Barks. Reprinted with permission of Coleman Barks and Maypop Books.

Langston Hughes: lines from "The Dream Keeper" and "The Negro Speaks of Rivers" from *The Collected Poems of Langston* by Langston Hughes, edited by Arnold Rampersad with David Roessel, Associate Editor. Copyright © 1994 by the Estate of Langston Hughes. Used by permission of Alfred A. Knopf, a division of Random House, Inc.

Book design by Claire Naylon Vaccaro

Library of Congress Cataloging-in-Publication Data

Birdsey, Tal.
   A room for learning : the making of a school in Vermont / Tal Birdsey.—1st ed.
     p. cm.
   ISBN 978-0-312-54730-1
   1. Birdsey, Tal. 2. Teachers—Vermont—Biography. 3. Teachers—United States—Biography. 4. Educators—United States—Biography. 5. North Branch School (Ripton, Vt.)—History. 6. Private schools—Vermont. 7. Junior high schools—Vermont. I. Title.
   LA2317.B4885A3 1996
   373.110092–dc22
   [B]   2009016934

First Edition: October 2009

10 9 8 7 6 5 4 3 2 1

For Henry and Calder,

who were there

contents

I.
a dream of a school

Possessing what we still were unpossessed by,

Possessed by what we now no more possessed.

Something we were withholding made us weak

Until we found out that it was ourselves

We were withholding from our land of living,

And forthwith found salvation in surrender.

· ROBERT FROST, *"The Gift Outright"*

Adim room in a gray clapboard house in the Vermont woods in winter. Ten adolescents, the entire school—my school—circled at present around two plastic tables littered with notebooks and markers, pencil shavings, orange peels and apple cores, a teacup, an opened newspaper, a hammer, jackets and boots piled by the door, a gas stove hissing on high in the kitchen. Outside the snow is piling up, pine limbs loaded and bending and spilling light crystals into the half-dark afternoon cold.

Nick leaned back in a spindly plastic chair with his head tilted to the ceiling, holding the edge of the table to keep from falling over. Doug obsessively doodled épées and scimitars on his paper. Mira hunched over the table edge with her hands trapped between her legs, presumably to keep warm, her eyes cast down, reading words she'd written across the cover of her binder.

I asked who wanted to go, who wanted to speak out a place for us to hear. A little journey of improvised words or dreams, a sliver of memory—somewhere to start the story. We would close our eyes and enter those places they held in mind. Going was how we went.

"Um, me!" said Zoe, her hand half raised, cupped by her ear. Her eyelids were smeared with glitter, her blond, frizzy hair bouncing in the light.

"All right, go Zo-Zo. Let her rip."

"Yay, I get to go."

"Close your eyes, you wing nut. Go back and get gone. Make sure you're there. Way back, all the way back to wherever you feel most alive. Got it? You've got to go back to make it come alive. Then you'll have what you need."

"Yes, sir."

"Nick, couldja turn off the lights?"

"Yup."

Nick scrambled across the room and switched off the lights. My students sat in the cold gloom as snow fell past the windows.

"Zoe, where are you?"

"In the snow."

"The snow outside?"

"No. Snow a long time ago."

"How old are you?"

"Six."

"Make sure you're feeling six. Really six."

"I'm gonna be six."

I waited, looking around the table. Tico fiddled with a length of red wire, trying to attach it to a small motor he had extracted from a broken CD player.

"Tico, close your god-dang eyes."

"I'm listening, Tal. I have to do stuff with my hands. It helps me."

"Jesus, all right. Just don't clang those flipping pliers on the floor. It screws up the mood, you know what I mean? The rest of you wing nuts, no squirming, and put your heads down. No peeking. You're all going into the abyss of your heavenly, vacant souls. You're looking at the vast expanse of the empty wasteland of your minds. The *wasteland*. You shore these fragments against your ruin. This is the last time school will ever feel like preschool. After North Branch it's all going to be crappers-town."

"Okay, Tal, maybe if you would stop talking we could do it."

They settled in, heads bowed in crossed arms, fingers pressed to their eyes.

"All right, Zoe, what are you doing?"

"I'm making a snow fort with my dad. He's packing the snow with his hands. He has huge leather mittens on."

"What do you have on?"

With her closed eyes in the stillness of the room she smiled. "I have on my purple snow boots. Those were my favorites. I had them until I had to give them to Zelie."

"Who's Zelie?"

"She's my little sissy."

"Are you mad you had to give them to her?"

"No, they got too small."

"Is she there?"

"No, sissy's inside because she doesn't like it when all the snow gets into her boots and she is so little she gets cold fast. She's kind of a weenie. It's just me and my daddy."

"What are you doing?"

"We're digging a tunnel through a snow pile. I see my dad's fingers wiggling through. I'm kneeling and smoothing the snow down and there is a huge wall of snow above me."

"Night or day?"

"Night. There's streetlights on our street so everything is kind of glowy blue. The snow is like purple and bluish. The lights are on in our house. I know it's warm in there but we keep working on our fort. We make rooms and little windows and we peep through them so we can tell each other if we're suffocating. I like to tell my dad that I can still breathe. We do the same things with the leaves in the fall, except leaves get in my mouth."

"What about right now on the snowy street?"

"I have my little shovel I got at Martin's Hardware. It's red and plastic. My daddy's doing all the big shoveling."

"What's happening now?"

"Now my feet are getting cold."

"What do you say?"

"I say, 'Daddy, I want to go in, I'm getting cold.' He says, 'Okay, Verg, let's go in.'"

"Verg? Who in the hell is Verg?"

"That's what he called me. My nickname."

"I got you. Keep going."

"So he says, 'Okay, Verg, let's go in and have some hot chocolate.' We always have hot chocolate after making snow forts. Sometimes he would stay out there for an hour after I got cold and went in and then he would come in all covered in snow and say, 'Come out and look at all the changes!'"

She smiled, remembering that moment and her father, who had the little kid in him, working in the snowy street at night to build her snow fort.

Those who no longer had their heads down smiled back at her. We stayed in her memory, our own toes freezing, our own hands in mittens, playing games and not suffocating at all, dwelling there for as long as she could, as long as she felt was right. That was the best possible place she could be, safe in her past, tender and inviolable, a momentary respite granted to her in the rush of growing up.

These kids, these teenagers—my students—wore dark hooded sweatshirts emblazoned with fiery skulls or "Volcom," branded with logos claiming "No Fear," always wanting to leave childhood behind, losing themselves sooner than they knew. They spent half their time running from themselves, away from their parents, their pasts, from each other, toward whatever *adult* was, toward whatever was unknown ahead.

Schools did not always ask children to speak to or treasure the past. Schools did not always foster an environment hospitable to tenderness, pain, loss, lament, or the delicate realm of memory. But for my students memory and nostalgia were the sweet, safe antidotes to growing up too fast.

In *The Brothers Karamazov,* Alyosha says, "People talk to you a great deal about your education, but some good, sacred memory, preserved from childhood, is perhaps the best education." Hours and days we passed in a small school in the mountains—meandering, talking, asking, feeling, preserving.

Zoe's sacred memory, so fully formed, so exquisitely beautiful, affirmed that the past claimed a luminescent and breathing presence. It was *her* history, her source. A history of love, of time passing, the story of how she created and *became.* When she navigated back to the blue-purple winter light she recovered a fragile thread of connection between her and her father, even as she moved into the tilting orbits of adolescence.

The kids loved it. They wanted to talk about it. Their hands were waving.

"My father used to do that exact thing," exclaimed Mira. "He used to stay out there for hours and come in all covered with snow and want to show me what he had done."

"I want to go. Can I go?" they asked, blurting out about their own snow forts and sledding hills and frozen hands and favorite mittens.

"But it was kind of interesting," Annie said, her voice rising from a state of wonder. "It was supposed to be a place description. But it was all about her and her dad. It wasn't about the place on the street in the snow. Well, it was that. But it was about being in a place with her dad, and being close to him. I mean, being there."

"Being there, with him. Why does that matter?"

"Well, it seems more important or something. But is that what you want us to do?"

"Annie, I want you to write whatever the shape of the feeling is."

"But I mean, it's kind of weird and, like, psycho or something. If we did this at my old school my teacher would have been hauled off to the loony bin."

"Annie, do *you* think this is crazy? Do you want to go back to crappers-town middle school? Maybe it was crappers-town at your old school because nobody talked and wrote about feelings or memories."

"Well, no, it was just, like, a little strange. But I liked it. And you are a little loony."

"Crazy's better than boring, Annie."

"Are you sure?"

"Hell, yes. You learn more. How are you supposed to find anything of your own if you don't go looking in strange places. I can't tell you what to write or believe, but I'm pretty sure I can show you how to find it."

They looked back at me, waiting.

"Listen, there's a book called *My Name Is Asher Lev,* about an Orthodox Jewish boy who struggles to become an artist. There's a part in the book where a great sculptor says to Asher, his apprentice: 'Asher, anyone can draw. Art is when it is connected to the scream inside you.' When you write about the real places or people in your life, your writing will be connected to something like that scream."

"You want us to scream in our writing?" Nick asked.

"Yeah. I want you to scream. I want you to scream about the things that matter. You know, love, jealousy, self-doubt, joy, equality, betrayal, belief, desire, death, hope, good and evil, and everything in between. Scream loud and long. In time you will comprehend your powers, both demonic and divine."

They were staring, and they were listening.

From such recovered treasure—landscapes of old tree forts, hiding places in dark closets, screened porches in summer thunderstorms, or the kindled memory of being held by a parent—I simply asked them to begin.

In our cold schoolhouse in the mountains, these were our materials, and this was how we made our school.

If I was going to devote my life to anything, it had to be a legitimate cause. My two sons were the most legitimate cause I had. If I was going to retire from being a stay-at-home dad, I had to do it for something extraordinary. A school, created from my hands and heart, was the greatest thing I could give my children—my gift to them and to the future.

But Henry was only in kindergarten, Calder in preschool. They were still learning the alphabet and the names of things. Adolescence and middle school was another universe, far away.

I frequently loaded them into our Plymouth minivan, which was littered with cracker crumbs, sticky juice boxes, peanut shells, and browning apple cores. I handed them helmeted Lego men and toy John Deere tractors, buckled them into their car seats, and hauled them to meetings concerning the school I hoped to start.

The meetings were informal, around kitchen tables and hot woodstoves. I met with parents who wanted to create a middle school in the Green Mountains in Ripton, Vermont. These parents, four mothers and one community member, were satisfied with and deeply supportive of the town's kindergarten-through-sixth-grade public school, a homey institution with fewer than sixty students. A community school worked for the town's children, so why not create a local, independent middle school and keep the kids close to home? Besides, said Mia, a mother of three, "I want a school where the kids can still go outside. Once they're in middle school they don't have recess and they never even go for a hike during the fall."

Calder and Henry were not concerned with recess, block scheduling, curriculum structure, middle school science pedagogy, or enrollment projections. They just wanted to know why their dad was going to all these meetings. They needed to know what was happening.

"Well, I'm trying to start a school," I said.

"Can we go to it?" asked Henry.

"Maybe one day you can. This school will be for teenagers."

The word *teenager* held mysterious power for Henry and Calder, invoking, I guessed, an awesome, possibly malevolent deity.

"How old will the kids be in your school?" Henry asked, his eyes popped wide open.

"Well, I haven't got any kids in my school yet. But if I get any, they will be twelve, thirteen, and fourteen years old."

One afternoon we lay on the floor playing amid a potpourri of Tinkertoys, Hot Wheels, Legos, wooden blocks, and Lincoln Logs. Outside the snow was blowing sideways and our furnace was roaring, trying to replace the warm air rushing out the cracks of our Vermont farmhouse. Henry and Calder were busy managing a construction site.

"What are you building?" I asked.

"We're building your school," said Henry.

"It's going to be Daddy's school," said Calder.

They erected a sprawling rainbow-hued structure of wooden logs, blocks, and plastic bricks. They made an arched doorway opening onto a maze of rooms. I gazed in, my cheek pressed to the floor. Calder leaned green planks over the top to make a roof.

Henry returned from his room with a handful of Playmobil figures.

"These can be the kids," he said. Calder formed them into seated poses and sat them at Tinkertoy tables.

"This one can be Daddy." Henry held up a bearded Playmobil deep-sea fisherman. I did not have a beard and I was not a fisherman. But maybe a beard and yellow mackinaw signified the authority needed for a headmaster of a nonexistent middle school somewhere in the Green Mountains.

The furnace clicked on and the snow kept blowing. I watched them build my school, their school, with no plan and no scheme, amid a scattering of toys. They went forward on intuition and imagination and whatever was at hand.

One afternoon I asked them what I should teach at my new school. Of course, they responded by talking about what they had been learning.

"You should teach them about Fort Ticonderoga," said Henry.

"Teach them to not knock other people's blocks down," said Calder.

"Good, okay. Is that all? What else should I teach them about?"

"Teach them about Martin Luther King," said Henry.

"Teach them about letters," said Calder.

"Teach them how to hammer nails," said Henry.

"That's great, boys." I was taking notes now.

"Teach about dairy farms and space," said Calder.

"Teach them not to smoke cigarettes," said Henry.

"Can you think of any more?" I asked.

"Teach about patterns," said Henry.

"Teach them that if a tree is falling on their head, to get out of the way," said Calder.

"Oh, that's a good one, Calder."

"Teach them to not hurt people's feelings," said Henry.

"Oh, yeah, that's another good one."

"Teach them that they should not interrupt when Daddy is talking," said Calder.

"And if one of them is talking, *you* should be quiet," said Henry.

"I see. Okay. Anything else?"

"Teach them to share," said Calder.

"Teach them if their drawings are not perfect, it's okay," said Henry.

"Teach them," said Calder, "that cats are very soft."

Henry and Calder's list showed me my first step: Toss out the text-books, standards, rubrics, theories, and philosophies—and start from what you know. The school had to come directly from the children in it and from what was in them.

It was the best curriculum I had ever seen. It contained everything necessary: art, poetry, history, social skills, manners, health, nature, respect, the manual construction arts, and common sense. All I had to do was make their list relevant and important to my students. Then one day I would be so lucky to have a school for my two boys.

I printed the list and sent it to every person I had ever known who had even the faintest interest in education, announcing that I was start-ing a school. *Here is what we'll be doing,* I said. It's going to be a one-room schoolhouse in the Green Mountains, in Vermont. It's going to be a hell of a great school. And could you please make a generous dona-tion? We have a lot of copies of *To Kill a Mockingbird* to buy.

When Mia Allen first called me and asked what I knew about teaching middle school, I told her I had no short-age of knowledge and experience, having taught seventh and eighth grade for ten years at the Paideia School, an established independent school in Atlanta.

When Mia asked about my interest in middle schools, I said, with-out thinking, "It's always been my dream to start a school."

"Really?" she asked. "Wow. That's great."

Really? My dream to start a school? What exactly was I thinking? I'd never attached the word *dream* to my work as a teacher. Teaching adolescents was grueling, exhausting, vexing, disheartening, mystify-ing, lonely, and *beautiful,* even occasionally thrilling, exhilarating.

But it was not a dream. Normal people dreamed about opening restaurants, starting nonprofit organizations, building businesses, or climbing great mountains. No one I knew dreamed of starting a middle school.

Mia invited me to a community meeting to discuss local interest in an independent middle school in a rural hill town with a population of 562.

I arrived at a meeting at the community house on a raw November night in "downtown" Ripton, a classic New England village—a general store and post office, an old blacksmith's shop, an inn, the town office, and the Methodist church, which met only in summer due to the fact that it had no central heat.

Two dozen metal chairs were circled in the middle of an empty high-ceilinged room. We took turns introducing ourselves and describing our interest in education. A few of the participants were parents. Some were teachers or former teachers. Only four had a direct connection with this new idea of a community middle school. Mia, who seemed to be in charge, had three children, including Sophie, who was in sixth grade. Mia had formerly taught science in Shoreham, a small town in the valley. Marcia Croll was a middle school guidance counselor with no shortage of knowledge about the complexities of adolescents. Najat, her adopted daughter from Morocco, sat by her in the circle, skittish and fidgeting. Anza Armstrong was one of two moms of Rosa and Grace, adopted African-American sisters. Rosa was in fifth grade, and she sat shyly next to Najat. Anza was a nurse; her partner, Jan, was a Head Start teacher. And finally there was Cindy Seligman, a retired adolescent therapist, looking wiser than any of the rest of us. "I am here," she said, "because I believe in the idea of a small school in the town of Ripton."

The discussion centered on the "feel" of the proposed school: What would it look like? How big could it be? What would distinguish it from the larger local union middle school? It was clear that these were not extraordinarily wealthy folks, nor did they seem to be politically connected. They were not motivated by any particular animus against conventional schools—no agendas about school choice, vouchers, No Child Left Behind, or higher state standards. They were not griping about bureaucratic mire, school accountability, teachers unions, per-pupil spending limits, prayer in schools, the achievement gap, increased rigor, more testing, or better use of technology. They had other, more elemental concerns.

"A school should be a place where kids are not afraid but want to go to every day."

"I'm not really concerned about whether my child does well on testing. I just want her to be excited about what she's doing."

"Kids should feel like they belong and like they have an impact on their school and their community."

"A school can be like a large family. That seems really important in adolescence, when they are getting to the age where their peers are so important."

"I love the feeling of preschools and kindergartens. They seem to be such places of joy and excitement, but the older kids get the more schools seem to close all that off. It seems like a middle school could use more of that preschool joy and adventure."

"A school should be a place where things can happen and change and be reactive."

"I just want my daughter to be able to go outside into the woods during the fall. That should be a part of the science curriculum. Science should include the kids being outside."

"I hated my years in middle school. Everything about it was forget-table. School should not ever be forgettable."

Those words—*school should not ever be forgettable*—rang in my ears. This was simple, inspiring idealism, an attempt to describe the school they imagined. They were groping toward a school that was more intimate, humane, nimble, joyful, authentic, and transformative. They were looking for a school they could hold in their hands, a school that would more closely hold their children.

My turn came.

"First, I would open the school to all the towns around here, not just Ripton," I said. "Because in a town this small it'll be hard to get enough kids to make it work. Second, you would need at least twelve kids, and you mix seventh, eighth, and ninth grades. You'd need two teachers. One for math and science and one for everything else. Basically you make it a one-room schoolhouse."

A few heads nodded. Mia was taking notes.

"But the main thing, beyond structure, or curriculum, which are superficial, is that the kids have to feel it's *their* school, that they built or are building it every day. The kids themselves are the text, which they have to read and write every day. They have to know that everything they do matters. They have to feel free. If they feel like they've been 'put in' the school, they won't possess and make it their own."

"What do you mean by 'possess'?"

"Mainly, the kids have to be free to say what they feel. What they feel and who they are is more important than what they know or don't know. Because they're adolescents and self-centered, the subject should be themselves and who they are becoming. If you continually suppress that for some abstract curricular standards, they will close off. They have to be given time to muck around in their feelings, be wrong, act silly, say dumb things, learn the difference between inner depth and adolescent superficiality. They have to be free to write what they feel. They have to set the standards for themselves and be given the responsibility to maintain respect for each other and their work. They have to be guided to govern themselves. If something goes wrong, the teaching becomes how they can learn to deal with what goes wrong. When they screw that up, they learn from the screwups. But always, they have to be trusted with their feelings. What happens in the classroom must always be at the center. It's their story and they want to talk about it."

"How do you motivate them to want to do it?"

"They're intrinsically motivated. When they're given the chance to possess themselves and their learning and each other they'll work hard and look out for each other and discipline problems will virtually disappear. When there's a problem you help them deal with it, insofar as it transgresses standards they themselves have set. You deal with everything—right then, right there—with all of them. No secrets, no separation of behavior from curriculum. Their acts, right or wrong, are projections of who they are becoming. They want to know how to make it right. They want it to be fair and safe and fun. The school has to be a place where they can always create that."

No one stopped me, so I kept going.

"As a teacher I start with three basic assumptions. First, every one of them has some kind of genius or brilliance that needs and wants to be called forth. Then I assume they all want to do well, to do great, to be respected and accepted, to belong. And finally, if those things aren't happening, they'll want to fix it. They have to be given freedom to start talking, the whole class together, about why those things aren't happening."

I did not know if these thoughts sounded radical, generic, or obvious. In truth, I didn't know if the school I was describing was even possible. In my past teaching I had operated with these same ideas, and my students and I had achieved something approaching what I described. But that had been in an established school where parents, students, buildings, and materials were delivered to me. I had no idea how to make it happen from scratch.

Still, these two dozen strangers were listening.

The discussion moved to other topics: What kind of space would a school need? How much should it cost? How could it be made affordable? What about diversity? What should the curriculum be? What kind of teachers to look for? How to get the word out?

No conclusions were reached other than there would be another meeting.

As we folded up the chairs, Anza approached me.

"If you were starting this school, what would you need—at the bare minimum?"

"You mean like stuff and equipment?"

"Yes. A space, and what to put in it."

"Do you want me to tell you right now?"

"Why don't you make a list and send it to me."

I went home that night and wrote:

1. Two classrooms

2. A bathroom

3. Two tables

4. Twelve chairs

5. $500 worth of books

6. First-aid kit

7. Paper and pencils

8. Copy machine

9. Plants

10. A cat

It was ludicrously bare, idealistically Spartan, and absurdly naïve—the educational equivalent of going into the Alaskan wilderness with nothing but three sacks of rice and a shaker of salt.

The message? The children and the experience they created was the heart of it.

In January I was hired to be the headmaster of a nonexistent school. After having stayed home with Henry and Calder for three years, I was now gainfully employed. For a one-hundred-dollar monthly stipend I was charged with creating a brochure, developing a curriculum, writing grant proposals, publicizing the school, and contacting interested families.

We had no students, building, books, or money. Though daunting, I relished the challenge of filling that void. Perhaps I was rationalizing when I told myself that the less a school started with, the better—more room, then, for us to fill it with ourselves. I had to believe a school could work if the students started with the richness and the truth of themselves, if they were allowed to make the school in their own image.

In my head I began to shape a pedagogical approach that necessarily included messiness and chaos—the chaos of huge questions, absurd propositions, wrong answers, incomplete philosophies. As one builds with clay, we would start and stop, mold and remold, push and sculpt, until it took the right form. A school could not be created from the tainted seeds of orthodoxy or politics. The school had to be made, as Henry and Calder had done, by kneeling down without a plan and following where the hands and heart would lead.

I spent a month writing a three-fold brochure that described a school that did not exist. I wanted to convey that this school was going to be different; yet it had to sound solid and rooted. If families were going to risk putting their children in a new and unproven enterprise, there had to be something more than wispy, hopeful intentions. There had to be a plan, a thrust, and a purpose. On the other hand, I also had to convey that the school would be a process of *becoming*, that it was incipient. The school I envisioned had to be an ecological, *ongoing* environment, a place of social and creative interdependence. If I set a curriculum too rigidly, if I adhered to a set philosophy, the school might already appear to be heading toward a state of calcification before it even began.

On paper I described the school in conventional terms—a framework of values, curriculum focus, a philosophy of assessment and discipline. I contacted teachers and heads of schools and asked for advice (*Twelve students is what you want—that's what Chairman Mao said was ideal*). I asked for help on how to raise funds (Have you contacted L. L. Bean?). Suddenly my simple list—in which a cat and copies of *To Kill a Mockingbird* shared equal status—was getting crowded with items I had not considered in my Spartan idealism. How much for tuition? How much financial aid could we offer? Insurance? Licensing? Nonprofit status? Who would rent us a house—and would they let us put fire-exit signs in the living room? Would we need a wheelchair ramp? Fire alarms? Computers? Supplies? Who would keep the books? What about a telephone number? And if we needed a telephone listing, under what name would we be listed?

In our naïveté we had forgotten to think about a name for the school. Not only did we need a name, we needed one that would evocatively capture the unique essence of a school that did not yet exist. Trying to come up with the perfect name was like trying to create the perfect egg without knowing what we wanted the bird to look like.

The location of the school—removed from the shire town of Middlebury, high in the heart of the Green Mountain National Forest—was central to our identity. I scanned a map of the Ripton area. The Breadloaf School of English and the Robert Frost homestead were up the mountain to the east. Robert Frost Mountain was to the northwest, its eastern watershed running down toward the settlement of Ripton.

As much as I would have liked to have been the founder of the Robert Frost School, we couldn't really claim a legitimate association with Frost. I squinted my eyes at the topography of Ripton. *Abbey Pond. Pine Hill. Alder Brook. Beaver Meadow. Blue Bank Brook. Peddler's Bridge. Sparks Brook*—these sounded established, natural, and eminently woodsy.

For the sake of practicality, I used the name "North Branch" for our mock-up brochure. The North Branch, a feeder to the Middlebury River, was in truth a mountain stream lined with huge ferns and hardwoods, filled with massive yellow quartz boulders and fingerling trout, alternately rushing and collecting in deep, shaded pools. It flowed briskly along the Lincoln Road, then forked from the village of Ripton into a deep gorge, where it roared and tumbled down the mountain into the valley. *North Branch* was local and sounded appropriately humble.

"We were looking at maps of the town," exclaimed Mia. "That's exactly what we were thinking."

"So North Branch is good enough for now?" I asked.

"Sounds perfect to me," said Marcia.

"It feeds into the Middlebury River," I offered. "That's the river in Frost's poem 'West-Running Brook.' We get glory by association."

"Sounds great."

"We have no school but at least we have glory."

Now we could only hope that the eventual location of the school was legitimately close to the river.

In the brochure I described the meaning I hoped inhered to the name of the school:

> The name of the North Branch School derives from the brook of the same name originating in the watershed below Robert Frost Mountain, near Ripton. From there it feeds into the Middlebury River, flowing west and north to Otter Creek and finally into Lake Champlain. As a rising spring gathers and grows to become part of a larger body, the North Branch suggests motion and confluence, a place of origin and a place of coming together. We see the school as a nourishing element, a way station on a vital journey, a process of living and learning that deepens and broadens in time.

As attractive as metaphors about schools and rivers were, my reliance on poetic or metaphorical generalities was consistent with my difficulty imagining anything remotely concrete about what the school would actually *do*. Yeats said, "Education is not the filling of a pail, but the lighting of a fire." Simple enough, I thought: Ignite whatever was combustible, innate, and natural within each of my students. I also considered John Keats's statement, "Do you not see how necessary a world of pains and troubles is to school an intelligence and make it a soul?" Keats's question reminded me of the difficulty of teaching middle-school kids, yet I loved its insistence that true learning was born from lived experience. School did not have to be antiseptic or pretty.

By March we had two officially enrolled students: Mia's daughter, Sophie, and Marcia's daughter, Najat. Two students were not enough to make me feel like I was headmaster of a school.

Once after discussing our lack of a student body I said to Mia, "Will *you* be around?" I was desperate to know that there might be someone I knew close by. But I had to convince strangers to enroll their children in a school that did not yet exist—a school with no building, no money, next to no students. I had to convince them to leave those children in the care of a formerly licensed teacher from Georgia who had never taught in Vermont, whom they did not know.

Because we had no school to visit, I traveled to the far reaches of the Champlain Valley to the homes of interested families to tell them about the school to be.

To be was the operative term, as I spoke with half hope and small grains of confidence about a school that existed only in a brochure. I had nothing to show, no proof or evidence, no quantitative measures of effectiveness, no testimonials from ecstatic parents. Driving around in my minivan with my two children, I felt more like an itinerant preacher or a bedraggled missionary speaking to doubters and the half curious.

"Where are you going to get enough students?" parents asked.

"We'll, we've got a lot of interest so far. We're looking to have twelve to fourteen students the first year," I said.

But the question ignited in my head: *What if we don't?*

"What do you have for a building?" parents asked. My mind flashed to dank church basements, leaky geodesic domes, barns, wood shops, mildewed yurts in the woods, traveling classrooms, schools without walls.

I cringed. "We're working on it," I said.

"Build it and they will come," I was told by others with more experience in the school-building business.

I thought: *What if we build it and they don't come?*

I remember Doug's father, Dennis, warning me. "He's not an athlete, he won't do so well in your sports program."

"Well, that shouldn't be too much of a problem. We probably won't have much of a sports program to start."

"What's most important to us is that he continue to love learning," he said earnestly. "He loves astronomy. He loves math. I want him to keep having respect for knowledge and to keep asking big questions."

"I think we'll be able to do that," I said, and that was the truth. I knew I could keep them asking questions. Always, more questions.

I drove out on snowy spring days or in the dark evenings of early summer, to Cornwall and Salisbury and New Haven and Shoreham and Lincoln. I took off my boots in the houses of strangers and asked that they trust this place I might create that I did not know how to create.

I proceeded to describe a few basic ideas: creative writing, literature discussion seminars, field trips, class government and problem solving, a close-knit community. There would be concern for the individual, independent work, interdisciplinary curriculum, hands-on and experiential learning. It would be homey and comfortable and informal.

But these were the features of many schools and, to my mind, essentially common sense. I could not yet articulate how our school would be different from schools I had known, except in the material fact that our school would be quite small and that it would be somewhere far up in the Green Mountains. And it would have a cat.

I visited the Rutherford family one summer night. When I walked up the driveway, Nick and his younger brother, Devlin, were kicking the soccer ball in the fresh-cut grass on a hillside in the shadow of the Bristol Cliffs. They gave me a tour of Nick's dad's shop, filled with vintage tools and intermingling smells of pine sawdust, wood stain, and machine oil.

In the house we sat around a scarred antique table. Nick was a seventh-grader-to-be in a high school senior's body, his deep voice able to bring forth only a few appropriate syllables in response to the mildest of questions. His mother, Donna, with her mane of white hair and quiet voice, nodded and smiled as I sketched out my idea of the school. She seemed to know, with an intuitive confidence I did not yet possess, that this nonexistent school was the right school for her child.

In June I visited Zoe in the town of Bristol. Her family lived on Pleasant Street, near the town green where neighborhood kids shot baskets at dusk under the broad maples and elms.

On the porch I knocked and waited. The door opened. There was Zoe, a stick-thin, barefoot, blond-haired girl in jean shorts.

"Take off your shoes," she ordered, in an attempt to welcome me.

The living room was taken up with a weaving loom the size of a small car. On the wall hung an enormous framed map of Vermont, circa 1840, yellowed and torn at the edges. Crowded on the floors, windowsills, and tables were glazed ceramics, plants in pots, and clay figurines. A faded Indian tapestry seemed to be collecting dust on top of a small television.

I told them about the school in my most hopeful way. Zoe sat with her legs curled up under her, her brief answers to my inquiries barely audible. She seemed utterly uninterested.

I visited Mira, a seventh grader who had been adopted from India when she was two. It was a school night, and she was slumped at the dining room table with her father, Tom, moaning about algebra. "I hate this frickin' stupid math, Dad! It doesn't make sense."

She was small, with shining black hair and beautiful golden-brown skin. We talked together for an hour. She told me how at her current school she felt friendless, caught up in tangled social dramas that distracted, confused, and depressed her. As I was leaving, she climbed into her father's lap. She said good-bye to me curled up there, with her dark head snuggled under his white beard.

His name is Tico," Anza told me after receiving a call from a prospective parent. "He's adopted from Honduras. He lives with his mom in Salisbury. They're very interested in the school but the problem is that he's really struggled in school and they don't think the middle school really knows what to do with him."

When I talked to Deb, Tico's mother, the first thing she told me was that Tico could not really read. Reading, however, was not her central concern.

"I guess at this point I'm not even sure he'll really be able to learn to read," she said, her voice that of a parent who had negotiated every possible path, every bureaucratic trail, every program, and had come up empty.

"He's been getting in trouble and he seems like he's shutting down. I guess I just want Tico to feel valued in the school community. I don't want him to constantly feel like school is about telling him what he *can't* do. I want him to know he has talents and that he can be a good citizen and contribute in his own ways."

"I think we'll be able to do that," I said. "I know we can make him feel like he's an integral part. He'll have to be. In a school this small there's no way to hide. They'll all have to contribute."

She sent reports from the Boston's Children's Hospital, where Tico had undergone exhaustive testing for cognitive processing. His sentences were nearly incomprehensible. He had no grasp of how number operations worked. In addition, he had recently gotten in trouble for vandalizing a town bridge and stealing. On the face of it he appeared to be a huge risk, the kind of kid a fragile, new school might want to avoid. But there was a hunger in me, and in the founders of the school, to figure out how our school might work for a kid like Tico.

I told myself our school did not necessarily have to replicate whatever past dynamics had transpired between Tico and his schooling. What and how he learned did not have to come in a conventional package. I could not let myself believe that just because six years of schooling had not worked for Tico, he was uneducable—that it was time to send him packing to the resource room.

Besides, we needed customers.

One early summer evening I went to visit Tico. In the valley I drove past dairy farms, crossed over the Otter Creek winding through wet, plowed fields, the Adirondacks glowing purple in the distance across Lake Champlain. With the smell of manure and silage blowing in the open windows, I wondered how I might get inside the head of this adopted boy from Honduras who could not read. I pulled up to a farmhouse in Salisbury, a crossroad village of farm fields and swamps in the south end of Addison County. I saw a small figure far down the road, pedaling toward me, his bike wagging back and forth and his legs pumping furiously.

A plump, light-brown-skinned boy in a tie-dyed Ben and Jerry's T-shirt skidded to a stop in the gravel. He removed his helmet, revealing a lumpy Afro. He ducked his head down and murmured hello. Inside the house we talked briefly, and then Deb left us.

"So, Tico, which of these paintings on the wall are yours?" I asked. It was clear that none of them were, but I wanted to see how he would respond.

He smiled. "These are not my paintings."

He proceeded to explain who each of the artists were, their relationships to him and his mother, and how the paintings came to be in their house. He was observant, interested in his world, and verbally adept.

I asked him about movies he had recently seen. He told me about the film *Castaway* with more clarity than the average film reviewer. His ideas tumbled out in rapid and surprising associations. He told me about the trouble he'd gotten into—setting fires in the neighbor's yard and spraying graffiti on the town bridge—not capital offenses but red flags for a kid heading into adolescence and failing in school.

"Do you know why you did it?" I asked.

"Yeah."

"Why?"

"I guess I was angry. I was alone. I was doing really crappy in school." He dipped his head in embarrassment and looked up at me.

"Is that a reason?"

"Well, no. But that's what was going on."

"You wanna show me your room?" I asked.

"Sure." He jumped up and took the steep stairs two at a time. The door to his room was covered with stickers of skiing companies, radio stations, Calvin and Hobbes, and the goofy cartoon stickers bank tellers give small children, and one simply stating, "Warning: Explosives."

The room was an unmitigated catastrophe. Open drawers spilled over with spools of wire, T-shirts, cables, lightbulbs, remote-control cars, screwdrivers, sheets of Styrofoam, and broken robot toys. Blankets were piled in a ratty knot on his bed. On the floor were skateboard wheels, dust balls, rolls of duct tape, a lacrosse stick with no pocket, pinecones, instruction manuals, wiring diagrams, snowboard magazines, key chains, loose change, tubes of glue, whittled twigs, goggles, batteries, plastic models, wire snips, and several opened sticks of deodorant.

I gazed upon the wreckage. "I see you tidied up the place," I said.
"Very funny."

"Yo, bro, you need to clean this place. It's kind of a dump," I said.

"This is how it usually is," he said, smiling at me.

He showed me a papier-mâché mask he had made, a design for a go-cart he was working on, and his remote-control car. None of these works had a thing to do with school. He showed me his tools and his boxes of spare parts—parts of him, I guessed, the loose wiring of his mind that he was trying to piece together.

"Damn. So I see you've got a lot of projects going on."

"I like making things with my hands," he replied. His voice was soft and he was serious. He was proud of his workspace and everything in it.

I realized then that I knew everything I needed to know that Tico Brighton could succeed in our school.

Later, Anza and Marcia asked, "Well?"

"Oh, hell yes. He's going to be great. He's gotta come to the school and we can get around the reading. We've got three years to work some magic."

"Yes!" Marcia shouted.

I could feel myself moving out on the edge where no one else was, doing what a teacher did, groping forward with inner sense and hope. I was alone with nothing but what I knew already.

When I greeted prospective students, they offered small, limp, tentative hands. They averted their eyes, recoiling into themselves like turtles. But never had I met any student anywhere whose first appearance was like Annie Holland-Levine's. When I stepped into her house I was stopped by a giant Lycra bag, suspended by bungee cords, hanging from the ceiling. Just the top of a head protruded, a mass of curly hair mashed down under a bandana, as she swung bouncing and swaying in what looked kind of like a giant, lime-green, writhing elastic scrotum.

"That's Annie in the bag," her mother, Colleen, said. "It's her cocoon."

"Annie, why don't you come out and meet Tal," said her father, Ken. "He's the teacher who's going to start the school."

We sat down and I explained about the school that did not exist. Annie slowly climbed out and meekly entered the room, sitting on the edge of the couch.

"How'd you like your old school, Annie?" I asked.

"Oh, you mean the prison. It was awful. The kids were horrible and bullies."

"What do you mean?"

"No one cared about school. Anyone who made good grades got made fun of. They called me 'sheep girl' because I have sheep and curly hair."

"What'd you do about it?"

"Nothing," she said, suddenly seeming suspicious.

"You could have fought them. You know, brass knuckles, nunchucks."

"I don't like to fight," she said.

"Well, our school will be pretty small so I don't think we'll have too many bullies. If there are problems, we'll talk about what's happening."

"How many kids do you have so far?" Ken asked. He had a gentle face, smiling and without a trace of cynicism.

With Tico and Nick, I knew we had four kids for sure. We had four others who were interested, five if I counted Annie. I wanted to avoid giving a direct answer. The truth—only four students—would surely discourage them.

"Well, we have quite a few coming and a few of those are still deciding. We plan on starting with about twelve. Chairman Mao said twelve was the perfect number for learning," I said, adding a little puffery for diversion. Another half smile. I remained committed to vagueness, blurring the facts, exaggeration, and the desperate hope that they would follow.

"And what are your numbers now?" Ken asked.

"Well, we're at around eight."

"That's great, that's a lot. You're really doing well."

I breathed out. Annie was scrunched down, burrowed into her mother's side.

"So what's the story with that big spandex bag, Annie?" I asked.

"Umm . . ." She looked around cautiously. "It's not spandex, it's Lycra, and it helps me be like, less anxious? I kind of am, sometimes I get, like, a little freaked out and stuff?" This statement, ostensibly declarative, was offered with complete uncertainty.

"What's it like in there?"

"It's really dark and it's calming and supposedly the textures of it help me with my thoughts. They say that it helps kids with obsessive-compulsive disorder, which they tell me I have."

"Is it fun to jounce around in?"

"Jounce?" she repeated.

"Yeah, you know, bounce around, jiggle and stuff."

"Uh, yeah, I guess so."

Her room was shocking. Not one magazine, not one dirty sock, not one poster. Her bed, with a single smoothed-down pillow, was made up tight, blankets taut, as though for a white-glove inspection. Her dresser was swept clean, the closet closed. It seemed that she possessed nothing—no mementos, no jewelry, no diaries, no deodorant.

"Uh, Annie, this is the cleanest teenager's room in the entire United States of America. Congratulations."

"Umm, I guess I like order?" she said.

She took me to see her flock of sheep. She gave me her brother's mud boots and led me out into early evening, which smelled of hay and wet grass, manure and mud.

"These are my sheep."

"That's their house?" I asked, pointing to a ramshackle lean-to of corrugated metal roofing and warped plywood.

"Yeah, I built it with my dad. Of course they only go in it when it's sunny out. They like to stand in the rain. They're not very smart."

She pointed to a small maple tree. "That's where the robins' nest was when it fell."

"What happened to the robins?"

"We saved one of the chicks. We still have it inside. You want to see it?"

Ken was in the kitchen. The robin perched on his shoulder and Annie fed it half of a worm. She offered the worm to the bird, saying, "Eat this, little friend."

"What do you do with it? Where does it live?" I asked.

"Well, we've been letting fly it around the house. Soon we'll be able to release it. Here, take him. He won't fly."

She set the bird on my finger and I stroked its beak and tail feathers.

Colleen followed me to the door as I put on my shoes.

"That's the first time Annie has ever told anyone anything about her anxiety and OCD. It seems like she trusts you."

I drove home through the low fog of the dark Cornwall swamp, where frogs were migrating across the wet blacktop and cracked frost heaves, trying to make it from one dark place to another. I thought about Annie, her bouncing Lycra cocoon, her place of safe textures, her neat room, sheep, and little robin. If Ken and Colleen would let Annie come to us, the school would be a place where fragility could grow to strength. If she needed a school where kids cared about their work and didn't tease each other, she could be the one to make it that way. If Annie was the kind of kid I could get to come to my school, we might actually make the school I imagined.

We would have no sports or committees, no mandates or paraprofessionals, no computers or custodians, no cinder-block walls or glistening waxed hall floors. Maybe my list for Anza was right after all: a couple of tables and twelve chairs, some blank sheets of paper, a few copies of *One Flew Over the Cuckoo's Nest* and *To Kill a Mockingbird*, and these kids. These kids—Annie, Tico, Zoe, Mira—were at the chasm between childhood and adulthood. At that threshold I should be able to hold them for a moment and give them something of themselves to take before they went. The gift had nothing to do with conventional subject matter and everything to do with helping them discover a clear sense of who they were, wanted to be, might become. That's what great teachers did, the great teachers I had known—they drew children closer to a clear vision of themselves. And that's what should be happening, always, for those kids sitting in the classroom, looking at the teacher, waiting, listening, longing, hungering for something that mattered.

Driving home that night in the dark landscape of Vermont, a few orange house lights spread far out in the blackness of the valley, I was already thinking about my students, how in a few months they would be sitting around some rickety tables I didn't know where we'd find, in some building I did not know where. Without a map or plan we would get them to that table, and we would learn how to learn together.

The parents of these kids, I was learning, were not choosing the North Branch School because the topics to be studied were so radically, spectacularly different. As in many middle schools, we would read *Of Mice and Men*, solve linear equations, and study local ecosystems. The first parents gravitated to the school, perhaps, because North Branch represented the hope, implicit in the act of creating a new school, that something entirely different could be made— that current political debates about accountability or state funding fell far short of meaningful discourse about the education of children. These parents, no matter their income, education, or political views, were seeking education that involved something closer to the heart. In particular, they seemed to want something more creative and free. *Creative* and *free*—certainly vague notions, but they stood in contradistinction to schools tethered to rigid, standards-based approaches or school officials bombarded with federal mandates to test.

The parents seemed to believe me when I said a child's progress and achievement could be gauged without conventional grades or testing every six weeks. Some *were* fed up with the ossified bureaucracy of school systems that marginalized them or limited their input to voting yes or no on school bond issues. Some *were* galled that discourse about learning and child development went no further than political bickering about merit pay, disciplinary procedures, or whether or not the state should fund police officers in the schools.

The concerns of the first parents centered directly on what happened, or could happen, in a classroom. Mia asked repeatedly: Why not allow more of their education to take place outside? Wouldn't studying photosynthesis be more meaningful if it was done under the canopy of the local forest, under the spreading crowns of maple trees? What if such study took place at the Robert Frost cabin, where students, in one day perhaps, read "Birches," made drawings of leaves, and walked along century-old logging roads? At various stages in American educational history such an approach had been fashionable. It seemed simple and natural enough, and kids hungered for something like it, but it happened all too rarely in schools. The large size of schools—their cumbersome, institutional nature, their necessary reliance on centralization and adherence to economies of scale—was a major impediment.

Other parents wanted us never to bring a computer through the door. Some wanted art all day. Others liked that we were in the woods, on a dusty dirt road, with no linoleum, concrete blocks, or school secretaries barricaded behind sliding glass windows. Anza, who with her partner, Jan, would be sending Rosa when she reaches seventh grade, wanted her in school where she was not ostracized or stigmatized for being the brown, adopted child of gay parents. Moreover, Anza and Jan sought a school that would openly celebrate their child's family and origins. Deb, Tico's mother, seemed unconcerned that I lacked the formal expertise to teach Tico to read. "If he learns to read, great. I just want him to know that he's good at some things and not feel bad about what he can't do. Having him spend his days in the resource room or helping staff pin posters on the bulletin boards is not my idea of an alternative."

These first parents sought an education for their children that was, simply, more dynamic and responsive. They wanted a school where their children would not "get lost," where children could not hide or slide through. They sought a school where the words and actions of their children would have the power to ring out and resonate every day. They wanted a school that felt bigger than a family but smaller than a system—an environment that was intimate, safe, and secure. They wanted a place where conflict would be dealt with humanely and openly, a school that, literally and metaphorically, centered around a round table; a school where there was a greater balance, where their children had the time to look inward and into each other, where collaborative sharing was more than a buzzword. They sought a sense of humor. They wanted a school in which children, whether they possessed conventional academic skills or not, would be a part of shaping the course of learning and making something important. They wanted their children eager to go to school and to be thrilled by what was happening.

Over and over, it became clear to me that what the parents sought had virtually nothing to do with whether their children mastered a particular body of predetermined knowledge or met certain "standards." Professional educators and politicians would point to an enlightened curriculum, improved test scores, beautiful facilities, or properly trained teachers as key determinants of success. By choosing a school with no tests, no curriculum, no facilities, and haphazardly trained teachers, the first parents implicitly sought a school outside of all systems of tradition, a place where their children could discover themselves in the act of creating their own, true community, and the great meaning of their lives.

I went to see a prospective student, Steve, up on the North Branch Road. His mother, Tammi, told me to look for the blue trailer with cars in the yard. There were *lots* of junk cars—rusted, hoods up, and wheels off, a Toyota truck filled with bags of trash. The yard was littered with transmission parts, hubcaps, empty soda bottles, Tonka trucks, deflated soccer balls, retired chain saws and piles of seasoned firewood hidden in the overgrowth of jewelweed. A pen held an assortment of bedraggled, rain-soaked chickens and a belligerent, menacing turkey. A small garden of red and yellow snapdragons marked the way to the door.

I sat at the kitchen table with Tammi, Steve, and his father, Brian. The ashtray between us was filled with ashes and cigarette butts. Steve was gangly, with a thin neck, acne, eyes sunk deep in bluish eye sockets, greasy hair hanging over his eyes, his silk basketball shorts hanging down over his knees.

"What subjects do you like?" I asked.

"Uh, history, I guess," he said slowly.

"What history?"

"Um, like, the Revolutionary War?"

"What about it do you like?"

"Um, it's like, I don't know, pretty interesting, all the battles and stuff."

"You like sports?"

"Yeah, basketball and baseball."

"Who's your team?"

"The Atlanta Braves."

"Really? Not the Sox?

"Nah, I like the Braves."

"The Braves are my team," I said, smiling. "I'm from Atlanta."

"Cool."

"Who do you like?" I asked.

"Chipper Jones."

"Sweet. Chipper's awesome."

"Yeah."

"So how was last year in school for you?"

"Uh, not so good." He half laughed. "The teachers didn't like me too much. My math teacher hated me."

"Steve didn't do so well on his report card," said Tammi.

"But he's going to do better, right, Steven?" said Brian, arching his eyebrow from under the bent brim of a Patriots cap.

As I explained the school, it suddenly seemed to be a ludicrous, self-indulgent fantasy of the overly educated. Experiential learning? Piaget and constructivism? John Keats? W. B Yeats? I was talking to a family that scuffled by with the stray carpentry job and hauling firewood in a rusted Toyota pickup. The chances of them wanting to send Steve were slim.

Tammi called the next day. "We'd like him to come to your school," she said.

"That's great. We'd be happy to have him."

"Do you have any financial aid?"

"We do," I said. "I'll have Mia talk to you about it."

I attended an official meeting for Tico at the local middle school. Walking down the halls I noticed that all the clocks were locked in wire cages, presumably to prevent stealing or tampering. *Time locked up.* What did that mean? A place where time stood still, where students marked time? Where not even time ran free?

Tico's old teachers were there, along with Deb, Tico, the vice principal of the middle school, and the guidance counselor. Tico sat quietly at the table, looking like he would rather have been racing his bike somewhere far away. The vice principal was concerned about the decision Deb was making, believing it ill-considered, since North Branch was unproved, particularly since we would not be able to offer Tico state-funded support services or, at that moment, a math and science teacher, or even a building.

"So tell us, Tal," queried the guidance counselor, "why you think North Branch is the right place for Tico?"

Though this question arose from genuine concern for Tico's welfare, I took it as a direct challenge. I wanted them to know the concept that was forming inside me—that we would hold Tico close, that his inner mind, the shape and direction of his dreams, the state of his emotional being would not ever be far from mine.

"Well, first off, it's going to be very small, twelve or fourteen kids. We'll know Tico and he'll know us. I'll know him, what he loves, his dog, his garden, what his life at home is like. He'll have to be involved in a school this small. He'll have to sit up at the table. There won't be a back of the room. He'll have to talk, he'll have to share, he'll have to be a huge part of the school. In that sense his learning will be about how to create his role in a real community. I guess, for Tico, the main thing is that he won't get lost."

The vice principal flared up, flustered and agitated.

"Well, I don't think Tico will get lost here," he blurted out. "The longest anyone has ever been lost here is for only about ten minutes and that's only during the first week of school."

I could see that my idea about Tico not "getting lost" was very different from theirs, and I wasn't sure if my idea of keeping Tico "found" was something I could explain.

Marcia offered the school her rental house, which was perched on the dusty Lincoln Road high above the North Branch River. Marcia, Mia, Anza, and I inspected it for school suitability. It was a classic Vermont farmhouse, with peeling lead paint and not one floor plumb, two big rooms downstairs with eight-foot ceilings, and two tiny bedrooms upstairs. The current tenant was a radical leftist professor at a local community college. He'd covered the windows with old sheets and wool blankets. Books, papers, magazines, and musical scores were stacked in columns from floor to ceiling. A poster calling for immediate revolution read "Eat the Rich."

We tried to climb down into the cellar, but the stairs were blocked by a waist-high tide of lawn mowers, empty beer bottles, garden hoses, and mildewed boxes of Communist Party pamphlets. The kitchen was mostly taken up with an elephant-sized antique stove surrounded by the parts of a dismantled Kawasaki soaking in buckets of motor oil. The screen porch sloped precipitously toward the river, which we could hear rushing through the trees.

"What do you think? Would it work?" Mia asked doubtfully.

"Oh, sure. Yeah. It'd be fine. We could make it work." I was willing to try anything. Just to have a place.

We walked upstairs to the bedroom. The plank floor sagged and cracked, then bounced back spongily. I imagined a half dozen rampaging adolescents, practically our whole student body, falling through the floor.

"Okay, maybe not," I said. "Let's go back downstairs."

Mia and I found another house in Ripton, just up the hill from the river. Joe and Betty Matkowski were moving away for a few years and, as retiring educators, they were sympathetic to our fledgling enterprise. The house was surrounded by towering hemlocks and fir trees, through which little light penetrated. A dusty gloom hovered inside. The ceilings and beams were low, the wide-plank wood floors rough and unfinished, with half-inch gaps between boards. A huge, black woodstove sat in the middle of the living room that, I imagined, could be my classroom. The sunroom contained a small bar and sink. I rationalized: A sink and a counter were enough to constitute a science lab.

A large pen-and-ink portrait of W. B. Yeats hung in the kitchen.

"I saw that you quoted Yeats in your brochure," Joe said as we stood in semidarkness discussing a rental agreement.

"Yeah, I saw your poster," I said.

"How about I leave that here for you guys?"

I took that, gratefully, as a good omen.

The Matkowskis rented us the house for a thousand dollars a month and granted permission to add one window, overhead lights, a fire alarm, and our very own fire-exit signs.

We found a science teacher, Eric Warren, who lived up the road on the hill above the beaver ponds from which the North Branch River flowed. He was a transplanted Californian, a pro-Sandinista, a former antinukes protester, a graduate of the Goddard College School of Social Ecology, a master wood craftsman. His family lived "off the grid" and he was committed to solar power, sustainable communities, and the concept of cohousing. He had virtually no teaching experience. Since I, the ostensible headmaster, had no experience as a headmaster, we most likely had assembled the least-credentialed middle-school faculty in America. It was a miracle that anyone at all trusted us with his or her children.

We collected chairs, tables, old telephones, and carpet remnants. We picked up an assortment of wooden desks from Middlebury College. Neighbors had heard we were starting a school and dropped off boxes of out-of-date encyclopedias, history textbooks, and tattered, marked-up copies of *Crime and Punishment* and *Lord of the Flies*.

I looked at my growing class list. My students came from ten towns spread over the county: the eighth graders, Steve, Annie, Najat, Zoe, and Mira—each from a different school. Sophie, Tico, Nick, and Doug were seventh graders. At the last moment we added Janine, a ninth grader from Pittsford, giving us an age span from eleven to fourteen years old. Annie, Steve, and Mira, by their accounts, had suffered through miserable seventh-grade years. Annie had been relentlessly teased. Steve had failed every class but language arts in seventh grade and claimed that if we were to visit the middle school locker room, we could find a large dent on a metal locker door exactly in the shape of his very own head, courtesy of a posse of eighth graders who had used him as a human battering ram. Mira had been overloaded with too much academic rigor and not enough spiritual or emotional sustenance. Doug was a self-described nerd, precociously intelligent, with his "Stellaphane" astronomer's cap, too-small sweatpants pulled halfway up his calves, and copious amounts of saliva shooting from his mouth as he expounded on *Star Trek* or string theory. Tico could not read or write. Annie suffered from extreme anxiety and OCD. In addition, her mother told me, she was dealing with the aftereffects of an incident of sexual molestation when she was four. Sophie appeared terminally shy. Najat, according to Marcia, was hesitant about plunging headfirst into the world of adolescence and still liked to play with Playmobil figures to relieve stress. Janine's primary homeschool education had been working in a farmyard raising rabbits and tending lame horses, goats, and miniature donkeys. Zoe had been homeschooled, half-schooled, or unschooled and had spent half of a traumatic year in the local middle school. Five of the ten were receiving financial aid. Three of my students were transracial adoptions—from Morocco, India, and Honduras.

We came from all over the place and we were strangers. The parents did not know each other. None of them truly knew me. By enrolling their children, they trusted my word and vision as I had sketched it out in the curriculum guide. There was no instruction manual and no guarantee—just a collection of odds and ends that appeared to have, at best, only a remote chance of fitting together. Entrusting their children to the North Branch School, a school with no defined curriculum or structure, "charter" school status or orthodoxy, at the precipitous moment when their children were entering the critical, tumultuous time of adolescence, could only be seen as an act of utter, eradicable faith.

What did we have? I surveyed our facility. It was pitifully gloomy, dark, cramped, with only one window on the north side of the house. The south side faced a steep, rocky, fern-covered hill. At the top of the hill the forest of towering conifers effectively prevented sunlight from ever penetrating the building except at high noon. The wood beams spanning each room seemed to press down, heavy and close and cobwebbed. The kitchen, which doubled as my "office," had a small gas heating stove and a dark closet, later dubbed the "hellhole," and an absurdly gargantuan 1950s lawyer's desk that must have weighed five hundred pounds. In the living room our two plastic tables sat dangerously close to a cast-iron woodstove. The staircase led upstairs to a warren of small dark rooms and closets. There was one bathroom—unisex.

I filled two sagging plywood shelves in the living room with a variety of old textbooks, the de rigueur *National Geographics*, dating back to 1971, dog-eared copies of *The Adventures of Huckleberry Finn* I had bought at yard sales, and a set of World Book encyclopedias donated by the Shelburne, Vermont, library. A heaping load of wood was stacked under the staircase where, as evidenced by the nest of shredded newspapers and cracked sunflower seeds, a red squirrel was making a comfortable home.

Joe Matkowski had left us his father's old butcher-block table on top of which sat our nine-sheets-per-minute copier and scrap paper bin. An old dish hutch contained shoe boxes of pencils, staplers, and masking tape. Eric cobbled together plywood boxes—closely resembling coffins—to double as benches and storage "lockers" for backpacks and coats. Incongruously, a framed print of Piet Mondrian's *Broadway Boogie Woogie* hung over the kitchen sink—an urbane, constructivist touch hopelessly out of place amid the detritus of dust balls, mouse droppings, crumpled papers, empty baggies, and dirty dishes. In what I took as a hopeful sign, a large iron bell sat mounted on a post on the porch. It was the only item on the whole property that suggested the idea of *school*.

In a fit of enlightened frugality and necessitated by our minuscule budget, we decided to pay into subscription membership for a "seconds" supply and equipment club, apparently the perfect way to equip moribund rural churches and small renegade schools. We deliberated carefully and finally made the plunge. For five hundred dollars we received a catalog each month through which we could enter into a lottery for tools and expensive equipment like oscilloscopes, Bunsen burners, and drill presses. As an add-on we could order office supplies, lined paper, safety goggles, and lab aprons—all the things any reasonable school might be expected to have on hand. Eric and I carefully filled out the forms, hoping to be the lucky recipients of a high-end microscope or a slide projector.

When the first box came Eric and I ripped into it like greedy children under a Christmas tree. Out came a box of 1,000 extra-small latex gloves (which we later inflated to use as trail markers); 2,500 paper plates with Japanese *manga* characters on them; 1,000 pencils labeled "Ridgeview High School," the lead of which, when put to paper, disintegrated into fine graphite dust particles; 7 spare bicycle tires; an assortment of paper sanding disks; and a diverse collection of nuts, bolts, and washers, none of which connected to any other. Eric assured me that we would be able to use these items in some kind of science project, and I believed him.

By late August we still did not have a Certificate of Occupancy: The lights and wheelchair ramp had not yet been installed. But there was work we could do ourselves to ready the school for an almost-dozen adolescents. The weekend before school opened we held a workday in order to bring our ragged band together and get to know each other.

We filled ruts in the driveway with gravel. We cleaned the bathroom, made two extra parking spaces, washed windows, threw out the garbage, painted some walls, and weeded the garden. Tico made a stone path leading to the deck. Sophie's dad, Freeman, smoothed out the driveway with the plow blade on his tractor. Tammi, Steve's mother, found a half-empty bottle of tequila under the kitchen sink and, judging from the expressions of the parents, it seemed to me that they thought I had left it there. The day ended with moderately level parking spots and all our Magic Markers sorted.

Along with asking the parents to bring shovels, wheelbarrows, and paintbrushes, I asked students to bring a special quote from someone whom they admired to inscribe or paint on the wall—their first assignment. I don't know why I thought it was a good idea to have as our first act in our new school the covering of an entire wall of someone else's house with sloppy adolescent graffiti. Was I not being overly permissive, giving the kids too much leeway, surely leading them to setting fire to the place within a week? I had no idea what the kids would even be quoting: Britney Spears? Rage Against the Machine and "We Don't Need No Education"?

I did know that I wanted them to begin to think of this school as someplace wholly different. So why not establish that difference by violating a most deeply held code of conduct in schools? *Deface it, make a mess of it,* I thought. *Write our names on it. Call it our own, begin to possess it.* Somehow deep down I had faith that they would understand the project as I meant it—that we were going to be rewriting the rules.

"Let's write your quotes on the wall," I said.

They all looked at me but no one stepped forward.

"Go ahead, it doesn't matter if we ruin the wall. And write 'em up there big."

"On *this* wall?" Najat asked.

"Yeah, go ahead."

They moved tentatively, then suddenly a noisy scramble—students and teachers with their scraps of paper with quotes, wielding brushes, paint dripping everywhere. We climbed on top of each other to put the words up.

When we were done the wall looked terrible—barely legible writing, misspelled words, shaky attempts to make rainbows, smiley faces, peace signs, yin-yang symbols, and smeared, fluffy clouds. No order, no sense of form. Paint smudges and lots of muddy brown. Quotes from Theodore Roosevelt, Louis Armstrong, and Picasso. Najat transcribed an entire poem by her grandmother. But it wasn't a disaster. I sent the kids outside so I could meet with the parents.

We sat in a circle on the deck on picnic benches, half-rotted Adirondack chairs, and rickety stools. I told them what I hoped we would be doing for the first few weeks. I told them that I would need their support and patient humor to make the school work, particularly since the school's families came from all over the area and many of us had never met each other: This was the great challenge—how to create a community where none had existed before.

Then I said, "I want to end this meeting with a quote, which explains my goal for this school. It's a quote from William Faulkner, and though he's talking about writing and the writer, I'm substituting for those words *teacher* and *teaching*."

I read: "'The teacher's only responsibility is to his teaching. He will be completely ruthless if he is a good one. He has a dream. It anguishes him so much he must get rid of it. He has no peace until then. Everything goes by the board: honor, pride, decency, security, happiness, all to get the student taught. If a teacher has to rob his mother, he will not hesitate; a good school is worth any number of old ladies.'"

I looked up. "And that's what we're after," I said. "Though I mean, we will do all those things to make the school work, not to rob old ladies."

I smiled. They laughed nervously. Perhaps my judgment was sketchy. Quoting a dead, white, hard-drinking Mississippian? Perhaps *their* judgment was sketchy. Sending their kids to a school in a barely legal house up in the mountains on a dirt road near nothing? Had they made a catastrophic mistake enrolling their children in the school of a teacher who appeared on the verge of violating innumerable codes of behavior— if not laws—in order to teach their children?

I wanted them to know that I had high goals, to reassure them that I was committed, if not institutionally, at least to education. I held Yeats's words in my head: "Heart-mysteries there, and yet when all is said / It was the dream itself enchanted me." I wanted them to know that I was establishing the school with a slightly anarchic but wholehearted dream—not to be just any school, but a Grecian Urn of a school. I wanted them to share the intensity I felt, that it was time to surrender to some undiscovered greatness we would find in ourselves. Starting a school was like having the power to remake the world. I wanted them to believe, as I did, that this school mattered greatly.

II.
fall

Cultivate a work-lust

that imagines its haven like your hands at night

dreaming the sun in the sunspot of a breast.

You are fasted now, light-headed, dangerous.

Take off from here. And don't be so earnest,

So ready for the sackcloth and the ashes.

Let go, let fly, forget.

You've listened long enough. Now strike your note.

· SEAMUS HEANEY, "Station Island"

In the days before school opened, my enchanted dream, so luminous in the previous months, was swept away. In the early morning hours as the birds sang awake, before the sun rose over the mountains, I dreamed scripts of entire classes, all of them disasters. In my dreams the students refused to listen, they walked out, they ran away with no intention of ever coming back. I chased them, dragged them down, held them in their chairs. I screamed at them to listen and to learn, and they shouted back, laughing at the whole proposition, laughing to each other as, one by one or arm in arm, they left the classroom. My voice, irrelevant and weak, was swallowed up by adolescent contempt.

I was afraid the first day that no one would show up. I was amazed when they did.

On the first morning I pulled in to see three electricians' trucks in the driveway. Parents stood together on the deck chatting, while kids milled nervously around the front door holding backpacks and bag lunches. I sent the kids out to my truck to unload two old bookshelves Eric and I had recently scavenged from a collapsing barn.

Mia, Anza, and Marcia stood waiting with Riptons' zoning commissioner.

"We can't go in yet," Mia said. "We still don't have the Certificate of Occupancy. The electricians got here at three o'clock this morning to hang the lights."

"What?"

"They said getting up this early was getting them ready for hunting season."

"Mia," I said, my heart pounding, "I don't give a damn about hunting season. We don't have the lights yet?"

"They say as soon as they are done in the science room, you can go in and they'll finish the other rooms this morning."

At 8:42, three minutes before school was scheduled to start, the first set of lights flicked on. The Certificate of Occupancy was issued and the North Branch School was in session.

I gathered my ten students around two wobbly metal computer tables for our first class. As we started, the electricians moved to the other room to hang the lights so we wouldn't be in total dark.

I was nauseous, and not only because I had no idea what was going to happen—in the next minutes, or the next year. I looked out the window at the ferns on the hillside in the morning light. I looked at my class, my school, squeezed around the tables.

"Uh. Okay, guys. I'm Tal. I'm the teacher. Zoe, what's your name?"

"Uh, Zoe?"

"Last name?"

"Um, Wright-Neil?"

"Are you sure? Because you say your name as though you weren't sure."

"I'm sure, I think," she said meekly. The others giggled quietly.

"Middle name?"

"Leora."

"What in the Sam Hill kind of name is that?"

"It means, um, 'light.'"

"Nice. Very bright, very sparkly. Did you know there is a lobster-woman in Maine named Zoe?"

"Uh, no." She was petrified.

"I read a calendar about her and it said that in Greek *Zoe* means 'life,'" I offered.

"I know."

"You know what? That I read a calendar in Maine, or that Zoe means 'life'?"

"Um, the second one?"

"Zoe. Life-Light. That's one of those names like the actor Canoe Reeves."

"Isn't it *Keanu*?" Mira said.

"Yeah, that's what I said. Canoe Reeves. He's a famous actor. Here's another one. Did you ever hear of the actor River Phoenix?"

They stared at me and shook their heads.

"He was a famous movie star back in my day, in the eighties. He was in a movie called *Stand By Me*. He once stayed at my house for a whole week. With all his scroungy, skeevy, slacker bandmates. He had a rock band when he wasn't acting."

"Skeevy? Scroungy?" asked Annie.

"Yeah, you know, rock 'n' rollers who don't practice personal hygiene. They invaded my house. They all had matted hair, wore the same clothes for days, and they slept till three in the afternoon. About twelve of them, draped on the furniture in my house like wilted, brown weeds. They were a bunch of complete losers, total cretins."

"What's a cretin?" asked Nick.

"Cretin? Look it up," I said. "Someone go get a dictionary." Janine scurried into the living room and brought back a tattered, duct-taped *Webster's*.

"Did I ever show you my high school dictionary?" I asked.

"Uh, no, especially since we've only been in school for ten minutes," said Annie.

"Someone look up *cretin*," I said.

We waited while Annie found the word and read the definition: "'Wretch, innocent victim. One afflicted with cretinism. A stupid, vulgar, or insensitive person. A clod or lout.'"

"That's what River Phoenix and his bandmates were, louts!" I shouted. "Greasy, unshaven, vulgar clods who talked all day about karma and played bad music."

I paused.

"A lot like teenagers."

A few of them giggled tentatively. The rest continued to stare.

"Are you implying that we're cretins?" Doug asked.

"Yes, I am. Okay. So that's our first vocabulary word: *cretin*. Can someone use it in a sentence?"

Doug volunteered. "On the first day of school, the teacher accused his students of being cretins."

Everyone laughed. Some of them wrote in their binders. The rest continued to stare at me with looks of apprehension.

I spoke to each student: What's your middle name? Who are your parents? What do they do?

"Where were you born?" I asked Tico.

"Honduras."

"Honduras? Do you know where Honduras is?"

Some of them nodded.

"Central America. Next to El Salvador and Nicaragua. But where, Tico? Where exactly?"

"La Ceiba."

"La Ceiba, Honduras. Did you guys get that?"

They nodded.

"Cool," said Nick.

"What about you, Mira?"

"Puna, India."

"Where's Puna?"

"Near Bombay. In the south."

"Goddamn, Mira. That's a hell of a long way. And what about you, Najat?"

"Morroco."

"Do you know where?"

"Not really."

"I'm asking you where you're from. It's important. Where you're from is going to be a part of everything we do. And I mean, *inside* of you. Where you are from, from what you are made."

They stared at me dumbly, off balance, at a distance, looking down, scratching a leg, waiting.

Then I asked the first serious, "academic" question in the history of the North Branch School: "Who knows what a mandala is?"

Mira raised her hand. "Isn't it like a Buddhist circle design thingy?"

"Yes, Mira, you're on the right track, especially about the 'circle thingy' part."

"Isn't it like some religious thing?" offered Nick.

"Well, it isn't *like* some religious thing. It *is* a religious thing," I said.

Then, without thinking, I blurted out, "Didn't your parents tell you this was a religious school?" I gazed at each of them. "North Branch is going to be a religious school."

"*What?*" Zoe mouthed, the word inaudible as she shrank against the back of her chair. The others stirred uncomfortably. A religious school? How much longer was the weird teacher going to go on like this?

"A mandala is of Hindu origin," I explained. "A representation of the cosmos, and also, sometimes, a reflection or microcosm of the soul."

"Micro-*what*?" said Nick.

I brought out Joseph Campbell's *The Power of Myth* and opened to pages showing mandalas from cultures around the world.

"Everybody come up here," I said, as I pushed the book to the middle of the table so everyone could huddle around, with our heads nearly touching. I wanted them close.

"See, the circle is the key," I explained. "It's a perfect whole. Not hole-in-the-ground. Whole as in what?"

"Complete," came the answer.

"Yes, complete, whole. Look. Here's a snake, in a circle, eating its tail, symbolizing rebirth and regeneration. And this is the rose window at Chartres Cathedral in France."

"Oh, I've seen that," said Nick.

"Is that a Buddhist one?" someone asked, pointing to an image of the Buddha sitting above a lotus flower.

"Yeah. And this one is a Navajo shield."

"That's so awesome," said Tico.

"Okay," I said. "That's what we're going to do. Doug, Tico, go get that box of markers and a stack of paper. We're going to make our own mandalas."

"Really? Coloring on the first day of school?" said Annie.

"But I want total silence," I said sternly. "Remember, this is a religious school. Be reverent. Heads down. Just draw. Start with a circle. It doesn't have to be a thing. Just whatever comes to mind. It can be random or divided into sections or total chaos. There's no right or wrong."

Some of them started immediately, with a clear idea. Others stared at their papers, or looked at me.

"If you don't know what to do, just start. Just make a mark and then another, and see where it goes," I said.

Soon they were all working, some within the lines, some outside. Nick made a geometric pattern with a compass. Doug worked on a Pollockian tangle of brown and black. Najat's was split neatly, like the yin-yang symbol, but with a sun and moon and a teardrop in the middle.

Tico colored so hard he tore through his paper. In the other room the sound of drills and clatter of hammers continued as the lights went up. At our tables, the soft scuffing of markers filling in open spaces.

After half an hour, they looked up. I asked them to take turns showing their drawings. It took some encouraging, since none of them knew if their work was right. They were timid because they were displaying, really, intimations of their souls, drawings of what each of them contained, a sort of free-form Rorschach. One by one they described the thoughts behind their images:

"The clouds are because sometimes I'm not clear about what to do."

"The crisscrossing lines are when I'm confused."

"Blue represents freedom from my bad thoughts."

"The tears coming from the eye are raindrops, because they're cleansing."

The conversation took all morning. We started in emptiness, in virtual dark, with nothing but ourselves and whatever I could draw out of them. By lunchtime, all the lights were on.

The second day I asked them to write speeches, short stories, really, to begin describing the school they wanted to create. I asked them to define what they needed to be themselves, openly and publicly, no matter if we crossed painful territory: *What experience has led you here, to this moment? What do you need here? What do you want to happen here?*

We sat around our two plastic folding tables next to the cold woodstove. With only two windows I felt as though we were conducting class in a dusty garage. The front door was wide open, and the bright woods beyond made a blinding patch against the dark wall. Brand-new track lights shone down over the heads of my school of ten students.

"Sophie, what do you want here at your new school?"

She spoke slowly and carefully, almost primly. "Um, I want to have fun and feel good in school." Her fingers were intertwined and resting neatly on her binder. She batted her eyes and her cheeks blushed red.

"Ah, so do I," I said. "I want to have fun too. But Sophie, is there anything slightly more compelling, something with a little more feeling, a little more pizzazz, that you can tell us?"

"What do you mean, 'feeling'?" Nick asked.

"I mean, Nick, like feeling. You know, like how you feel, man."

"Uh, okay."

"Uh, everyone join with me in song. Ready, a one and a two and a one-two-three—*Feee-lings, whoa oh oh fee-lings,*" I sang out in an off-key twang.

They looked at me with raised eyebrows and mild disapproval.

"*Fee-lings, whoa-oh-oh fee-lings!*" I sang again. Without a doubt I was the most idiotic teacher in New England.

"Stop!" came voices from around the table. They were perturbed and baffled.

"What is *that*?"

"It sounds like a dying cow."

"What it is, you guys," I said. "What I'm talking about is feelings, is—hey, how come you didn't sing with me?"

"That's the worst song I've ever heard," said Najat.

"Stop criticizing and listen. I'll tell you why you didn't sing. It's because you're self-conscious, you're scared, afraid to stand out, afraid to be different. It's easy to think you're different when you wear the same bitchin' skateboarding sweatshirt that ten million other teenagers are wearing, talking about 'no fear.' But as I always say, which of you nuts has got any guts? So let's try it again. A one and a two and a three— *Feeee-lings, whoa-oh-oh feee-lings.*"

They moaned and half mumbled along, not quite willing to go to such absurd lengths to please.

"Ahh! Could you please stop? *God.* You're breaking our eardrums," Najat complained, but she was smiling.

"Ah, Najat, I see your smile. I think you are starting to get the feeling, yes?"

"Yeah, right."

"Okay, look, Sophie, what I am talking about is this: What have you felt in school that was good that you want to feel *here*? What have you felt in school that was bad that you don't want to feel here? What I mean is, what depth do you have inside you besides wanting to have fun and feel good?"

"Umm . . ."

Silence followed, a silence I wanted. In it something real might emerge, something all the kids needed to hear, or might even be feeling themselves.

"Do you mean, like . . ."

"I mean, like, anything that you remember that you never want to feel again. Or something you believe you should *always* be feeling in school."

As she began to talk her lips quivered and a tear dripped out of her eyes.

"Go on. Keep talking. If you feel like crying, it's all right to cry."

"Last year my teacher got really mad one time at another kid and tipped his desk over and threw everything in it and shouted at him."

"And that scared you?"

She nodded.

"And did you think the kid deserved it?"

"Well, kind of. He never did his work. That's why Mr. J was mad. But it was only about spelling or something."

"So you understood why he was mad? But you didn't agree with what he did?"

She nodded again, with tears still tracking down her smooth cheeks. Annie placed a box of tissues in front of her.

"Feel free to use the special North Branch snotsy wipes that Annie has so generously placed before you."

She smiled and pressed her fingers against her eyes. "Thanks."

"But it scared you. Why?"

"Tal," said Mira. "Um, she's crying."

This defense, ostensibly altruistic, was in truth Mira's attempt to protect herself.

"Um, thanks for your input, Mira. I noticed she's crying. But the tears are where her knowledge is. Or I should say, the knowledge will come after the tears. Go on, Sophie. You said it scared you. Why?"

"Because I was afraid he would get mad at me. It felt like he didn't like us. It felt bad all the time. Well, not all the time, but that got into my thoughts."

"So your teacher made you fearful."

"Yeah."

"Rightly or wrongly?"

"Wrong, I guess. Well, he never got mad at me. But he just seemed angry, like he was out of control. It's like all he ever saw were things to get mad at."

"He didn't notice the good things?"

She shook her head.

"Were there any good things to notice about him?"

She shook her head.

"So for you, joy and happiness were sometimes hard to feel in school."

She nodded.

"And that's what you want to feel: joy, happiness, security?"

She nodded again.

"Why are those things important?"

"Because learning should be a good thing, a happy thing."

"Why?" I asked. "It's school. It's supposed to be rigorous and preparing you for life."

"Maybe," Annie offered, "it should prepare you to be happy?"

"Well, maybe. Sophie, I think you shouldn't fear your teacher in that way. Do you believe that?"

She nodded.

"I agree that you should feel some joy in school. And your teacher should be able to see other things besides what kids do wrong. And you don't want to feel fear, is that right, Sophie?"

"Yep," she said, as though she was all finished.

"So Sophie, that little story is what you write. That episode, that experience, Mr. J, the desk, the shouting, the fear you felt, all of it. That's how you come to know what you want to feel. And if you can show the feeling, you can make us believe it too. If you make us feel scared, if you make us feel how you cried, we'll also feel the need for joy and safety, and we'll work for it. We'll feel that what you say matters. Do you understand this?"

She nodded, and some of the others did too.

"Spiffy. But was that the only time you felt bad in school?"

She shook her head, and tears started again.

"When else?"

"I made fun of the same kid."

"Why? Was he mean? Ugly? A dork? A tool? Popular? Unpopular?"

"Um, he was really poor. We made fun of him because he didn't do his work, how he talked, and about his clothes."

"Didn't do his work? Isn't that the same reason Mr. J threw his stuff around."

"Yep."

"Did you make fun of him to his face or behind his back?"

"Behind," she whispered. "He always wore sweatpants with holes in the uh . . ."

"The crotch?" I said with an idiotic smile. "In the area of the midsection? In the area of the scro—"

She broke a little smile and wiped away some tears. "Yes, Tal."

"In the area of the scrotal sac?" I said gleefully.

"Tal!" they shouted.

"Okay, okay. So, Sophie, what does that have to do with feeling good here at the old alma mater, good old North Branch?"

"Tal, we have only been here for two days," said Mira. "It can't be our old alma mater, or whatever."

"Right. How true that is, Mira, how true that is. Go ahead, Sophie."

"I felt like a bad person. I felt bad because he couldn't help that he was poor."

"Why'd you do it?"

"I don't know."

"Were you the only one?"

"No, other kids did it too."

"If you felt it was wrong, why didn't you tell them to stop, or stop yourself?"

"Well, when we were doing it, it *was* fun. I wasn't even thinking about it. I mean, he didn't hear it. But I know it was bad. I kind of knew it then. I felt bad. Because I didn't want to get made fun of either. So I said it about him."

She was crying, but she smiled and looked up.

I smiled back at her. "Now do you know why you did it?"

She nodded, still smiling—the beautiful, relieved smile of a kid who has begun to understand something about how to mend herself.

"Because?"

"Because I was afraid. And I didn't say to anyone to stop because I was afraid."

"So, let's see. You want to feel like your teachers are mentally stable, fair, and like you? You want to not tease people. You know you yourself don't want to be teased like that boy was teased, no matter how poor or unfashionable. Perhaps you want to be in a school to find out why you teased him? You want to feel safe and feel joy, and that's what you need to feel good in school and have fun."

"Yeah."

"That, and you want to make sure everyone who wears sweatpants has the crotch part sewn—"

"Very funny."

"Then that's your speech. Does everyone in here understand this?"

The others were watching and listening with an intensity I'd hoped for but had not expected. What was happening inside Sophie and around our table was real, true, and interesting. If my students could feel what she was saying, then perhaps they would begin to feel their own stories inside of themselves too.

"Listen, you cretins, she knows what she wants. But she's got to tell us the story of how she learned it. First come the feelings, then the knowledge. Then we can believe her, or even follow her."

"So Tal, you want us to like, get all psycho?" asked Mira.

"I wouldn't say like psycho, Mira. I would say: Tell a true story that matters."

As Frost suggested in "Mending Wall," we sometimes must go behind the wall, to search behind the first, simple words. In the beginning of North Branch, that's all I knew to do. I didn't have anything else except the students in front of me. The first simple words and the feelings from which they were born.

Harry Crews wrote in his memoir *A Childhood*: "Only the use of *I*, lovely and terrifying word, would get me to the place where I needed to go." The only stories that mattered were the ones born from lived experience. I asked them to embrace the personal pronoun *I* so that we might come closer to what was sacred inside of them. Those truths—*their* truths—would bring us closer to what mattered.

Tico wanted not to be made fun of because he couldn't read. Doug wanted to be free to pursue knowledge without being called a geek. Mira wanted to have a friendship that wasn't based on power. Steve wanted to know that he would not have his head bashed into a locker. Nick wanted to stop following the popular kids and making fun of his friends, mainly Doug. Janine wanted to know what it felt like to have a friend. Najat wanted to feel comfortable as a brown girl in a place where there were not many others who looked like her. And Sophie wanted to feel joy.

These were the first stories, and that was how we began to know each other.

The next day we gathered around the tables, leaning back in chairs against the sagging plywood bookshelves. Notebooks and scrap paper lay scattered under Nick's gargantuan feet resting on the table.

"Nick, get your feet off the table. It's time for class." He dropped them to the floor. Tico bounced through the room like a pinball, bumping into chairs.

"Tico! Goddammit, let's go!"

When they had all settled we started up again.

"All right, you little teenyboppers. What did you think about yesterday? How do you like your new school?"

"Uh, I guess it's pretty neat," said Annie.

"That's real in depth, Annie, and very fascinating. Whaddaya like about it?"

"Well, it was weird that Sophie cried. But it was good. I mean, that would never happen at my old school. You would be, like, harassed until you met your gruesome death by roving bands of bullies."

"You mean that people would not show their feelings like Sophie did because it would leave them vulnerable?"

"What's vulnerable mean?" asked Nick.

"Open to being wounded."

"You'd be killed at my school," said Tico.

"Killed? You mean, like whacked? Popped? Iced? Gunned down?"

"No. You know what I mean." He was glaring.

"No, I want you to say what you mean."

"You would be teased. You just didn't do it. You could never cry."

"But Tico, I have noticed that you yourself are sometimes walking around with your hat pulled down low and wearing your wicked cool shades and sagging your pants like some wannabe gangster. Is that like, your disguise, so you can hide from the thugs, or pretend to be one, or not ever have to cry?"

"Very funny." He pulled his hat down lower over his eyes.

"Yes, it was very funny."

"Whatever."

"Uh, Tico, don't say 'whatever.'"

He looked at me sullenly.

"Listen, you dimwits: Saying 'whatever' means you've stopped thinking because you're afraid of what will happen if you *keep* thinking. Or of what will happen if you start feeling."

I waited for a moment. They didn't argue.

"So look. Annie, you mean to tell me that you would never cry in school? You mean no one cried? That's crazy. Crying is part of being human, and there's a reason everyone does it. It's how we cleanse out what is gritty and hurting inside of us."

They stared at me.

"I cry every day. Especially when I come here."

"Ha-ha," said Najat, staring at me with her lips pursed tightly.

Steve raised his hand. He looked scared, slouching there with his baseball hat askew, his basketball shoes untied, his hair greasy and un-combed, but he was polite.

"*I* thought it was okay that she cried," he said.

"It wasn't strange? Wrong? Uncool?"

"No, I thought it was good."

"Why?"

"I guess because she was telling us something important. If she didn't cry, we wouldn't know anything important. Or about her."

"And Steve, if crying happened at your other school?"

"If anything happened, the person went to the resource room and everyone gossiped about it because no one knew what happened."

"I feel like that sometimes," said Zoe. She sat crunched down in her chair with her shoulders folded in, her face pale. Her lips were bright with lipstick, her eyes heavy with mascara. She did not look bright or free. "Like Sophie, I mean. Like Steve said. There's nothing *wrong* with crying."

"Sophie," I asked, "did you feel embarrassed that you cried?"

"A little. I guess because I didn't know what people were going to say."

"How does hearing what Steve said make you feel?"

"Good. Like crying was okay."

"So it turned out okay? Any bullies assault you?"

"No, not yet."

"Tico, did you assault or harass her because she cried."

"Ha-ha. No, Tal, not yet." He tried to look tough but he was suppressing a smile.

Steve raised his hand again. "I appreciated that we didn't have science so we could keep talking. I mean I know science is important. At my old school we could never change the schedule.

"You mean like how we talked the whole afternoon about your stories for your speeches?"

"Yeah, it was like you let us keep talking because that was what was important. It was like we were freer or something."

"Can we do that now? Keep talking and skip science?" Nick asked brightly, with a big phony smile and dancing eyebrows.

"No!" I said. "Go to science."

L ike animals in new territory, the kids were bound to try to establish some kind of pecking order. It began predictably, with Mira gathering Tico, Steve, and Nick by her side at lunch and proceeding to cut glances at the geeks—Doug and Annie, who sometimes talked into imaginary watch-radios on their wrists.

As I was about to start class after lunch on the fourth day, Annie did not come in when we rang the bell.

"Can someone tell me where Annie is?" I called out.

"She's out in the woods," said Najat.

"What the hell is she doing out there?"

"Mira said something to her and she got upset. She's up in a tree in the woods."

"Up in a *tree*? What the hell is she doing?"

"Mira said something. Like Annie doesn't even know what masturbation is or something."

It could have been, *God, you're such a fag.* It could have been, *She's so fat* or *He's so fucking dumb*—anything that marked a difference, anything that established a hierarchy or closed off one person from another.

Having a student disappear into the woods on the fourth day of school was not an auspicious beginning. In fact, it portended disaster.

"Go get her. Hurry up. Everyone else, get your asses in here." Sophie and Najat dashed out to bring her in. They returned escorting Annie, who had her head bowed and her face pressed into her blue bandana.

When we were up to the table I asked, "What in the hell is going on?"

Annie still cradled her face, hunched over the edge of her chair.

"What's going on? We need to know, now. We don't have a lot of time so let's get to it."

We had plenty of time, we had all day—and there was no way I could send them home without some sort of resolution. They had to know that some kinds of behavior could not, and would not, be tolerated.

"Mira," I said.

"What?"

Najat raised her hand. "I think Mira said something that upset Annie. I mean, I don't think she meant to make her upset. Um, but Annie heard it. Annie and Doug were playing, I don't know, some game. I don't know what Mira said but it was something like 'she doesn't even know what touching herself is.'"

"I appreciate your forthrightness, Najat," I said.

"We were playing a game and it totally didn't involve you, Mira," Doug said with a fierceness I had not seen before.

Mira rolled her eyes.

"Mira, you must have said something, something like what Najat said. Maybe it wasn't exactly what she said, but it's probably close enough. Don't roll your eyes. It's ugly and makes you look satanically possessed and not very smart."

"I was just joking. *God.* I didn't mean it for her to freak out."

"But whatever exactly it was didn't exactly make her feel like, you know, the champion of the world."

She stared at the table and pulled her hair behind her ears.

"Were you trying to make her feel bad? Did you want her to know that you were the one who could make mean remarks while she played innocent, playful games at lunch?"

"I don't know. I wasn't thinking anything. I wasn't really even talking to her."

"Were you kissing up to Tico and Steve?" I asked.

"What?"

"I mean, kissing their butts. You know, their asses. Trying to impress them. Sucking up to them. Trying to sound like you know it all. Trying to be cool. Doing the things that make you popular, which is another word for having a lot of friends who are either afraid of you or are using you to get popular."

"I wasn't trying to be cool."

"You all were sitting out there on the porch talking, and Annie and Doug are running around in the woods. They're geeks, and maybe you're feeling like you're the wicked cool kids. Know what I mean?"

"I don't know. Why do you have to analyze everything? God."

"Because I'm smart. Because if I don't, you won't learn. How many times have you said, 'I don't know'? You keep saying it because you *don't* know. You have power but you use it wrong and without awareness. So I'll analyze, and you tell me if I get something not quite right. Okay?"

"Okay." She was irritated and uncomfortable.

"So Mira, maybe you weren't thinking this, but it's a feeling inside you. Here you are in a new school, no one is sure who is friends with whom, and you're thinking, 'Who will be my friends so I won't be alone?'"

This exposed Mira, but she was looking and listening.

"Maybe you, maybe all of you, are a little afraid in this new school. You don't know what's going to happen, so you put up defenses, you know, like teenage mutant porcupines or something. You're talking to Steve and Nick, and you don't know them, but they're not total geeks, and you don't know what to say, they don't know what to say, so you take the most convenient path, and you pick out a weakness in someone or something else. You go for the first available target."

The others looked at me and nodded. Mira stared.

"I'm wondering why, Annie, if it was just the words that were said, why you're so upset. Something really freaked you out, more than Mira possibly could have intended. But you still could just have ignored her and kept running around in the woods with Doug, right?"

Annie was bent over, her head buried between her knees. She nodded.

"But you couldn't ignore it?"

She nodded again.

"So what's going on, Annie? Something struck you. Mira's comment struck you, much harder than she meant to, to the point where you're hiding in the trees and burying your head."

I had to pursue it, knowing where it was headed. Unraveling social upheavals, defusing trauma, pushing for the truth, making them cry, letting them cry, making them say what they were feeling, however uncomfortable or inconvenient, was the only way to engage them, disarm them, teach them. Otherwise the walls would only get higher, the truth untouched, and whoever they were, or could be, would remain hidden.

Annie mumbled something.

"I can't hear you, Annie, because you are having an intimate conversation with your knees and a tear-soaked bandana."

Everyone laughed. Annie's body shook a little, but I wasn't sure if she was laughing or sobbing. She mumbled again.

"Can you please say it in a way that I can hear, Annie?"

She lifted her head and whispered, "I was sexually molested when I was four."

The room was absolutely still.

"Did you guys hear what she said?"

They nodded.

"Do you all know what that means?"

They nodded.

"It means someone did an unwanted sexual action to Annie. Violated her and her space."

They sat silently.

"Did any of you know that before now?"

"I heard about something happening to Annie," Doug offered. "But I never really knew what it was."

"Annie, when Mira made the comment, do you think she knew about what happened to you?"

"No."

"Did you, Mira?"

"No."

"So there was no way for her to know that she was saying something that would make you so uncomfortable about something from your past, right?"

"But," Doug said, "she still shouldn't have said it because it was rude and mean and wrong."

"True. But the reason for being rude and mean, the bigger reason behind it, we can figure out. We can figure out the source of it and the consequence for being rude and mean, and we can even decide whether we will tolerate it. But sometimes we say things without realizing that those things are bombs. They hurt in ways we couldn't imagine, far beyond our intent."

They nodded.

"Annie, the thing that happened, one time or more than one time?"

She was wringing the bandana for all it was worth.

"One time. A girl who was babysitting me. She still lives in Branbury. When my dad was giving a guitar lesson."

"So Mira's comment hit a raw feeling. So Mira is partially guilty, but not totally, for how you're feeling now."

"Is it that big a deal?" Mira asked.

"It's a huge freaking deal if you were putting her down to bring yourself up. Showing off your knowledge, whatever. It's a big deal if the thing you put her down for is something you yourself are uncomfortable about, or to gain social power or status. It's a big deal if you're Annie. Apparently a lot of things make her extremely uncomfortable. It's a feeling that she can't control. And as far as I can tell, she hasn't done one thing wrong. Not here, not when she was four. She's never done anything wrong, but here she is on the fourth day of school crying and climbing up trees. So yeah, it's a big deal."

"Well, I didn't know," Mira said.

"I know, Mira, I know you didn't know. How could you?"

She dipped her head and twisted her black hair in her fingers.

"Annie," I said. "You are great. No matter what some kid did. You are still good. Angelic even. You never did anything wrong. So you're still afraid. That's okay. It's even okay to say, 'Hey, goddammit, nobody is going to make me feel that way here.'"

She nodded in her bandana and mumbled something.

"What'd you say?"

Nick answered for her. "She said, 'I don't curse, but I understand.'"

"So you understand: This was not sex or love. Sex is gentle, intimate, caring, loving between two people who know each other, who love each other, who feel safe with each other. What happened to Annie was something else, something hurtful and unwanted."

They nodded silently.

There was so much more to do. We had only barely begun to talk, to listen to each other. Mira was somewhere deep inside herself. She looked at Annie, and then toward me. That was enough for now.

On the first Friday we hiked to Lake Pleiad, a glacial depression nestled among the downhill ski trails of the Middlebury College Snow Bowl. We ate our lunches in the sun on a massive granite ledge sloping toward the glittering water. Then I sent them into the woods to make sculptures out of whatever they could find.

"Once you find your spot, not a damn word, you cretins, or you'll break the spell. The only sound I want to hear is the cracking of twigs and the wind in the trees." Still, I imagined them going off into some shady glade and just saying, "To hell with making these lame-ass fairy houses—we're teenagers now."

They scattered along the shore and into the woods. I walked among them, watching as they knelt on the ground between roots, staring at the woods around them, then scurrying about looking for materials. I *could* hear twigs snapping and the wind in the trees and the soft footsteps of my students on the pine-needle floor. And they *did* build moss-covered fairy houses, or teetering towers, or spiraling designs of brilliant red leaves curling into the shadows under rock ledges. Janine wove grasses among limbs of a goosefoot maple. Tico built an entire human-sized lean-to out of fallen limbs speared into a rotted stump. Zoe built a winding staircase with twigs the size of hairpins. She crouched at the foot of a fir tree, hunched so close to the ground that her hair dragged in the dirt.

They worked with the innate intensity of small children in sandboxes, as though they had telescoped themselves back in time. Their sculptures were mandalas in three dimensions, constructed beyond the walls of any room, beyond dictates, entirely outside the lines. They stopped only when I told them that we were running out of time.

We toured each structure. On a September afternoon in the heart of the Green Mountains they told each other tales about little queens who lived in fairy kingdoms, whose minions walked along gold-leafed roads under arching fern fronds and golden lichens. They told stories about imaginary civilizations whose fortunes depended on protecting Earth from cataclysmic doom. We kneeled down to peer into the doorways of little sanctuaries furnished with fully set tables, downy moss beds, and acorn bowls filled with seeds.

It didn't take much for them to forget how old they were.

I told them they were going to write the North Branch School newsletter.

"What news?" Annie asked. "We've only been in school like, seven days."

Annie could get wound up and chattering about anything from

aliens to Revolutionary War surgical techniques. Often I had to tell her to be quiet and sit on her hands. I'd figured she'd have a lot to say about what we were doing.

"How about the news that we started a school, you wing nut. Everything we're doing. A bunch of teenyboppers in the woods."

"We're not teenyboppers," said Mira. "And who would want to read it? No one is going to care about what we're doing," said Mira. "I mean this is like the freakiest place ever. It's like, not even a school. We don't even have a clock. We don't even have a computer."

"Listen, I don't give a damn about a computer. I don't give a rat's ass about what we *have*. What I'm interested in is telling people what we're *doing*. We have supporters out there who want to know what their money is getting them. You know, the big donors."

That was partly true—we did have many people who had made small donations. Pretending we were swimming in money made me feel like the school might actually be succeeding and that more than ten of us cared about what was going to happen here.

"Tal, that's pathetic," said Doug. "How can someone who presumes to be all about learning be so corrupt?"

"My power knows no bounds. We'll send the newsletter to all the people who gave us money before you guys even signed up to come here. You may not believe this, but there're a lot of people who have a deep interest in what happens at this school."

I told them about a former student who had sent us a ten-dollar bill to buy a copy of *To Kill a Mockingbird*. They were moderately impressed.

We set about recording our first week's activities: hiking the Long Trail, constructing our Andy Goldsworthy sculptures, and our "egg drop" competition, when we climbed onto the porch roof to launch our egg-protection devices onto the mossy deck. We reported on a relatively rare and endangered carnivorous plant, the sundew, we'd found growing on the big hill; our discovery of a wily mouse in the kitchen cabinet that had eaten an entire bag of Cape Cod potato chips and eluded our attempts to capture him. We wrote about marking out our nature trail, the clay masks we were going to make, and our speeches on "what we want in a school." We wrote about making our school sign, on which Sophie had originally misspelled "North *Branh*."

"That's great, Sophie! When people visit our school they'll see that we can't even spell the name of our school," I said.

"Hey, that's not a bad idea," said Doug. "They'll feel sorry for us because we can't spell and then they'll donate large sums of money."

We reported on the answering machine at the school that, unknown to us during the first week, announced: "You have reached Astrid Menya, certified deep tissue massage therapist. If you would like to set up an appointment, please leave your number." No appointments were made, and we changed the message.

We wrote about our class time capsule, which included each student's descriptions of "one important thing I did for someone else this week." They thought this an odd question to ask but they relished discussing it. Doug had helped his mother with her piano practice. Zoe had combed her sister's hair before school. Mira had given half her lunch to Steve, who didn't ever seem to have one. They suddenly had a glimpse into each other not only as schoolmates but as complex constellations of needs and attributes, which included an awareness of others.

Compiling nice deeds done was not part of the State of Vermont school standards. In fact, nothing we did the first weeks would fit any school district's curriculum rubric. I understood the state's standards but didn't care much about them. I cared about understanding my students and learning who they were and how to make them feel they were making something new and important. I cared about what they yearned to know and understand.

When the articles were written we sat in a jumbled half circle on the deck in rotting Adirondack chairs among the dried-up remains of shattered eggs. I figured they were as interested as I was to see what form we were taking, so we read our work aloud as we sat in the afternoon shade. They responded as though they were hearing a tape-recording of themselves: curious, smiling, a little embarrassed.

"So," I said, "what are we going to call this fine work of literary reportage? What do you all think of 'The Compass'?"

"Uh, that's okay, Tal, but . . ."

"Don't you think 'The Compass' is good?"

"Well, uh . . ."

"What are your ideas, then?"

They tossed out possibilities. "The North Star." "The Reporter." "The Ripton Times." "The North Branch Globe."

Then Doug said, "How about 'The Current'? You know, the *current* news events, and also the *current* of the North Branch River, the flow of events? Pretty tricky eh, eh?" He was delighted with his suggestion.

We voted and *The Current* won unanimously, to great acclaim. They loved it because it was theirs.

When the single greatest historical event of the previous forty years happened on September 11, 2001, the North Branch School was hopelessly unprepared to follow events. Alone together, tucked away in the shade of pines in a mountain hollow, we were virtually cut off from the entire world.

We gathered on the deck for morning meeting. The breeze and early sun filtered through the pines. The phone rang. The message said two planes had crashed into the World Trade Center towers, which I announced to the kids with enough gravity in my voice to suggest that it was important, though I had no idea—and didn't care much—about what had happened or what it might mean.

They all immediately wanted to see if it was on television.

"Plane wrecks are a dime a dozen, you guys. Come on."

Undeterred, they moaned, "Pleeease."

After all, what could I teach them that might compare to history happening?

We found an old black-and-white television in a closet, but when Tico turned it on we got only static. Nick ran through the house looking for a radio but there was no radio. So all ten kids and I piled into my Plymouth Voyager. We found the public radio station and heard the first-person reports from dust-filled apartment buildings in New York City.

My students would one day become a part of the world beyond these mountains. And I taught with all my heart so that my students would want to be a part of it. I wanted them to be excited to let themselves grow up and live. But I never felt more isolated than I did then, sitting behind the steering wheel with my whole school in a rutted driveway, wondering if I'd ever want to let go of them at all.

Seamus Heaney, the great Irish poet, wrote about his notions of artistic self-expression, about his own nascent understanding of himself as a writer, maker, and seer in the poem "Personal Helicon." He reminiscees on his childhood curiosity about wells, how he loved to peer into the darkness, to listen to the sounds, and how he "loved the dark drop, the trapped sky, the smells / Of waterweed, fungus and dank moss."

The meaning of wells for him resided in their aural, tactile, olfactory, and visual richness. The world reflected through his senses so acutely that the well became a mirror, a field of vision, a penetrating power—a space that "had echoes, gave back your own call / With a clean, new music in it." The poem concludes:

Now, to pry into roots, to finger slime,
To stare, big-eyed Narcissus, into some spring
Is beneath all adult dignity. I rhyme
To see myself, to set the darkness echoing.

I wanted our school to become a place where "prying into roots"—of matter, belief, idea, and ourselves—was the essential ongoing activity. As a teacher I did not so much want to impart some body of predetermined information but to present the world as a realm to be sounded, charted, and uncovered.

We did this when writing their goals for themselves and the school; debating concepts of loyalty, honesty, and self-understanding; or by establishing the principles upon which they wanted to be evaluated. They pried into roots when they explored their beliefs and experiences, or when they drew and analyzed mandalas. They set the darkness echoing when they built sculptures from found materials in the woods under the shade of pines, kneeling on the soft earth—at just the right remove from all adult dignity.

I looked back on our first dozen days together. On the second day I had asked them to draw their hands—something close, something integral—the hands with which we would make this school. We spent the afternoon doing some preliminary drawings, spread out around the school, some sitting in the warm light of the sunroom windows, others in the Adirondack chairs on the deck. Though not particularly enthralled doing a difficult task, they worked diligently and amiably. There was quiet talk and laughter and lighthearted moans of despair.

"This doesn't look like my *hand*," said Annie.

"Tal," Steve called, "my thumb looks like a dead stump."

"Just draw what you see, Steve," I said.

Those first images were mostly rendered small and timidly—small hands, thin fingers drawn lightly in the corner of a page, with a wide field of paper all around. My students were holding something back, cautious about making too many wrong marks, not sure what the hand could do.

I wanted to believe that they would learn to feel safe enough and be bold enough to enlarge the expression. Then the drawings would take on nuances of tone, emotion, perspective, depth, and grace. I told myself: *They will learn to surrender and see, listen, and shape the reflection looking back at them.*

I listened to the quiet scuff of graphite on paper and gentle erasures. I strolled outside, hoping in silence, watching them work with their heads bent, creating tentative echoes of themselves. The sun was warm, the sky a deep clear blue, wind blowing through the hemlocks on the top of the hill. It occurred to me that the school I had imagined *was* happening—a physical place, concrete and real, existing after nearly a year of making.

E ach morning I drove to school from New Haven, a farm town in the valley, a half-hour drive. Each morning I listened to the music of John Coltrane. Of the manifold glories of his art I was mesmerized by the way he had continually pushed his tradition to the furthest edges, creating dimensions in sound that had never before been imagined. I felt a kinship with that process, not because I was creating great art but because I felt keenly the loneliness of being out on the edge doing something that no one, not even me, truly understood.

When I listened to "Brasilia" or "Soul Eyes" I did not consider lesson plans, standards, methodology, or even our subject. I thought about what it was like to be feeling forward in the dark. What were we going to do to make it through the day, or to the end, when I didn't know exactly what the end should be?

My answer had nothing to do with standards, pedagogical rubrics, econometric measures, or test-score improvement. I would think instead about what story I could tell to confront whatever problem was infecting our class. Were they working hard? Why weren't they prepared for discussion? Were they taking care of the building? Why weren't they being generous with each other? When they were in the presence of something beautiful, could they feel the beauty of that thing?

"Have you guys ever heard of John Coltrane?" I asked them one morning.

"Who's that?" asked Steve.

"He's a god of the alto saxophone. He's a great jazzman. He's a genius."

"Cool, Tal," said Mira.

"He was as good a jazz musician as Hemingway was a writer."

They looked at me dumbly.

"Did you know that Hemingway rewrote the last paragraph of *The Sun Also Rises* twenty-nine times until he got it exactly the way it needed to be?"

"Wow," said Annie.

"Do you have any inkling about or appreciation for why he did that?"

"Because it was important?" said Janine.

"Because he didn't want to make any mistakes?" said Tico.

"Of course he didn't want to make any mistakes, you nimrods. Of course it was important. Every word, every tone, every sentence mattered. His life—life itself—depended on it. That's how come when we read him seventy-five years later we feel life coming from the page and holding our hearts. He was making something that was new in the world."

"Whoa, don't get all worked up, Tal," said Najat.

"Najat, this is what's worth getting worked up about. Someone who gave his heart to the world, a gift to us. Coltrane practiced for five hours a day, even when he was playing better than anyone else had ever played in history."

"That *is* cool," said Nick.

"You're goddamn right it's cool. When I was little, and I couldn't sleep, my dad would read me parts of *The Sun Also Rises*. He would read me the part about when Jake and Bill go fishing on the Irati River in

Spain. I can still remember how I felt when I heard that part of the story. I remember the trout, and the pools of water, and the wet ferns where they kept the fish they caught. It was music to me."

Hemingway had no meaning for them, but they listened, and I hoped they heard.

"Coltrane's song 'Naima' is the same. He wrote it for his wife. It's a love song and it's beautiful. Perhaps one day you will grasp the profound meaning of it."

"Tal, you know who is like, so great?" Najat said. "Christina Aguilera."

"Oh, that's so typical, Najat," said Doug.

"It is not. She is so great."

"Wonderful, Najat. But Christina Aguilera is not John Coltrane."

"Well, to me she is."

I promised myself I would bring in "Naima" to see if they could be changed.

Later, I read to them Richard Wilbur's poem "The Writer." Surely they could hear the music in the beauty of a father's wish for his child and, perhaps, even, their own parents' wishes for them.

When we read it aloud, the words of the poem hovered in the air, and then disappeared.

"What're your reactions?"

"It's pretty cool," said Steve.

"Cool? Cool? Do you see anything in the poem about the weather being cold?"

"You know what I mean. Like how the guy is listening to the girl type her story."

"My mom has an old typewriter," said Najat.

"Goddammit, you guys. This poem is not about a typewriter. Poets don't write about typewriters. They write about the feelings that matter. What do you think this poet is trying to tell us?"

"So, like—" Nick started. But he had no idea of how to enter the discussion.

"Go on, Nick. Try. Say something."

"Well, there's the bird. Is he saying that the girl and the bird are the same?"

"That's a decent start, Nick."

"Um, maybe—" His idea, whatever it was, was stillborn.

"Maybe," offered Steve, "he means that her writing is like a ship of words she rides into the future."

"That's great, Steve." Yet as I listened he seemed to be doing no more than reading an old recipe. His heart, wherever it was, was not in his speech.

I could ask a hundred questions, but I could not make them become ecstatic or possessed. They might understand "The Writer," but they did not believe in it. The words and the prayer that the poem was— it did not move them.

I railed at myself. I concluded I had not taught the poem well. My method was wrong. What words should I have used? Did I provide an emotional context or reason for us to engage it? "See better, Lear," Kent implores his king. How could I make them hear and see better?

The space I had to fill was so huge and empty. I never knew whether we were putting the right sounds or words in the right places, with the correct emphasis or tone. How to give harmonic structure to something so unformed? How was this song going to resolve itself?

We traveled alone, utterly stranded, often blind, among the whispering pines in the heart of the Green Mountain National Forest. The unavoidable fact was that every single day was like writing a new score. Every day was a test, the same test that each of us confronts once the artifice of schooling ends: We had to learn how to live with and love each other and move ourselves forward.

I wanted social studies to be tangible, real, and local. I chose Vermont history not because I knew much about it but because I thought it would give us the greatest number of reasons to take field trips. As much as I liked the freedom we had in our new school, it was small and lonely with ten teenagers every day.

Before our first trip I was afraid of what might happen, afraid my students would be the unruly wild ones, the ones for whom the rules were made, terrorizing kindly bespectacled tour guides or infecting quiet museum rooms with vacant, apathetic gazes.

I struggled to explain how I wanted them to comport themselves.

"Listen, when we go out to the museum, you gotta give something. If we go all the way there you better not piddle around. I mean, you have a choice. You can sit there on a bench being bored, like brain-dead dimwits, or you can look at the stuff and learn. Do you cretins understand what I'm saying?"

Doug raised his hand. "You want us to be sponges of knowledge."

"Exactly! I want you to be sponges of knowledge. If you aren't, I will kill you dead with my bare hands."

"You won't kill us dead."

"I will. I will kill you dead if you are a brain-dead dimwit."

"How can you kill us dead?" asked Janine. "Isn't that like doing the same thing twice?"

"I will kill you dead if you aren't sponges of knowledge. Then I will kill you dead again."

It was easy to jump in two vans and head off on field trips. My Plymouth Voyager, which Doug had dubbed "the Golden Chariot of Knowledge," could carry half the school if we tossed the car seats into the back. Mia often brought the other half, along with the dog hair, hockey equipment, muddy cleats, and empty tomato boxes that littered her van. We visited Mount Independence, a Revolutionary War site, picnicking under the giant maple trees. We viewed the collection of

Impressionist paintings at the Electra Havemeyer Webb collection at the Shelburne Museum. We toured a replica of a classic English barn and took turns using an eighteenth-century adze and drawshave.

In science Eric had them study local tree species and forest succession. We climbed to the top of the Skylight Pond trail, observing the differences between varieties of maples and the way the deciduous trees thinned at the higher elevations. We learned terms that applied to our local landscape: *switchback, goosefoot, star moss, vert mont.* From a ledge on Bread Loaf mountain, we gazed over Ripton, to the broad, green patchwork valley and southern Lake Champlain as it stretched west in the haze to the Adirondacks. We visited a logging site in the hollow, tasted and spat out the silt in mountain streams in order to identify soil types. We walked down to the North Branch River to eat lunch on the boulders, and someone always fell into the clear, rushing water.

We hiked the trails around Ripton and made a time line of the history of Earth scaled down and compressed into one kilometer, each millimeter representing 4,600 years. Each student was given a prehistoric time period like the Precambrian or Jurassic, and as we ticked off the meters, each student posted a sign on the trail to mark the beginning of each epoch. The whole way Doug sang a dirge for the woebegone Silurians, and at the end we discovered that the historical span of Vermont's statehood amounted to one-eighteenth of a millimeter in relation to the previous thousand meters, and my students' own lives were equal to the width of a human hair. On the walk back to the vans we all discussed what might have come in the infinite kilometers before the one we had just walked.

We had visitors: Jon Gailmor, a musician, who played a song for us called "Geek Mythology"; Landon Smith, a retired dairy farmer, who shared portions of his collection of eight thousand Abenaki artifacts. A local ceramicist brought clay she had extracted from the banks of the Winooski River—the same source of clay that would have been used by the Abenaki—for a day of pot building. The "Thomas Jefferson Lady" visited and brought a grab bag of items for us to pull from a burlap sack, each one connected to Thomas Jefferson.

Tico later wrote: "History is not my favorite subject. If someone told me that we were going to study Thomas Jefferson, I wouldn't think that would be fun. But, when the Thomas Jefferson lady came in with a shirt like the American flag and a cloth bag that she asked us to pick things out of, it got interesting."

Eric's wife, Su, taught us to fold origami cranes and we spent a week making hundreds of cranes as part of our decorations for a fund-raiser for the Middlebury community food shelf. Tico knew the story of Sadako Sasaki, the young girl who was two at the time of the Hiroshima bombing and ten years later died of leukemia. He told the whole story: how Sadako had attempted to fold one thousand paper cranes (*senbazuru*), believing she would get well by doing so, and the Japanese legend that folding senbazuru would so please the gods that the folder would be granted a wish. Tico told us how Sadako had wished to get well. Afterward, with the memory of September 11 still fresh, we all wrote what we hoped the peace cranes might mean. Tico wrote: "It's kind of like a prayer you can see."

We built a short nature trail that wound through the woods and ended at the top of the hill looking down on our small, dilapidated school. Another day I brought an atlatl, a spear-throwing device used throughout prehistory by indigenous peoples from around the world, including Vermont's Abenaki. We spent several lunches hurling the steel-tipped spear over the fern-covered hillside, attempting to skewer a cardboard box—which I told them represented a woolly mammoth—in violation of numerous codes, safety regulations, and common sense. Throwing spears in the woods with teenagers was the antithesis of headmasterly behavior, but it was a way to engage them, to get to know them, to rattle the cage of convention.

At times it seemed that we had *all* been let out of that cage, and we were standing around in bewilderment, overwhelmed with newfound freedom—no schedule, no demands from administrators, no new laws with which to comply, no tests to administer, no assemblies to attend, no curricula to adhere to, no bureaucracy to circumvent. Morning break or lunch could extend if we were hunting a woolly mammoth, or if the sun was warm on our backs.

E arly in the fall, I decided that we would make ceramic masks, knowing that even adolescents loved playing with clay, rooted as it is in some of our most basic impulses—the need to make and destroy, the freedom to poke, twist, and mold—the whole unbounded universe of mud pies, puddles, and sandboxes—and the joy of trying to make something out of nothing.

I knew little about teaching with clay, but I asked Zoe's dad to bring up two bags so we could start. After we had pounded on the clay for a bit I announced a contest.

"Okay, you hoodlums," I said, "here's the deal. Everyone has a ball of clay about yea big to build a tower. Whoever builds the tallest tower wins, but it has to stand up for ten seconds. I will do the official measuring."

"Tal, what is 'yea big' and why do you call us hoodlums?" asked Janine.

"Yea big is about this big, my little friend." I held up a ball of clay the size of a baseball. "I think you know the answer to the other question."

"Tal, Sophie's lump is bigger than mine," Najat moaned. Sophie stuck out her tongue at Najat and then gave her a smidgen of extra clay.

"Tal, I am going to like, *so* win this contest," said Tico. "Tal, I am going to like, open a can of whup-ass."

They howled with laughter.

"It's just like you disgraceful adolescents to be worried about whether you can win," I announced. "You spend too much energy on superficialities and not enough on substance and meaning."

"You are a hypocrite!" said Doug. "I do recall that you made this into a bloody competition."

"Start building, you adolescent freaks! Or Tico's going to open a can of whup-ass on you."

The room filled with a noisy flurry of clay pounding and laughing. They poked, twisted, and molded. They tossed little balls of clay and marked their cheeks with brown smudges.

"Look, Tal," said Mira. "I made an evil snake. Look, he's got fangs and he's smiling."

"Tal, I've got it," Nick shouted. "Look! Tal, I'm going to win. Quick, measure my tower!"

"Nick, you idiot, stop shaking the table!" Tico shouted.

"Tal! Where is the tape measure? I want an official record!"

"Nick, goddammit, can't you see I'm busy with my own tower. I'm trying to win this competition. I'm opening a can of whup-ass!"

"All males are disgusting competitive creatures," said Zoe. "Competition is for mental midgets and Neanderthals. I am trying to make a Happy Little Tower. See, Tal, do you see my tower? I made it with this teeny ball of clay."

On the table in front of Zoe was a tower the size of her pinky.

"Isn't it cute!"

"Zoe, we do not want cute towers. We're trying to build *up*, for God's sake! Get with the program."

Steve's tower, thin as a stick of spaghetti, slowly drooped over and dipped to the table.

"I suck at clay!"

"Nobody can suck at clay," said Mira, who was busy stabbing her lump of clay as though it was a voodoo doll. "Maybe you just suck at building towers."

"Well, I think I suck at clay. My tallest tower is only seven inches. It won't stand up."

"You don't suck, Steve," I said. "You are a wonderful youngster. Keep trying."

"You have to give it a buttress, if you had been listening to Tal," Doug said, as though all the rest of the world were ignoramuses. "You know, the architectural structures that hold up cathedrals."

"Are you kidding? Nobody knows what a buttress is," said Janine. She was no longer building. She was compulsively sweeping up every fragment of clay we dropped on the floor—the superintendent of schools we didn't have.

"Tal, your students are making a mess," she added.

"Tal, Tal, come here! I need an official measurement!" Nick was apoplectic, his face red and veins popping out.

Amid the ruckus, Annie, who was working quietly beside me, looked up.

"Tal, is it okay if I don't make a tower?"

"Why not?" I looked at her hands, in which she held a wet, perfectly round ball of clay. Her hands were completely coated in silky slip and she was repeatedly smoothing and caressing the glistening ball.

"Sure, Annie, but is it okay for you with all this mess? I mean, are you feeling overwhelmed? Is it too dirty?"

"Yeah," she said, with awestruck wonder in her voice, in the middle of the festival of chaos. "I'm really kind of liking the way it feels."

My training in poetry taught me to see likeness in things that are not alike, to find meaning in unexpected, synaptic correspondences. In this instance I knew what was happening: Annie was okay here, safe enough for her to plunge her hand in mud, safe enough to let the mess of it seep into her. If germ-covered doorknobs had once terrified her, here was a place where she could open the door.

T he next day we flattened our clay lumps into slabs and draped them over our faces.

"I can't breathe!" came muffled voices. "I have clay in my mouth!"

"Poke a hole where your nostrils are and then push in the eyes," I said. "Make it exaggerated and dramatic! And don't eat the clay, for God's sake!"

We built up the brows and eyes, adding horns, beards, and fangs—Doug gave his Spock-like ears, and Steve's was a laughing elf. We decided to do a pit firing, about which I knew nothing, except that we would cover the stoneware masks with a smoldering pile of extremely hot combustible material to create smoky heat in order to "glaze" the masks.

We stood in the wet grass on the morning of the firing. I held four shovels and a pickax.

"Okay, here is where we'll dig the pit," I announced, pointing to a patch of grass. "Who'll dig it?"

"Tal, what exactly are we trying to do here?" asked Tico.

"Tico, please, your enthusiasm is overwhelming me. I explained this. We are going to cook the masks in a pit of wicked high heat and smoke in order to make them look cool."

"I don't think this is going to work," he said.

They stared at the ground. I held a shovel out to them.

"Okay, come on, let's go! Let's dig."

I had thought they would leap at the opportunity to dig a hole, as opposed to sitting in the dark room around our broken tables.

"For Christ's sake, you guys, come on."

Najat stepped forward. "I'll do it," she said cheerily.

She plunged the shovel blade into the rocky soil. Then Nick took up a shovel, and Janine followed. Tico took on the role of directing and offering running commentary as he stumbled over tools and stones. The rest went into the woods to collect pinecones and lichen, bark, pine needles, dry moss, anything that would burn. From my truck I brought newspapers, sawdust, a jug of used motor oil, and a variety of flammable chemicals. I had asked Janine and Sophie each to bring sacks full of dried animal manure and hay that, I had heard, burned hot and long and created great effects, particularly mixed with sawdust and spent fossil fuels.

Now we had before us a heap of environmentally destructive combustibles—to go along with sheep shit, horse turds, and goat pellets. We gathered around to place the masks in the mixture.

Doug ceased arguing with Tico and conducted a ceremonial dance. I threw a dried turd at him.

"What are you *doing*?" Najat said, her eyes popping.

I tossed one at her head, and she tossed another back. I threw one at Sophie, and she ducked and threw one at Najat.

"What kind of school is this where the head teacher assaults students with animal dung?" Doug shouted.

"Let's go, you jackass." We drizzled black motor oil over the mixture, lit the paper, and watched the fire spread and smolder down. Smoke rose out in delicate curling wisps.

"Hey, Tal," said Tico, "can you say *Hello-oo, fire warden*?"

For the rest of the day it cooked, with the kids checking the pit periodically to blow on the fire and reposition the masks so they sat closer to where the flame might be. Occasionally Tico and Nick "helped it along" with some unknown chemical remnant.

"It's working, it's really heating up," they said as they came running back into the class.

"Is it still burning?" I asked.

"Yeah, we poured more oil and stuff on it. You should see mine. It looks so cool. It's smoking all over the place."

"Yeah, Tico the little pyromaniac was like, making sawdust explosions."

By the end of the day we were able to pull out the blackened masks, balancing them on sticks. We laid them out on the deck side by side so we could see what we had made. They were dusted with ash, beautifully smoked and mottled, shades of pale white, faded gray, and dusky black. No two masks were alike, each formed in the inimitable shape of its maker, having emerged, despite our fumbling ignorance, or perhaps because of it, from a bizarre and illegal fire of our collective creation. Looking at the masks—the flared nostrils, horns, beady eyes, and ridged brows—was like looking at the perfectly imperfect reflection of ourselves, our renegade band, a school still in the rough heat of its formation.

One day I looked at them and said, "What are we doing here?"

"You mean, like today?"

"No, I mean like, what are we doing *here,* in this school? In *school?* What is the purpose? What do we want to happen? Why do we go to school at all?"

"Well, the basic answer is we have to get an education," said Doug. "The law says we have to."

"Okay, true. But what else? What's beyond that, what's beyond the visible, or physical, or law?"

"I need to get a good education so that I can grow up and be successful and make a lot of money," said Nick, without a trace of irony.

"Nick," said Mira. "Come on!"

"Okay, that's true too, I suppose. Although, Nick, that's kind of depressing. That's a shit-bucket answer. It's boring because it doesn't get us anywhere *now*. What are we doing here? Now?"

Annie raised her hand. "You mean, the larger purpose. What were we born to do?"

"I guess. Something like that. Why not?"

"What do you think?" she asked. She emphasized *you* as though she was willing to set aside her answer, if she had one, to make room for mine.

"I think we are in school to find the god within us," I said.

"Okay."

"I don't mean Jesus or the Buddha or Allah. I mean, we are trying to find the part of us that is like a god and bring it out."

"But how are you supposed to know it when you find it?" Annie asked.

"I think you feel it. School is for helping you see it and say it. School is the mirror you use to look into as you search."

"Cool," she chirped.

"So who has found the god within them? How will you know?" I asked.

They looked at me over their open binders. The spotlights shining down made their pages appear to be bright blank portals. I did not know how we would know, or if it was even possible. I *did* know that, like King Lear, we needed to learn to see better before we could see anything at all.

At the second parent meeting I realized again how small the school actually was, a total of twenty-one parents circled up in front of the woodstove. I didn't want to talk about what their children were going to do, or even why we were doing it. I only wanted to show them what their children had already done.

I read the speech Najat had written in the first week of school. Najat was not a conventionally great student, and even as an eighth grader, she still played with Legos and dolls—just like my four- and six-year-old sons. She was courageous enough, however, to speak directly from her fears and to her most basic hopes. She wrote about wanting to fit in, wanting to have good friends, wanting to be seen not for how she appeared, or whether she had gotten her period, or had acne, or had the right clothes. She had put her interior world out in the open without shame.

I read her words:

"The most important thing is to feel safe in school, to feel safe to be comfortable to be myself and not worry about what others might say.

"I want the respect to feel safe, so that if I do some work, a project, my artwork, or my math, people will not think I am bad. In math I'm worried I'm not as smart as other people and that others will judge me on that and think I'm stupid. In art, I'm not that good. When I see the artwork of my friend Alicia, at first I say, 'Wow, that's incredible, like, really professional drawing.' My second reaction is, 'I wish I could draw that well.' Then my third response is, 'My work is awful, it's terrible, and it looks like it's been done by a two year old.'

"Some people may say that I say this just so that people will say, 'No, Najat, yours is great.' But in fact, even though I know I've tried my best, I also sometimes know it is not any good and I do feel bad. I want to feel safe knowing that if I do well in art, I can feel proud of myself, and if it isn't that good, then people won't say it's terrible. I also want to feel safe from people judging me for the shirt I wear, even if it isn't the greatest shirt. I don't want people to think I am awful or wrong or that I can't be a good person just because my shirt is dirty or not in the right fashion.

"Sometimes I have pimples, and I don't want people to make fun of that.

"I also sometimes worry that because I'm brown, people will not want to be friends with me. That's how I felt sometimes when I was little. When I go to the mall in Burlington with my friend Alicia, she blends in perfectly. Everyone clings to her because she is so cool and hip and has the right clothes. Because I am the only brown person in the whole mall, I feel like an alien, like I am visiting Earth and I'll never blend in. Sometimes I feel like no one sees me. In the mall, Alicia will be nice to me, but I don't feel like I am the center of anyone's attention.

"At school I don't want to feel this way. I want to feel safe and comfortable, and equal. 'Equal' to me means that people don't judge me by my math, the color of my skin, or the style of my clothes. I want to be judged by how nice I am, and not unimportant things like fashion. When I know that school is like that, I can focus on other things without worrying if I am 'smart.' I think every kid should be treated as an equal, especially in school."

Through open and direct address, Najat was author and architect of the world she wanted to inhabit. Her conception of a just environment was authentic and undeniable. Above all, she wanted to be *seen*. In two handwritten pages, she constructed a moral and ethical manifesto that, when it echoed in a classroom, could become a kind of communal elixir. I wanted the parents to know that having a school where the kids could speak directly and movingly to each other in this manner was the necessary first step, and that we had made that first step.

Her essay was not a masterpiece, but it was a soulful disclosure fluent in the language of the heart and adolescent experience. If the words were not entirely beautiful, they were certainly valuable. When I read her words for the parents, I hoped they would be able to see our origins and understand that ethical order evolved not from me or an educational system, but from the students.

E ric and I told the kids to bring their bikes to school. Our school was going mountain biking. How many middle schools could say they took the entire student body mountain biking? There weren't a whole lot of directions for us to go, as all roads—all of them dirt—headed steeply *up*. We could go toward Breadloaf Mountain or we could go north toward Lincoln. We decided on Lincoln, which would take us to Eric's house, at the farthest edge of Ripton. Since Eric's house was off the grid, our ostensible purpose was to see the solar panels he had mounted on his workshop, another outing that, I hoped, might bring us closer together.

We rolled and wobbled out of the pine-shrouded driveway, ten kids and two teachers, up the Lincoln Road. The maple trees lining the road were already deep into their changes. We pedaled through the "hollow," past old farmsteads, houses with peeling paint or no siding, trailers on rusted wheels, yards littered with plow trucks, bags of garbage, woodpiles, tractors, snowmobiles, and ATVs—the detritus of a working community in a rural Vermont mountain town where, even on an early fall day, smoke rose from rusty stovepipes. We pedaled past garages decorated with moose antlers and rusty crosscut saws, past sheds where chain saws hung from rafters, yards with stacked tires filled with rainwater and sodden leaves, overturned fishing boats, engine blocks, truck beds hidden in dried goldenrod, barbed-wire fences, defunct chicken coops, gas cans, scattered stone walls, and a few shrunken pastures where cows were grazing in the dying grass. It could have been 1940.

Tico, Nick, and Steve raced ahead, skidding hard on the dirt road, bursting with energy and testosterone. The road followed the North Branch River, and when we came to the first bridge I made everyone stop.

"This here is the North Branch River. Gaze upon it."

"We're gazing, Tal," said Mira. She was panting.

"Do you know why this here river is important?"

"This here river?" asked Doug.

"Yeah, this here river."

"No, Tal, please tell us," said Sophie with her singsong voice and sarcastic smile.

"This here river is where we got the name of our school. Pretty cool, huh?"

"Great, Tal."

"I thought of it myself."

"Great, Tal."

"It's a river of meaning."

"That's real cool, Tal."

"Okay, let's move out, sports fans." Tico, Nick, and Steve reared up on their bikes, popping wheelies and showing off.

"I am *not* a sports fan," said Zoe.

"Oh, Tal, can't we rest a little more," moaned Mira. "I'm freaking dying."

"Mira, I'll ride with you in the back here. Zoe, you and the rest of the sports fans move out. Let's go."

While Mira projected a fiery confidence and precocious intelligence, in this matter of physical endurance she'd reached her limit amazingly quickly. She could not keep up with the others and was almost hyperventilating. She masked her panic with irritation and complaining. It was hard to imagine that this sloping mountain road could present such a physical challenge, but it did. She labored as I slowly spun my pedals. The river, glinting in the sun, ran alongside us over black stones and the forest rose sharply to the west. Eric and the rest had disappeared. Staying at the back was where I had to be, sweeping the borders, shepherding the edges, making sure that the least of us was coming along.

I thought of being a teacher not only in terms of who needed to be brought along intellectually or scholastically but also who needed to be kept close to the heart of the community. The elemental fear of children in school is being left out, of being dumb, inept, awkward, or unpopular—whatever exposes weakness or difference. I knew that for these kids, as for all students, the fear of being left out or left behind was an iron shackle on learning. On the other hand, feeling a sense of the embrace of the community was the prerequisite for all good growth and learning. If our school community was going to work, they all had to feel that they were held close as a vital part of the whole.

We pushed our bikes up to Eric's house, high on the hill above the river and the fir trees, which pointed up like dark slender steeples against the blue sky. The kids romped through overgrown grass and dying summer flowers. We looked briefly at the solar panels arrayed on the roof of Eric's shop, but information was not what compelled them— activity did. We jumped back on our bikes and began the long easy ride back, coasting along the river, the sound of the North Branch in our ears. When Mira and I pedaled into the driveway of the school, the boys were doing jumps over rocks down the fern-covered hill, all of them hot, sweaty, red cheeked. We leaned the bikes against the side of the schoolhouse and in the grass, where they stayed all through the fall—as it got darker and colder, as wet leaves piled up on the deck in the freezing rain—a reminder of warm days on the mountain.

Since we were a financially shaky operation on a minuscule budget, we thought we could keep heating costs down by utilizing the large woodstove in the main room. In Vermont's earlier times, tending the stove in the schoolhouse was an essential part of the contractual duties of the schoolmaster. The idea of having a woodheated schoolhouse up in the Vermont hills appealed to my sense of aesthetic history. I imagined arriving on early mornings and stirring the coals to bring a true, earthy warmth to our studies. We would sit with our open books discussing great literature and important ideas as the stovepipe ticked. It dovetailed nicely with my Yeatsian ideal of education simply being the lighting of a fire.

One morning I arrived to find a huge heap of cordwood, which Mia had delivered, dumped by the side of the house. I was looking for things to do to keep us busy, active, and together. I did not care whether there was an academic component or not: As long as we were working at something even vaguely constructive, I was satisfied.

We spent a chilly morning in the dark room, with Sophie and Mira zipped up in down jackets while they worked with x and y variables.

After break I announced: "We're headed outside, you damn teeny-boppers. We've got some firewood to stack. Got to put up the old woodpile!"

As soon as I uttered the word *outside,* Tico was gone, dashing and stumbling, knocking over chairs, as if he would die if he were not the first out the door, his black skater sweatshirt dragging behind him. These moments represented for Tico a gasp, literally, of fresh air, a way out, an escape from all the ways school had imprisoned him. *Outside* meant no reading, no writing, and no failure. *Outside* meant that the suffocating walls of school had been removed.

"Move out, everyone!" I shouted. "Set up a bucket brigade and move this wood. Just like in the olden days."

"Olden days?" asked Annie. "Didn't you just move here from Atlanta?"

"We had olden days in Atlanta."

"And Tal, why do they call it 'olden'? Why is it not just 'old' days?"

"Great question, Annie. That's the kind of inquiry that will lead to success."

"Aw, Tal, do we have to do this?" Mira complained. "I don't care about the olden days. I don't want to get dirty."

"Yes, Mira, you have to get dirty. Yes, we have to. Do you want to freeze your heinie off this winter?"

"We're going to freeze our heinies off no matter what."

"Come on, let's go." Behind us in the dark room we left our heaps of open binders, papers, and pencils scattered on the floor, backpacks spilling carrot sticks, Cheeze-Its, and crumpled assignments.

Nick took charge, organizing the filling of the garden cart, the wheels of which were falling off, the plywood sides rotting, the tires flat. One rule of thumb with middle-school kids: If there is something halfway broken within their reach, it will be completely broken within the hour. Our landlord would never use his cart again.

Steve and Tico stood on top of the woodpile commanding and directing. Zoe and Mira staggered over with armfuls of wood.

"Jiminy!" I shouted. "Look at that load—these girls are strong!"

"Here, take it, hurry," screeched Zoe. She stared madly at a brown, gelatinous mass of lichen growing on a chunk of firewood.

"What kind of school *is* this?" she asked, flinging the question to no one in particular. "God. Disgusting!" She poked the jellied mass with a twig.

"Tal," Annie queried, "shouldn't you be sued for using us as illegal child labor?"

"Tal," called Janine, "what if the commissioner of education sees you doing this? Big, big trouble."

"Who's the commissioner of education?"

"You're a terrible man. Do you even have a license to teach?"

"Once I did."

"Oh, my God."

The heaping pile by the driveway shrunk while the stacks on the other side of the school grew into teetering walls. In one hour we moved and put up two cords. We stacked the last half cord under the porch overhang to keep it out of the rain and snow. This had the effect of closing off our doorway almost entirely, barricading us behind a firewood wall.

"Hey, Tal," Nick said. "This'll be an awesome fort for when we have snowball fights." Nick clearly exhibited forward thinking, an awareness of possibilities, and an irrepressible, positive mental outlook.

I called that a good lesson.

I tried to keep a fire in the stove. Invariably, though, I would became distracted and have to assign someone, usually Nick or Tico, to tend the flame. Fire-tending abilities of male adolescents, I found, were inconsistent at best. During a discussion about forest succession the room would suddenly fill with smoke. While grouping like terms in algebra we'd have to peel off all our layers down to T-shirts because the room had become a dry sauna.

Tico was hunched over by the stove and pitching in balls of newspaper on top of roaring flames.

"Yo, bro, can you get that thing figured out? Turn the flue back! Christ almighty, it's hotter than hell's kitchen in here."

Tico clanked the door of the stove shut.

"You try!"

Eventually he too would forget about the fire and by the afternoon we'd all be freezing again.

Education was not as simple as lighting a fire.

From the beginning we wrote. No poetry, no fantasy, no fiction. The subject was ourselves.

Before they could begin to learn to *write* well they first had to see and listen well. We started with places they had known, the small knotholes of memory where they kept their clear, undisturbed, original selves. By going back they could see where they came from, the first candescence, the origins of their dreams.

We spent a great deal of time talking about the senses. Whenever someone told a story, I asked the class what part of the story was most alive—what could they see, feel, taste, or hear. Over and over I asked them to say the textures of a thing, a place, a memory. They had to say it first so that the shape could begin to take form.

We closed our eyes and walked step by step through their memories. I turned off the lights and made them put their heads down so they could see the places inside themselves and look somewhere else besides an impersonal school system, me, curriculum, books, or each other. I wanted to slow them down, create a mental pause so they might begin to cultivate the habit of thinking more deeply about what was inside and construct meaning from *that* source. I repeated Keats's words, which were becoming my inner catechism: "Do you not see how necessary a world of pains and troubles is to school an intelligence and make it a soul?" I did not want to teach them simply to absorb my ideas—they had their own.

With Tico, I had an intelligence that could not read or write. Early on, I found trying to teach Tico—even having him in class—was like having an electrified mouse jumping around in a box. He startled, he leaped, he looked frantically under the table, he exploded out of his seat at the first ring of the phone. If there was a sound he blurted out, "What's that?!" with hyperalarm, and he heard things we couldn't. He always had his backpack with him, which was filled with an assortment of electrical parts, tools, spent batteries, scratched CDs, and notebooks filled with half-finished drawings. He was constantly tinkering. We teased him, saying that we could always track where he had gone in a day by following the trail of snipped wires, alligator clips, Phillips head screwdrivers, and broken motors he left behind. If other children had learned how to use writing implements in school, Tico had mastered the manual arts of pliers-wielding and duct-tape repair.

Perhaps the essential thing he had learned in elementary school was a vast repertoire of ways to avoid being humiliated and exposed. He hated to write in class and had numerous strategies to weasel out of doing it. And why wouldn't he feel this? He could barely read. When I asked the class to write a response to a question, he invariably had to dash to the bathroom, answer the phone, or rummage through his backpack. Sometimes he'd claim, "Tal, I already figured this out. I know what I want to say." Other times he told me he was just going to draw his ideas, handing me an occasionally legible scrawl of Basquiat-style graffiti. A complete sentence might have only three intelligible words. At least those times he was trying, with his pencil on the paper. If he began with a clear statement, his thought would disappear into clusters of letters: *I thot hhis ihm fvrme iitret vrogtrt thas,* he might begin, able to sustain his effort only for a moment. He would finish by drawing or doodling while others wrote down the page.

Tico participated in class discussions about place descriptions, but he did not want to talk about his own words. Even my mere mention of his possible writing topic caused him to act wounded and defensive.

"What are you going to do, Tico?"

"I already know what to do," he said quickly, as though pricked.

"What? What are you going to do?"

"Never mind," he said, ducking his eyes to his blank page.

His mother, Deb, was intensely focused on helping him succeed. Six years of one-on-one aides, specialists, and tutors had not gotten him where he needed to go. But whatever assignment I gave him, she agreed to work with him on it. He would dictate, she would type. Without fail, on the day a piece of writing was due he would turn in a handwritten draft and three typed drafts, each draft slightly more complex and alive, evidence of her work with him. Though he could not construct the written product by himself, his mind was amazingly fertile and nimble. He saw things that the rest of us did not know existed, as if he were a hunter hearing and sensing signs all around to which the rest of us had grown deaf.

Early that fall he turned in this piece of writing:

One day last year my science teacher let us wander in the woods alone and there was a fire drill. We missed it. The school missed us. The principal got really angry with our teacher. But that day reminds me of a lot of things.

It reminds me of winter coming because it was in the fall and I was sitting so quietly that I could hear the soft tap of leaves falling. This was the first time a teacher had ever asked us to do a "quiet sit" and observe things around us. We did sketches of what we saw in front of us and what we saw in our peripheral vision. Some people drew pinecones. Some people drew needles in a clump. Some people drew trees, and some of us drew nothing but just sat there and listened to the different sounds and took it in and shared what we thought with the class. When people shared their ideas it was really interesting because we were all learning something different and at our own pace.

It is much easier for me to do things independently outside than to have people tell me: "Sit down and write this and read that and look at the chalkboard and copy that." It's not something you want to do. It's just something they want you to do. You may get an education, but another kind of education is like what I did that day in grade school. That was a time I felt good about myself because I knew I was learning something.

Tico was one among those "who drew nothing but just sat there and listened." Yet schools asked students to *do*. And if they ever asked students to listen, they asked so that students could hear the instructions for *what* to do. Schools rarely asked students to listen as an end in itself, as though the institution of school did not trust the students to be able to hear meaningful sounds. Schools almost never asked students to close their eyes and sit in the dark to re-create memories, go silently into the woods, or listen to the soft tapping of leaves falling to the forest floor. School had not asked Tico to do what he *could* do. But on the one day a school did ask him, he discovered what he needed, he saw what he felt, he heard what he knew. Tico knew how to listen, and we had to listen to him.

As I read his short sketch at my lawyer's desk, my hand was shaking. I wanted to cry out in celebration and amazement. I called the class in from break and gathered them around my desk to read it to them. They listened and clapped politely.

"Do you see what he's telling us? Can you hear this? *He hasn't given up.* He's still trying. He's telling us what he needs to live, in school and in the world."

"Yeah, Tal, we get it. Don't go psycho on us," said Annie. "But that's really good, Tico."

"You're goddamn right it's good," I said. "It's better than really good. All of you ought to be carrying Tico on your shoulders and dumping a cooler full of Gatorade on him. Tico's the savior of education in America. He's the only one telling us how schools should do things. It doesn't have a damn thing to do with tests. He's telling us what *we* have to do. We have to listen to *him* and make a way for everyone to listen and see and write what they feel. Otherwise we'll learn, but *what* we learn won't be our own. And he's telling us we all do it differently."

They looked at me with glazed eyes.

"Yo, bro, this is what I'm talking about!"

I wanted them to see what it meant to make something beautiful, to be listening to winter coming. I wanted them to understand that the anguish and repeated failure Tico had experienced in his years of school had not eroded his desire to listen, observe, and see into the nature of perception. That was what we were given, our chance to remake the world from what we knew. Tico was giving us the world he knew—pinecones, clumps of needles, the movements at the edge of vision. Like a silent tracker in the woods, he had led us to the place we needed to go.

I sometimes felt a hundred miles from normalcy. Often I dreaded the day ahead, the hours alone with ten teenagers in a cold, shabby house in a mountain hollow, trying to invent a school. But the only near disaster was inviting an experimental trumpet player in to do improvisational music. I presumed it would be easy enough. Everyone would bring an instrument and we'd have a jam session. *How could that not be fun?* I thought. The day the instructor came, all but two kids forgot to bring an instrument to play—clearly an act of blatant adolescent passive aggression.

"Tal, I forgot my guitar," Mira said. "Nobody remembered."

"Well, tough. Speak for yourself. Go get something that makes noise."

"Like what?"

"Anything. A pot, a spoon, a sack of nails to rattle, wooden blocks. I don't give a rat's ass. You need to be ready for class."

She rolled her eyes acidly.

Wooden blocks? My suggestions most likely had the effect of making the idea of improvisational music seem more absurd and childish, especially to a group of self-conscious adolescents who barely knew each other and did not have the remotest desire to make fools of themselves.

When the instructor broke out his miniature trumpet and began to toot and squeal, the kids stared at each other, mouths agape in terror or disgust. He asked them to play back to him what he had just played. They gazed vacantly at him, perplexed and sluggish, banging on their pots in halfhearted, broken rhythms. Sophie strummed an out-of-tune

G chord on her guitar. Najat played a wobbly measure of "Amazing Grace" on her clarinet. Two spoons tinged. A tambourine rattled intermittently. Tico fiddled with the batteries of a Casio keyboard.

The instructor told them to play all at once, then stop and listen to each other and the silences between the sounds. This was a mystical injunction far beyond their creative abilities, leading to a cacophony, followed by a sullen, embarrassed silence. I was afraid even to look into the room, for fear that there would be a mass rebellion, followed by the instructor packing up his horn, never to return.

I did peer in. My students were turned around, half snickering, completely disengaged. A few more toots and bangs. Another faint rattle on the tambourine.

I was so upset by this miserable foray into music education that I lay awake all night trying to fashion a response. The fact was that it was not the instructor's fault. He had been given an impossible task, at least with this group of students. Making music out of nothing was creatively complex, requiring liberation from self-consciousness, which was the air my students breathed. I had not yet moved them to the place where inhibition dissolved in the joy of making. All I could do was try to push them through improvisational jazz class and try to get what we could out of it.

The next morning I gathered them around the stove. I told them they were rude, that their actions were unacceptable.

"If someone comes here to give you something, you better open up to receive it, and you better damn well give yourself back. I don't give two flying shits if you think it's weird. I don't care if you are narrow and afraid and think it's dorky. You give something and you make something. You appreciate what you have. Your job is to do the learning. There's an opening that's been made for you and you have to walk through it."

There was a momentary silence.

"I *like* the dude," said Najat. "I like how he toots."

"Good. Maybe you're the only one who is open-minded. Thank God someone is. The rest of you are pissing me off."

They sat silently, looking at the floor.

Then I told them the story of how I had first encountered the music of Sun Ra, the avant-garde jazz bandleader, how initially I thought his music to be absurdly cacophonous and hopelessly incomprehensible. I told them my inability to comprehend Sun Ra was not his fault; it was mine: I was in a state of ignorance—musical, historical, and cultural. I told them how I continued to try to understand the music over a period of years, forcing myself to grasp Sun Ra's mystery and accomplishment, until I finally understood—maybe not everything, but something. I told them of attending a Sun Ra concert where the audience, the band, and gold-draped dancers paraded around the club while Sun Ra played "Zippity Do Dah." I told them how Sun Ra played staggeringly complex variations of Duke Ellington compositions, until the entire club was in an ecstatic frenzy and the man next to me stood up on his chair and repeatedly shouted toward the stage: "You're better than Mozart! You're greater than Mozart!"

"It was a miracle. I was seeing something majestic, and I understood it."

They liked my story, and they tried a little harder the next time, but it did not turn us into great improvisational jazz musicians.

In the classroom I could direct the discussion, create the activity, and stir up the energy. If we needed a light story, a joke, a true story, a stern lecture, an angry harangue, I could deliver. If we needed to wake up, I could require them to practice kung fu in the cold morning air. But at lunch, as they separated to play and eat, the energy dissipated. Annie and Doug often played imaginary games. Mira and Zoe were deeply concerned with lip gloss, downloading Eminem's new songs, and who knew whom at the high school. Steve was "going out" with Mira, but their relationship consisted of Mira critiquing Steve about his personal hygiene and constantly telling him that he should eat more. Sophie and Najat spent lunch wandering in the woods on the nature trail. Janine used her lunch break to tidy up the school and remind me of how many school safety codes we were violating. "You know, Tal, if the governor of Vermont saw this school, you would be fired."

At lunch I'd sit at my desk and a few kids would sit in the kitchen by the gas stove talking about music, arguing, complaining, or asking me what we were going to do next, and often, I couldn't really say.

In the scramble to fill up our days with interesting and serious experiences, I let the kids trample over traditional school norms. When Annie asked if she could bring her lame lamb to school, I said yes. We spent a day taking turns holding the little lamb, with his foreleg jutting out in a plaster cast, which we all signed. When Janine asked if she could bring some baby bunnies to school for pets, I said sure. *What's wrong with having bunnies at school?* I thought. It seemed appropriate when during a literature class on *Of Mice and Men*, Sophie was holding a cute, fuzzy bunny while Lennie dreamed of rabbits. But when the bunny cage began to reek and the bunnies were forgotten and left foodless over the weekend, we had to send them back to the farm whence they came.

We entertained ourselves trying to catch the renegade red squirrel which, nightly, ransacked whatever lunches we had left around the house, leaving for us scatterings of peanut shells and cracker crumbs. In the middle of a literature discussion about Lennie and George and the meaning of friendship, someone would call out, "Uh, Tal, there he is." The whole class would jump up as though they had never seen anything so exciting as a red squirrel running for its life over a dark, dirty kitchen floor.

We were not so unlike Lennie, George, and Candy, plotting to get our little cabin and a hutch full of bunnies. Steinbeck wrote: "We'd jus'

live there. We'd belong there. There wouldn't be no more runnin' 'round
the country. . . . We'd have our own place where we belonged and not
sleep in no bunk house. . . . We'd have a little house an' a room to our-
self. Little fat iron stove, an' in the winter we'd keep a fire goin' in it."
The school was a ragged, strange family, half pulled up to a table, writing and talking about the school we wanted. Maybe we couldn't keep
an actual fire going in it, but our schoolhouse was where we belonged.
We just had to stay long enough for the feeling of hope we read about to
become our own.

I n November I told them we would begin to write stories.
    "What do you mean, *stories*?" they asked.
    "I mean whatever happened to you that made your thoughts, be-
liefs, and ideas. Whatever you have inside you that is important to you
to write about."
    "Like, what?" said Doug. "You mean true?"
    "I mean I will not read a load of crappy sci-fi, made-up fantasy crap.
No 'Xanthrax and the Sword of Ravensclaw' crap. No phony made-up
crap."
    "So you mean nonfiction," said Doug, with a trace of disappoint-
ment.
    "Like I said: true stories."
    They looked at me, waiting.
    "I mean whatever real feeling you have screaming inside you, like
Asher Lev's teacher said. Whatever confuses you, troubles you. The big
stuff. Conflicts, hard times, things you don't understand. No fiddle-
farting around with rainbow crap or 'I have a dream' essay junk."
    "Oh, we did essays last year," said Najat.
    "I'm not talking about essays. I'm talking about your *stories*."
    "What kind of stories?"

"Your *stories. Your* stories. The things stored inside you. The events of your life that made you who you are. Or made you know who you want to be."

"You mean, like, we have to write a *true* story?"

"Um, like, I mean, yeah. What's the point of making up a not-true story? You've got to write about what matters. When you know what matters and can write it truly, then maybe you will be ready to write not-true stories."

"How are we supposed to know what matters?"

"That question, if you can learn to answer it, is where you will begin to learn, you know, some important stuff."

"Some stuff?"

"Yeah. You make meaning out of your life. You take the stuff of your life and turn it into art."

"What?"

"Tal, my life is boring. Nothing has ever happened to me."

"Look. Then you have some choices: be boring and write a boring story. Or you can make a boring story interesting by lying a lot, or even being creative. Or you can look harder at your life. But here're two pearls of wisdom: There's no such thing as a boring life, and all of you can create art."

"Tal, I don't get this," said Najat.

"Why does it have to be true?" asked Mira.

"Because, Mira, the only important thing I can teach you is to learn how to discover what *is* true, true to you, what is true *of* you. If you can do that, you'll know what is beautiful. You will know what is right. You will know what you need. The only way you can learn that is to look at what you know to be beautiful, right, and necessary in your own life."

"But why does it have to have a conflict? Do you mean like a fight?"

"Listen to this: 'Now that my ladder's gone / I must lie down where all the ladders start / In the foul rag and bone shop of the heart.' That's from a poem by W. B. Yeats. 'The Circus Animals' Desertion.' Now do you understand?"

"No." A sullen refusal, or inability, to understand.

"I'm talking about the place where everything begins is inside you. I don't mean a *fight*. I mean you have to start climbing by going down. The place you go is inside your heart. Sometimes it's a foul place, a place of tension and conflict. Because conflicts are the points at which you learn things. You weren't born with what you know. You went through experiences to gain what you know. A story is a dramatic and artistic representation of that experience. Writing it down is how you learn it and make it part of your soul and begin to see yourself."

"What do you mean, *soul*?"

I pushed my hat off my head and ran my hand through my hair.

"Um, Tal?"

"Yes, Najat?"

"How long does it have to be?"

"Oh, for fuck's sake! You go from soul to rules. Why don't you ask: How great does it have to be?"

"Because I need to know how long it has to be."

"It doesn't matter how long it is if it's true and great. But usually somewhere between twelve and thirty pages."

"What?" they all shouted, leaning forward. "Thirty pages!"

We could talk all day about the meaning of existence or the key to getting into heaven or souls and truth, and they could lean back in their chairs gazing at dust balls on the floor. If we approached authentic work they came alive, they were apoplectic.

"I can't write thirty pages! How am I going to write thirty pages?"

"For God's sake, you wrote three pages in your last place description about your tree house where you played when you were five. Tico wrote a page and a half about sitting in the woods. So why're you all worried about writing twenty pages about something important in your life?"

"I don't think I can do this," said Janine, shaking her head emphatically so that her curls brushed her cheeks.

"Don't worry. I'll show you a few tricks I learned in the army. Then you can write the important stuff."

"You weren't ever in the army."

"I was too. And I know a lot of tricks. How else did I learn a lot of tricks if I wasn't ever in the army?"

"God, whatever," said Zoe, rolling her eyes and laughing at the same time.

"So here's what you have to do: Write your story idea in a page and no more, no less. It has to be about what is beautiful, right, and necessary. Make sure you sketch out the beginning, middle, and end. Make sure you describe the conflict. And you have to be able to say what the resolution is in one sentence. If you can't tell me the idea in one page, it's a crap idea. If you can't tell me the feelings that are in the story, it's going to be a crap story."

"Whaddaya mean, the 'resolution'?"

"You know, the epiphany. The revelation. The realization. The 'closure.'" I put emphatic and sarcastic air quotes around the word *closure.*

"Give me your story ideas tomorrow. Typed and double-spaced. Get cracking, goddammit!"

We spent the next two weeks discussing story ideas. We'd sit around the table and read one, and then I would lead them into exploratory, Socratic questioning. I wanted them to answer my questions, but I also wanted them to learn how to ask the questions themselves, to let their own sense lead them. I tried to push to the point where a raw and true feeling began to emerge, the edge between where they were and where they needed to go. This often involved tears. They got used to the tears and they learned to read the feelings behind the tears. And then they learned to talk to and about those feelings.

"Zoe, I don't get what you want to write about here. I mean, I see that your story is about your sister, but I don't feel the conflict or see the feeling. You say you played dolls and played in the garden, and you say she is annoying. What the hell is that?"

"I don't know. We used to play a lot. I think we just stopped."

"Don't think about it," I said. "Feel something."

We waited.

"Close your eyes and don't think."

She closed her eyes and we sat quietly.

"Maybe you miss her," said Najat. "I mean, I don't have a sister. I have a half sister, and I miss her, but if I had a sister and then we stopped playing with each other, I would be really sad."

"Yeah, I miss her," said Zoe, still with her eyes closed.

"But why don't you play anymore?" I asked.

"Um, I don't know." Here her voice was a whisper.

We waited in the quiet of the room.

Annie raised her hand. "Maybe you got busy with other stuff. Like how you said you were talking on the phone and instant messaging all the time. Maybe *you* stopped playing with her, instead of it being that you two stopped playing."

"Is that the story, Zoe?" I asked.

"Yeah, I think that might be it."

"Does that make you sad?" I asked.

She nodded, an acknowledgment of her flight from childhood and her longing for a return to intimacy with her sister.

"And guilty," she said. She opened her eyes and gazed down at her hands, which were curling up the corners of a blank sheet of paper.

"Zoe," I said, "you didn't commit a crime. You're growing up. But maybe you can't grow up without her. You're growing into your own person but you don't want to leave her?"

She nodded.

"The beauty and glee of your playing. The knowledge that it is ending. Wanting to hold on to it. To go back sometimes. Something you want to say to your sister."

She nodded again.

"As my old friend Auguste Renoir used to say, 'The pain passes, but the beauty remains.'"

"Tal," said Sophie. "I don't think Renoir would want to be your friend."

"Sweet put-down, Sophie, but Renoir knew the score. Zoe, go write your story idea right now, right now, on that paper that you are mutilating. You can sit at my desk. Lemme see it when you're done."

By lunchtime Zoe had her story idea.

Over and over, the process was the same. Always, that gentle pressure had to be brought to bear, a little leaning on them to bring hazy generalities into the shape of defined knowing.

"I don't get it, Doug. You say you want to be free of fear. You want everyone to get along in the school. That's your holy grail. I understand that. But we don't know *why* you want that. I mean, what's the experience that makes you choose that above all other things?"

"Well, sometimes in sixth grade it felt like we weren't all together."

"Instead of saying the general and meaningless 'we,' say who you mean."

"You mean—"

"I mean, who are you talking about?"

"There's Nick—"

He glanced at Nick, who was leaning back in his chair next to him, barely listening.

"Nick," Doug blurted out, "you are a warthog."

"What? What are you talking about?" Nick looked like he had been caught in a snare, hanging from his ankle and not knowing why.

Doug spoke again, and this time he was crying. "You are a warthog because you betray me. You were my friend, but as soon as there are other people you leave me behind. When we came to North Branch we were friends and now all you do is hang around like some teenage bum talking about skateboarding and idiotic trendy music and whatever the cool people think is cool and you totally forget me. And we have been friends for ten years. It's the same thing you did last year. You thought Cody was cool and you ditched everyone who was your friend."

Nick tried to answer, but he shook his head. His voice quavered. "I know. I don't know why I do that. Why do I do that? I just, I don't know." Tears ran down his face. No denial. He was asking himself the questions that might lead to something like his own divinity, or at least new knowledge.

"You should know, Nick," Doug said bitterly, gazing straight at Nick.

"Easy, Doug," I said. "I don't think he's denying it. He's listening. He's asking the same questions of himself that you're asking. So what happens, Doug? You feel connected and then he leaves for bigger, better, more glamorous things?"

"Yeah, and the things he leaves for are superficial, moronic things," said Doug. "How can he put those things higher than friendship?"

Nick was looking hard at him. His cheeks were shining and wet—tears on the face of this powerful, muscular thirteen-year-old boy. "But Doug, those things are not superficial or moronic to me. Those things are part of my friendships."

"Okay, but you don't have to ignore everything that is *not* those things. I mean, we are all still here. You have to care about other people, and people are more important than being popular."

"I know, I know. I don't want to not be friends. I want to be friends with everybody. I just forget."

"You were old good friends, right?" I asked.

"Yeah, Doug and I used to play all sorts of games."

"How do you remember it?"

"It was the most fun I ever had in elementary school. Making up games, imaginary worlds. A game called Captain Rover that Doug made up. We'd hide things and then make up mystery plots and go find the things we hid."

"It was so much fun," said Doug.

"Nick, do you know why you left Doug for them?"

"Yeah. I mean, they made fun of everybody, especially the nerds. I didn't want to be some nerd they made fun of playing games like Captain Rover. I was afraid they'd make fun of me."

"So what'd you do?"

"I ditched him."

"So you wouldn't get made fun of?"

"So I wouldn't get made fun of."

"So you ditched Doug to protect your own sorry ass?"

"Yeah."

"Do you want to forget it, Nick? Those times of playing Captain Rover?"

"No, of course not. Not ever."

"Then tell him."

He half glanced up at Doug, then said to the table: "I loved playing those games. I felt terrible when I went to hang out with the cool kids and Cody. Those guys were jerks. I wish I could not have done that."

Doug look at him and shrugged.

"Nick," I said. "It's partly you trying to be cool, partly growing up and changing. Maybe you do forget your past, even sometimes maybe part of yourself."

"I feel like a total idiot now."

"So feel like an idiot. Feel idiotic, absolutely and completely, like a total dumbass, and be mad at yourself for what you did and keep it in mind. What you're doing now is exactly the same."

"Whaddaya mean?"

"Next time you're hanging around Mira or Steve or Tico, look at yourself instead of them. Think about what you're afraid of saying next time you're agreeing with some dumb trendy bullshit. Remember what it feels like to be an idiot, remember that you are one, and then you'll be smarter. Even better than that, remember what it felt like when those guys made fun of you for playing with your friend. Then you'll know what Doug is feeling."

No matter how much Nick scolded himself or how much I pushed him to look at himself, I knew he would do it to Doug and others again. He was a soul devoted to the good, but he transgressed against his soul. Like all of them, it took time for him to learn.

"So now both of you have your topics for your stories. Doug, that divine place where we do not ever forget each other, where we hold friendship as sacred. Describe it, let us know why we need it. Nick, how to grow up without losing or forgetting the past or turning into a trendy suck-up in the process."

"I think I get it," said Nick.

"You've got to tell us why you did it, how you felt, what you were afraid of, and what the consequences were when you were afraid."

"I will, I'll try."

Their stories, their struggles, and their quests became the subject, *our* living text. Mira wrote about her failure to fit in at her old school and about having no friends whom she could trust. Doug wrote about the difficult life of a nerd. Nick wrote about being teased by the "cool" kids in fifth grade and then trying to be cool in sixth grade, the consequence of which was turning on his old friend Doug, the nerd. Janine wrote about memories of her father, whom she no longer saw. Sophie wrote about life as a "popular" girl, which led her to tease the poorest boy—the one with holes in his pants—in her school. And Annie wrote about her anxiety and obsessive-compulsive disorder, a monumental topic, and a monumental step for her.

Reflection was a way for them to see the world—through themselves, through me, through each other. I was teaching them to hold the mirror before them—not to check the complexion or hair, glossy lips or menacing sneer, but to look inside.

They began to pile up the pages—descriptions, scenes, dialogues, interior monologues. Long paragraphs of self-reproach, self-deprecation, questioning, wondering. Whenever anyone was stuck, I would read part of the story aloud and we would talk about how to move it forward. *What's missing? How did you feel when she said that? Shouldn't you put a scene here to show that you were afraid?* Sometimes I read old stories from former students whose stories were fully realized and legitimate works of art. My students listened in awe because these stories, written by kids their age, were whole and full of wisdom.

I told them again and again that they were entering a tradition, that they had much to add. Their stories were their most important possession—the origin of their beliefs, the cornerstone of their knowledge. If they possessed their stories, then they possessed themselves.

I ranted: Don't say what you think, say what you feel. The feeling comes first; the feeling is the power, the illuminated core. The telling of the story—the art—refines the feeling, shapes it, clarifies it. The feeling, thus purified, emerges as understanding. The beauty in the story then becomes the beauty of the maker.

Maybe such theorizing was half-baked, half-cocked. At least it wasn't timid or tepid. At least we were driving for something great.

My assumption was simple: My students could not know themselves until they had comprehended or expressed the concrete reality of their lives. Anything else was at best hazy abstraction, at worst a shameful form of avoidance.

So every day I asked questions that centered on the idea of emotional intelligence: What do we know? What do we feel? What feelings do we hold? What feelings elude us? Should emotional learning even be a part of school? How much play should we give to the exploration of feelings that might be provocative, discomforting, profane, or taboo?

I told them to write about their relationships with their parents, siblings, friends, members of the opposite sex; how they saw themselves as learners and people; myriad issues around adoption, growing up, divorce, body image, substance use, identity; their experiences, good and bad, in school; their anxieties, embarrassments, failures, fears, guilt, hopes, impulses, emptiness, loves, and dreams—in short, all the issues that consumed them.

Certainly conventional intellectual knowledge was important. How else would they grow up and be able to enter the world to *do* rewarding and meaningful work? Mastery of facts, logic, and reason, and facility in linear and critical thinking were essential. But I was talking about fluency in the language of the heart, which emerged from willingness to speak from deeply felt experience. Yes, I wanted them to be able to say things well. Even more, I wanted them to have something valuable to say.

I read to them Ted Hughes's description of Honoré de Balzac: "When Balzac, the great French novelist, was writing, he used to rave about his room, shouting and muttering and pouring with sweat. On one occasion, imagining the anguish of one of his characters, he tore a bedspread to pieces with his teeth. He gave everything he had, you see, though that is not the only way to do it."

"You see, when Balzac wanted to get to the truth, he tore up stuff like a wild animal."

"Is that what you want us to do?" they asked.

"Yes. Yes. Yes. Tear stuff up. Tear stuff down. Rage and give everything you have."

They had never before been asked to commit so much. They had never been led consciously to believe that school and the world could be made into a more righteous place through their own words or ideas.

I watched Annie manage her anxieties. She had to leave the room sometimes and enclose herself in the giant green Lycra bag her mother had suspended from a beam in the kitchen. Other times she perched on the staircase, looking down on the class like a frightened bird. I watched Mira alternate between tenderness for her classmates, fierce resistance against any kind of conformity, and adolescent torpor. I listened to Nick announce once, without any sense of irony, that he had come to North Branch as a seventh grader so that he could prepare himself to get a good, high-paying job when he grew up.

Sometimes I felt a little like a matador with a red cape, luring them, I hoped, from where they were into a dance of indescribable beauty. To get there, I had to enter the ring with them, where they could argue, bellyache, and kvetch. As I anticipated, they complained to me about my choice of books we read for literature.

"Why can't we read something happy?" complained Najat one day as we started literature class.

"Because, Najat, happy books are crappy books."

"I want to read a *good* happy book!"

"You mean some jolly tale with happy, sugar-coated bunnies and little rainbows?"

"No. I mean maybe a book where not everyone dies!"

She had a point. In many of the books we were reading that year—
*Of Mice and Men; Roll of Thunder, Hear My Cry; One Flew Over the
Cuckoo's Nest; The Old Man and the Sea; Fahrenheit 451*—death figured
prominently.

"Najat, the books we read are the books I teach. When you start
your school, you can pick all the crappy, happy books you want."

"*God*, you're such a poopy head." She rolled her eyes.

"Najat, what's the point of reading books that have happy endings?"
I asked. "Life is about suffering and enduring. Life has death in it. If a
book does not have those things, it's not about life. Life ends with
death. Death helps us know why we live. Death is always there reminding us that the life we have is unspeakably precious."

"Who cares about dying? It's just so, so depressing!"

"Yeah, and your grandmother—who just happens to be a poet—are
her poems all about cute little squirrels collecting nuts and hopping
through the woods? No! Najat, your grandmother writes about the real
things of life. She's going blind, and guess what? She writes about *guess
what*? Going blind! She's not afraid."

"Tal, *we* are not going blind, and *we* are not dying!"

"Oh yeah, snap!" said Zoe. "I think we should read *Dancing in My
Nuddy-Pants*. That is the bestest, greatest book ever written."

"*Dancing in my Nuddy-Pants*?!" I raved. "You want me to waste our
valuable time here at the North Branch School reading a book by some
English ding-a-ling teenybopper called *Dancing in My Nuddy-Pants*?"

"Tal, we've got to read *Ender's Game*!" Doug exhorted, his eyeballs
popping out and little flecks of saliva raining down on the table. "It is *so*
cool. See, it's about this kid who is being trained—"

"Doug! I do not have seven millennia to hear about the entire plot
of some freaky sci-fi fantasy book written for creepy teenage boys."

"Tal, you would love this book. It would be the perfect lit book. It's
full of really serious themes and conflicts. It's got just what you love:

issues. We have to read it. . . . Please, please, please. If you have the class read it I will retract my previous comment that you are a false god."

"Doug, I already know that I am not a false god. We are not reading cheesy time-warp sci-fi crap. And, in case you were not aware, Ray Bradbury is the big cheese in the sci-fi department and we *are* reading *Fahrenheit 451.* But if you want me to look at *Ender's Game,* bring it in and I will read it. But I sure as hell ain't taking your word for it."

"Tal, you are such a butt head!" said Najat.

"False god, false god," Doug chanted, pointing at me.

"Tal," Janine reminded, "*ain't* is not proper grammar."

"*Ain't* is in my trusty *Webster's,* my little friend. Look it up. Listen, you little bunch of shit muffins. As I told Najat, when you guys start your own school with a *new* bunch of superficial teenagers, you're free to have them read any crappy, happy books you want them to read, and I am sure it will be a really popular school. Until then, we're reading the books I pick. You got it?"

"Fine Tal, what*ever.*" This was Sophie, imitating a vapid teen, rolling her eyes, but with a great smile. Her hands, as always, were clasped tidily over her binder.

"Nice eye rolling Sophie," I said. "That's real talent. Do that again. That was really cool. You've been taking lessons from Mira."

It was an absurd discussion, but it was fun. They were asking: *What is important?* Why is *this* important? Why are you teaching us *this*? Would it not be better some other way? They were asking me why I was so obsessive and relentless and intense. Who *was* I, and why did we have to do school this way?

I imposed my predilections on them. I even oppressed them with serious, grave works of literature. But that's what was needed in school— to be reading and discussing serious literature, serious ideas, every day, books around which we could hold meandering discussions to assemble our own meanings. At least they were free to question and free to discuss. In truth, it was the discussion they needed. They were talking about the books they loved, the things they wanted from books, and from me.

Walter Benjamin, in his essay "The Storyteller," wrote that without stories, *true* stories, dark or tragic tales, we risk becoming people living "in rooms that have never been touched by death, dry dwellers of eternity. . . . What draws the reader to the novel is the hope of warming his shivering life with a death he reads about."

I did not want my students to be dry dwellers of eternity. I was going to teach them what I believed, with as much fire and élan as I could muster. We would draw close, I would draw them close, to see how a book, or even death, could warm their lives. I hoped that in time they would understand.

With all the current talk about test scores and high standards, and with my credibility and the survival of the school on the line, I worried that we might be seen as some kind of "free school" without demonstrable standards and where nothing of quantifiable value happened. The public—or the parents—might legitimately ask: Where were the measurable results, the rigor, the organizational orthodoxy? Given the culture of politics around education it would be all too easy for the North Branch School to be dismissed as utopian fantasy.

I sometimes worked myself up into a state born of both despair and curiosity: What are we doing this for? What is school for? Why had I started a school in the first place? What was supposed to happen, what could happen in a school with twelve-, thirteen-, and fourteen-year-olds once the old system was discarded? The word *school* comes from the Greek *scholē*—"a lecture or discussion." Another etymological shading of *scholē* means "leisure, spare time," which later passed on to mean "otiose discussion"—that is, futile and functionless discussion. It could be said that I had led a functionless discussion about what books to read in our literature class. Socratic dialogue was the perfect fit for my students because they were questioning so much. I was realizing that school *was* a place where such meandering dialogue could happen, where we could create something like a Greek symposium, where the discussion was given time and honor. Our work was that constant interplay of question and answer, speaking and listening, searching and finding.

I thought of my own children with their towers of blocks—things got built up, knocked down, and then they started all over again. It happened every day in every kindergarten in the world. Perhaps school *was* meant to be the place where children were held back from the world for a short time so that they could play and build with ideas, words, argument, even their hopes and dreams. There would be enough time to climb around inside words, inside books, and inside their own lives to have the chance to see which words, books, hopes, and dreams mattered.

We did not read *Dancing in My Nuddy-Pants* and we did not read *Ender's Game*. We did read Elie Wiesel's *Night,* the heart-rending memoir of his experiences in the German concentration camps at the end of World War II.

I wanted to disturb them, shock them, infect them, or at least cause them to forever allocate a small part of their hearts to what happened in that story. By choosing *Night,* I was putting the agony and the enormity of the Holocaust before my students' eyes as no generic history text ever could.

I wanted them to see the traces of Wiesel's experience, to feel the power of memory and words, and to recognize the value of committing those traces to *their* memories—not to control memory (as the Fascist would), but to see how a memory could be sung out, horrifying though it was, to see and hear how the artist drew out the contours and shadows of lament. To discover how words, literature, and art could speak, and to feel whether any beauty remained.

I was once teaching *Night* at the Paideia School in Atlanta in late spring, a glorious time in the South, with Bradford pear trees, dogwoods, and azaleas blooming in profusion along every street, yard, and park. As I began the class one late morning, I couldn't help but look out our windows into the green leaves fluttering in the breeze. Suddenly I wanted to flee the ashes of Auschwitz and be far away and released from the burden of witnessing, even if it was only through the lens of a book. I found myself having doubts—parents raised objections often enough to make me doubt—about whether young adolescents should be subjected to the horrors described in Wiesel's book. I had tried to put some context around the story so we could see it as a historical event, but I could not help feeling that I was committing a vaguely criminal act by asking students to stare into the pitiless depths of evil and suffering while we sat in the comfortable splendor of spring's radiance. Wasn't I making the suffering continue? Why put it before them at all? I found it nearly impossible to read certain passages in *Night* each year, not only because of the grotesque injustice and unmitigated suffering, but because so much of the book was so heartbreakingly sad. Why make my students sad? Why show them, to use Yeats's phrase, "tragedy wrought to its uttermost"?

That spring morning I found myself wondering aloud to the class, "Why should we read or see these things? It's so depressing. Should I have you reading this stuff?"

Without pausing, Delilah Haverman, an eighth grader, stared at me without blinking: "How could you *not*?"

She instinctively knew what I was coming to learn—that pushing to the extreme edges was my responsibility, a necessity, if we were ever going to learn.

Ｗe read *Night* despite Najat's protests. I required them to read the assignment for each class twice and to write a two-page typed response of their own thoughts and questions. I didn't want to have to tell them what was important: I started each class with an invitation for them to tell me.

"So, reactions? Re-ack-*she*-ons? That's French for 'reactions.' I'm multilingual."

"That's great, Tal."

"So who wants to start?"

Hands went up tentatively.

"I thought Juliek was important," said Mira

"Aw, I was going to bring that up," said Tico.

"If it's important, there'll be more than one thing to say about it, bro," I said. "Go ahead, Mira."

And we were off.

I had a teaching postulate: A good teacher will ask at least one hundred questions a day, eighteen thousand per school year, half of which might be philosophical, theoretical, ambiguous, or otherwise mystical in nature. *Why is Elie telling us this story? How does he know the god within him? For what purpose does Elie live? If we pray to God for the strength to ask the right questions, then what are the right questions?* I asked for responses and they sat shifting silently in their seats. They weren't sure what I was asking for. They were not accustomed to such questions or doing the hard work. They expected the lesson to be laid out prior to class with questions they could answer and activities they could carry out. They had been conditioned to receive answerable questions and to give tepid responses. Maybe they were used to never having to venture any ideas at all, staying within the pages of the book and never involving themselves in the interpretations, as though literary study were somehow divorced from experience. They were not trained to open a book and ask, "Why has this book been written for me?" They were more than willing, or only able, in the beginning, to sit looking at me, waiting for something to happen.

"What the hell is the matter with you?" I asked. "Wake up. You have Elie, who believes profoundly, and all you can do is sit there doodling a note on your binder. Nick, where's your book?"

"Uh, at home?"

"You think it's at home?"

"Uh, yeah. I must have left it there."

"Nick, did I tell you that you have to have your book in class?"

"Yes."

"Nick, you don't know where your book is, do you? But I will tell you this: It's not at home."

"It's not?"

"No, it's not, because you left it in the kitchen, on my desk."

"Sorry."

"Nick, goddammit, come to class prepared. We have a book sitting in front of us that tells us something about why we live. Elie has relived it so we can learn it, and to you it might as well be reading the goddamn telephone book."

It got warm, but I figured they'd rather have an interesting class than a boring one. If there was one thing I wanted them to know, it was that reading these books mattered more than anything else. I did not want them to be indifferent. The book was sacred. They would know that I was serious. If they weren't, I was going to prick, pry, curse, harass, and rage.

"When I come back in here every damn one of you better have your hand raised and be ready to talk." I stormed out the front door, slamming it behind me. As I walked around the nature trail, I was not sure my act would work; they might still be sitting there with glazed looks on their faces.

When I opened the door, the room was quiet and every hand in the class was held high.

Over the weeks, their responses began to show an astonishing range and depth. They wrote suites of poems, did detailed drawings of major characters, or posed their own philosophical questions that they tried nobly to answer. They wrote comic strips of major scenes, portraits of characters speaking important words, letters to dead characters, letters to those who would censor the book, and letters to themselves.

Once, after reading the scene in which Juliek, the violinist, plays Beethoven's concerto to a roomful of dead and dying men, I got this:

> But Juliek is something more. He is attached to himself insofar that he knows his life like music and he can play it as that. He is detached from the world around and completely within himself, living everything one last time, connected to his soul and beliefs. That is what religion is: It is the quest for detachment of worldly things and attachment to whoever you are inside, whatever of yourself you love, whatever journey you have been on, to be able to play that journey, even for dying men, in the hope that it will give them life. Even though Juliek died, he never lost that peering forward. He is able to find the hope under the layers of decay; to recover the fire from the embers and bring it flaring back to life, to embrace that life and never detach himself from it. That is what "being whole" is. It is having what you need to drive you forward and the knowledge of how to drive. That is what Juliek has and knows to the core and what these people are discovering through their experience. What seeing and living death gives them, what life is; finding those things within you, like the air to breathe by.

That peering forward—that was what I wanted my students to have.

"Do you all know what that means?" I asked.

They nodded unsurely.

"That response, that's the definition of living beautifully, playing the music until the last note, playing it against all the tragic and evil forces of the world. That's Balzac raving in his room or Hemingway writing the paragraph twenty-nine times."

"I tried to imagine what the sound of the violin would be," said Doug.

"The violin was his soul," said Sophie.

Najat raised her hand. "Which they never could take from him."

I held the paper out to them.

"That's an amazing response, you guys." We spent the rest of the class trying to understand what the violin meant, to Elie, to them, and what it meant to embrace life, to find oneself in the deepest part of life, even in despair, and to play beautiful music in the darkest place.

Later we discussed the passage in which Wiesel writes of his first "selection" ordeal, by which Jews were chosen to live or die with the wave of a baton. I knew that the scene would be the focus of our discussion.

Hand in hand we followed the throng.

An SS came toward us wielding a club. He commanded:

"Men to the left! Women to the right!"

Eight words spoken quietly, indifferently, without emotion. Eight short, simple words. Yet that was the moment when I left my mother. There was no time to think, and I already felt my father's hand press against mine: we were alone. In a fraction of a second I could see my mother, my sisters, move to the right. Tzipora was holding Mother's hand. I saw them walking farther and farther away; Mother was stroking my sister's blond hair, as if to protect her. And I walked on with my father, with the men. I didn't know that this was the moment in time and the place where I was leaving my mother and Tzipora forever. I kept walking, my father holding my hand.

Behind me, an old man fell to the ground. Nearby, an SS man replaced his revolver in its holster.

My hand tightened its grip on my father. All I could think of was not to lose him. Not to remain alone.

I asked them, in the stillness of the classroom, what this passage was about.

"How do you feel when you read this?" I asked, after Doug had read the passage aloud. "What does it make you feel? What's happening in you when you hear these words?"

"It makes me sick. I feel nauseous," said Janine.

"I felt guilty, because when I read it I felt lucky this never happened to me," said Steve. "I shouldn't have felt that. I should be angry."

"Maybe you are," I said.

"I guess I just felt, I don't know, sad." The room was filled with a huge quietness, the kind that lives in churches.

"I just wanted the book to stop," said Mira. "But I shouldn't have wanted that. Because Elie couldn't make this just stop. What he was living through is a lot worse than us reading a book about it."

"So," I said, "that brings up this question: Why are we reading this book, if it makes us feel so terrible? Or: Why did Elie write it to us? Why did *he* relive it and go back through it. Because we have to know that it's a lot more painful for him to write about it than it is for us to read about it."

"Because he wants us to feel it. If we don't we could become like the Germans, who feel nothing, or don't know what they feel," said Mira.

"Choosing to not read this would be a form of cowardice," said Doug. "This book is something that should not be avoided."

"Bringing us this close is how he makes us feel what he felt," added Steve. "So that we will know about it."

"So why should we know about it?" I asked.

"It shows us what really matters in the world," said Sophie. "Like, Elie knew that the only thing was his father's hand. Before that he was detached from his father. When he is holding his father's hand he knows his father is the most important thing in the world."

"Even more important than his religion, maybe," said Anna.

"He saw his mother stroking his sister's head. That was the thing that mattered. That's what he's telling us," said Nick.

"And why should he tell us that? Why is seeing his mother's hand on his sister's head important?"

"It's physical connection," said Sophie. "The ability to protect someone or give them comfort. That's what we have in the world."

"Well, it makes me think about my dad," said Nick, and he began to cry. He tried to wipe the tears away, smearing them across his cheeks.

"If the book makes you sad, Nick, let it make you sad. If it makes you cry, let it make you cry."

He tried to talk, but his words seemed jammed up, his understanding shaky.

"I don't know, it just . . ."

"Why do you think about your dad?" I asked. "What do you feel about him when you read this or talk about it?"

"I guess it makes me realize how much I need him. It makes me think about what would happen if he was gone. Like, how I don't always appreciate what he does for me. He works hard and he cares so much about what he does."

"That's beautiful, Nick," I said. "That you should appreciate him more, here and now. From that I can begin to feel something like what Elie felt."

Najat raised her hand. "Well, I think about how I don't have a dad. And what if my mom was taken away from me? I worry about her driving over to Stockbridge every day. I'm so scared when there is a snowstorm." Her lips were quivering.

"It makes me want to go home and hug my mom and dad," said Annie. "I mean, I appreciate them, and I tell them that I love them, but it makes me think I should show it more. Or mean it more."

"These things you all are saying, these are true things," I tried to explain. "Look at what Elie's story is making us feel. Not only horrible and disgusted, but also that tenderness and love are the most precious things. He is showing us, reminding us, what the Nazis forgot, what anybody can forget. Elie's mother's hand on Tzipora is more powerful than all the Nazi batons in the world."

My students, warming in the embers of such tales, imagined losing their own parents. They sensed how dearly they held their parents, no small thought for thirteen- and fourteen-year-olds hell-bent on forming their own identities. When they read this and felt these things, when they said how a book could make them feel, I no longer questioned the rightness or wrongness of teaching *Night*.

Neither I nor any of my students could ever comprehend the scope and depth of suffering experienced in the death camps of Nazi Germany, the same nation that gave the world Beethoven and Goethe and Rilke. Still, an inquiry into that suffering yielded something that would not have come into being otherwise—a fleeting glimpse of an inmost philosophy, a way of countenancing suffering, an image of wholeness, a way to make sense of a tragic story.

My most invasive and nettlesome concern, what kept me awake at night, the plague of my half dreaming, was to figure out how to help my students break free of self-consciousness in their writing. Seamus Heaney used the phrase, "ungoverned tongues," denoting that rare state in which the poet-creator attains heightened creative liberation: "A plane is—fleetingly—established where the poet is intensified in his being and freed from his predicaments. The tongue, governed so long in the social sphere, by considerations of tact and fidelity, by nice obeisances to one's origin within the minority or majority, this tongue is suddenly ungoverned."

At times my students seemed wholly ignorant of their abilities, disconnected from their potential, laconic, remote, and obliviously distracted by their own distractions. Someone's new haircut or ear piercing could always be counted on to elicit more fascination and excitement than would the structure of a poem or a cell. How, then, to sever their dependence on fleeting irrelevancies and jettison tact, fidelity, and the dictates of the social sphere and so ungovern their tongues? I knew they *could* do it, but it was a matter of leading them to *want* to do it, to raise their self-consciousness. I wanted them to believe that their words should be used as a crowbar, adze, sledgehammer, or compass—that they could not live or grow without the clarifying power of a language they already possessed but as yet could not freely wield.

My curse and my blessing was that I believed that every kid in the class—that year and every year—could achieve the power where words broke through the barriers of decorum and would awaken us, as James Wright wrote in a letter to James Dickey, "into dreams that include and surpass the data of [our] experience." This belief was a blessing because it drove me to have faith in them and so kept me working; a curse because I had to figure out how to help them find the words, how to redeem that faith.

A former student of mine had written a short poem:

I am a stranger to myself
With puzzled emotions lacking a foundation,
I've traveled so far and do not know my destination
nor my beginnings.

I cling to what I perceive as truth
and scold my decisions.
I bask in the temporary,
questioning every moment.
I wonder what my purpose is
and debate my feelings.
All I have to believe in are my intentions.

His words were muscular and at the same time tentatively groping. There was no prettiness or subterfuge. He had neither physical moorings nor clear direction, and even his intentions remained undefined. And yet his authority was clear: He spoke for the questing adolescent, the seeker. He articulated what it was to stand before the opened window, to be poised at the threshold, plagued by stasis or unrealized power. For the adolescent is often a stranger to himself, puzzled, unknowing, anguished, questioning, wondering, debating, to the degree that it is possible for him to simultaneously scold himself with self-doubt, bask gloriously in the moment, and gaze unsurely into the future.

I wanted to bring my students to that threshold at every moment of every day. I constantly changed angles of approach, varying the combinations, throwing out flurries of questioning, jesting, puzzlement, exhortation. I harassed, I harangued, I shouted. I spent whole class periods handing them back their stories, reading them back passages that were clumsy, tepid, or shallow.

Once I handed Zoe back her story. "It's not there, Zoe. Not even close."

"What? I worked so hard on it," she said, as she started to cry.

"Zoe, it's too easy, too pat, too glib, and it doesn't have *you* in there. It has what you *wish* you felt, not what you really feel."

"But she worked hard on that story," chipped in Najat.

"Who the hell are you, Najat, her lawyer? She can listen to you and end up with a crappy story, or she can listen to me and maybe do something great."

The story was about how she felt "at peace" with Mira, who, she felt, sometimes humiliated and controlled her. But Zoe's voice was hidden behind following, cowering, playing it safe, and wanting a happy ending. In truth, the story was not terrible, but I had read the same story many times before. It was decorous and timid. I wanted her to write with more madness and shamelessness, to be frenetic, whirling, contradictory, unhinged. I wanted her to rave in her room like Balzac, to tear down curtains trying to find the glorious self she had submerged or masked. From *that,* poetry and vision might arise.

"I don't get what you want me to do."

"I want you to write a great story, Zoe. The story of the only girl on Earth named Zoe. I want you to put it all out there. Right now you're essentially saying you're at peace with feeling controlled and humiliated. That's terrible, and it's not enough. You have to go all the way."

"How do I do that? What's all the way? What else do you want me to do?" She was wilting.

"Look in the mirror, Zoe, and tell everything you've been through and make us feel why you were willing to feel it. Why did you accept being mocked, imprisoned? Where did your own voice go? What did it feel like to have Zoe almost disappear?"

"So what should I fix?"

"It's not fixable. You've got to start over."

I did not know what her story was or whether she could even find it. All I could do was offer her my absolute unwavering belief that she had depths we—and she—had not yet known.

One night I lay on my couch with a stack of their stories on my chest. I thought, strangely, of Hamlet's rage at his mother. In her chamber before her he clutched her locket, which held pictures of both his father and his uncle. There and then Hamlet became the daggers in her ears. "What devil was't / That thus cozen'd you at hoodman-blind? / Eyes without feeling, feeling without sight, / Ears without hands or eyes, smelling sans all."

He wanted her to see and to feel. He himself wanted to feel and by feeling *become, to be,* to live fully. As I waded through two hundred disjointed, meandering, artless draft pages, I knew I had to be the daggers in my students' ears. I wanted them to become and to be. I had to make them look upon whatever counterfeit they had tendered and turn their eyes toward the souls they had not yet revealed.

I carried the stories back to class with circled comma splices and misspellings, arrows, underlining, notes in the margins. I read back to them what I had written. *I don't understand this. Show, don't tell! Uh, any feelings here? What were you thinking?*

"Nick," I said, as I tossed his story out to the middle of the table, "I read this last night. It made me sad because of what it *didn't* show. No pulse, no passion. Where is your intensity, your gratitude for this life, your love for what can be known?"

He looked down at the story. "I don't know."

"Roethke said, 'We think by feeling.' But there is no feeling here, so there is no thought. There is nothing gritty or graceful in this. There is a topic and a plot but no feeling, and so the story is empty of you."

"I guess I didn't know what I was trying to do."

"I can tell you didn't know what to do. Goddammit! How many weeks have we been working on these mother-freaking stories? Nick, how many hours did you work on this?"

"Annie, I have no idea what you are talking about in this last scene. It's the ultimate moment of your story and it's a horrible string of clichés. That's all it is and nothing else."

I told them these things in our dark classroom, in the gloom of approaching winter, during the shaky beginnings of our school. I knew it was against all decorum—a teacher's tongue ungoverned. But I told myself the situation demanded it; my students needed and wanted it. I believed they longed for this push, this faith of mine, because they desired no less than anyone else to come into a closer communion with themselves—desiring, as Eliot wrote, "another intensity / For a further union." And if I did not push with a depth of love, faith, and fury, what would they be but a lot of timorous halfhearts?

I was here, and they were here with me—so that they could become changed, so that they could see vistas stretching out inside them, so they could *become*. We were here so I could help them learn to create beauty, kindness, gratitude, hope, and love.

I put myself at this gunpoint imperative: We had to make something great or we were, at best, merely competent; at worst, a true failure—making nothing at all.

They were afraid to read out loud, but I wouldn't let them bury their words. If Annie wasn't comfortable with her sketch, or Steve dug in his heels and wouldn't read his, I read for them. Sometimes the students felt more comfortable if whoever sat next to them read it, as though a different voice gave a protective cushion. Other times I read their work without asking permission; I read their work against their whining and wishes. If the poem was good, if there was poetry in it, I was going to bring it out. The atmosphere was positive: The effort to read, to participate in the conversation, to offer something, was met with affirmation and acceptance. If the piece was silly or shallow, we called it that, mirroring back what we heard and felt.

Because they spent four hours a day with me, I kept looking for ways to add new dimensions. I brought in music for them to listen to while they wrote—John Coltrane, Duke Ellington, Sun Ra, Coleman Hawkins, Woody Guthrie, Leadbelly, Billie Holiday, Bob Dylan, Jimi Hendrix, and Robert Johnson—anything that moved me. That was occasional filler, and they still sometimes sat before me in silence, not smiling, not applauding, void of visible positive response.

Zoe and I arranged for one of her grandmother's college students, Molly May, to come visit our class. Molly and I would teach a poetry seminar together. On the first morning, she introduced herself and then read to the class poems from her senior creative writing thesis, *Geography of a Plum*. One of Molly's poems was about feeling ugly and out of place as an eighth grader.

"Any of you guys ever feel like that?" I asked when she had finished.

"Uh . . . yeah, sometimes," Nick said dutifully, but he looked as though the idea pained him. "But I'm not a girl."

Najat was waving her hand madly.

"Yes, Najat? Did you want to say something? I think I could tell because you were indicating that you wanted to say something by the way you are saying 'Ooo, ooo, pick me!' and waving your hand around like you are drowning."

"Well, I was going to say—"

"In fact, you are saying it, right now," I said.

"I am SAYING, if you'll stop interrupting—"

"I'll stop interrupting now—"

"—that I know exactly how she feels!" she blurted out. "I hate being this age! I was in fourth grade when I started to develop. Do you know how awful it is to get boobs and you're only in fourth grade when it happens? Nobody else had boobs. I was like the *boob* girl. And I got my period when I was in fifth grade. And all the girls were mean and were always backstabbing each other and talking behind each other's back and you had to have a boyfriend if you wanted to be popular. It was AWFUL!"

Whatever had governed her tongue for so long was suddenly dissolving. We listened in amazement as she ripped through the miseries suffered as a teen and preteen. The whole class was laughing, not only about what she was saying but also because somehow her rant was liberating, pulling us along with her. Her story rose up and took shape before us, and she didn't care if anyone thought it was wrong.

"You tell 'em, Najat!" I said with a tinge of awe. "You go, girl! Uh-huh, yeah!" I felt delight and also relief. She said it, and it was okay.

In poetry class we started with Stevens's "Thirteen Ways of Looking at a Blackbird." That poem required them to take multiple looks at an object and encouraged the imagination to range freely, even joyfully. The poem required a second and third look—in fact, those multiple looks were the only way to see the whole. It blew monolithic concrete-ism to bits. I figured they would like the poem because it was about possibility. The mind did not have to be confined to one way of seeing. If there was one thing these students needed to do, it was to try to look at things in new ways.

We read the poem several times and then began our discussion.

"I don't get it," Najat moaned. "This is weird."

Innuendoes? Barbaric glass? O thin men of Haddam? What the hell was this? We read the poem again, and again. From confusion, little fragments began to cohere; from each part, a way toward the whole. They understood *twenty snowy mountains*—that was our familiar home. Our own dark November days—they understood how it could be *evening all afternoon.* They knew the shadows of cedar limbs and they knew moods traced in shadows and in falling snow. We lingered over those details. We talked about rivers, and euphonious sounds, and the sound of euphony. We bantered about harmony, symphony, and cacophony. We listened to the poem again. Then, suddenly, they loved the poem. They loved the liquid flow, the shifts, the mystery living in the deep gloom. They were caught up in a pantomime of thirteen fleeting, lucid glances at one beautiful bird—and one beautiful poem now beginning to live inside them.

Then we practiced on an object. I put a candle on the table, turned

out the lights, and they each spent a few minutes trying to write different ways of looking at it. Was it just wax and wick and fire? Or was it
more—movement, time, shadow, heat, or hope? Molly and I gave them
the assignment to go home and write a "Thirteen Ways" poem about
something important to them.

Two weeks later we sat down for poetry class. "Okay, get your poems out." There was a rustling of papers, binders unzipping, running
to find stray backpacks to get at tattered pages.

"Who wants to read? Let's hear one of these puppies."

"Tal," offered Annie, "poems are not puppies."

"Poems are puppies. We're gonna read these puppies. Who wants
to go?"

"Uh, Tal, do we have to read?" asked Mira.

"No Mira, you do not have to read, but wouldn't our class be more
interesting if we did read? Then we would have something to think and
talk about. Know what I mean? Or we could just sit here, afraid of the
thoughts we have tried to express, afraid of *any* thoughts, and we could
look at each other and wonder about what a poem might possibly be."

She rolled her eyes.

"Uh, Tal." It was Tico. He slid a sheet of paper across the table to me.
We had worked out a little unspoken procedure. If he had something he
wanted to share, he would simply hand it to me for me to read.

"All right, you weenies, Tico has volunteered to let me read his. Now
all teenagers and preteens, shut your traps. We've got a puppy to read."

I read the poem, called "Ten Ways of Looking at a Mind."

"1. *We are invisible to our mind's eye.*
    Our minds are invisible to us.

"2. *If you lose your mind I can tell you:*
    It's not under the couch.
    It's not under the chair.

"3. *You can mind your manners*
    You can mind your p's and q's
    But that won't help you:
    It's all in your mind.

"4. *You can't touch it;*
    You can't smell it.
    You can't hear it.
    You can make up your mind.

"5. *You are strands*
    Connecting your mind to the world.
    When you are out of your mind
    All but one strand is broken.

"6. *It's what's behind you*
    That makes you go forward.

"7. *If you had a big rock to push up the hill*
    You could put your shoulder to it,
    You could put your mind to it.
    I'd put my mind to it.
    But it might stay there.

"8. *Three minds sat under an apple tree.*
    When the apples fell
    One complained about getting hit in the head,
    Another thought it was food,
    The third said, 'Eureka. It's gravity.'

"9. *Three minds are better than one.*

"10. *Do you mind?*"

As I finished, I looked up at the class with my mouth half open.

"Did you hear that, because I'm not sure I got it. I'm gonna read this again, okay?"

"Okay, Tal," came the lackluster assent.

"Go easy on the enthusiasm, you guys. You're overwhelming me. Listen up. Here it is."

I read it again and I began to see. Tico was telling us how his mind worked and how many ways he could know himself and his surroundings. With leaping wordplay he demonstrated an ability to get inside a thing and become it. He told us that his mind was holding on by only one strand, barely keeping him in place, while others seemed to glide along unburdened, all abilities flourishing. He knew he could put his mind to a task, but he also knew he might likely fail. The tasks school had required of him were truckloads of Sisyphus's stones, deadweight he felt doomed forever to push up the hill, weight his mind could not ever move. But in his poem, he showed us plainly: His mind was more than able—it was heroic. He told us with impish, lilting delight—*I know quite a few things you didn't think I knew. Do you mind?*

I hoped the class got it—how could they not?

"Tico, this is amazing. I love this. I mean, this is incredible. Whatta you think?"

"That's pretty cool, Tico," said Nick.

"Yeah, what I like is how he put in the part at the end about Newton," said Doug, taking his chance to let us know he knew something while completely avoiding what Tico was telling us about himself.

"Who's Newton?" asked Tico, a little perturbed, sensing, perhaps, what was happening: They were moving away from his poem, perhaps partially because they knew it was better than theirs, perhaps partially because they did not understand it. Doug's intelligence and facility in school was a constant thorn to Tico about his own difficulties. They picked at each other constantly. Perhaps Doug could not yet understand an intelligence that came in an unconventional form.

"Uh, the famous scientist. . . . He discovered gravity? Hello," Doug said. The condescension was not disguised.

"Uh, Doug, you don't have to brag about how smart you are," said Mira. Zoe rolled her eyes, not at Mira but *for* Mira, to show she approved of what Mira had said. In her mind, Doug was nothing but a hopeless geek, therefore deserving of scorn.

"Oh, for Christ's sake, you guys. You're not even thinking about what just hit you over the head with a goddamn two-by-four. Why the hell are you bickering over whether Doug is being an intellectual snob when you should be talking about how great Tico's poem is?"

They looked at me in stupefaction.

"Is this what you do when you hear something good, something true, something that brings serious ideas into our class? Come on!"

They looked at me and then at each other.

"Tico just gave us something that he has probably never given any class. Maybe the best thing *you've* ever gotten. He told us something about how hard school is, and how he learns, and what his mind can do. When that happens you put all your petty crap to the side and you give something back. Understand?"

They nodded.

Tico was saying, *Here I am*—finally able to tell us about the shape of his struggles and the flow of his thinking, and we were not ready. We had a long way to go before we knew how to really listen.

Throughout the fall we had brief glimpses of the fiery blaze of autumn trees. At the school it was a shady solitude with the cool hush of wind in the firs. We heard no voices in the halls or announcements over intercoms and saw nothing but the woods and each other. Often we looked out the windows to see dead pine needles drifting down, a multitude of minute amber splinters falling silently.

As the weather changed, there was a shift in the locus of our gatherings. We migrated from outside, the site of rambunctious play at lunch, fort building, and games of tag and tackle. We spent more time around the stove in the kitchen. The ten of us could circle around it, and there we read poetry, held a mock trial, and had discussions ranging from the war in Afghanistan to Metallica to Irish bodhráns to the most humane practices for catching and eradicating mice. It was there we had folded our 165 origami peace cranes.

My students were discovering that there was no way to hide in a clique or become an anonymous part of the crowd. Gathering around the warmth on cold mornings, then, had the effect of pulling us all together, of bringing us nearer and closer.

Since we were studying Vermont history, Nick brought in an old diary his dad had bought on eBay, a delicate, leather-bound daybook with all entries penciled in a light, graceful hand. The diary concerned the daily activity of a Salisbury, Vermont, farmer by the name of Silas A. Bump in the year 1876. On one cold morning we circled around the stove to look at the journal, taking turns reading entries from each of our birthdays. *"Nov 7 Pleasant Visited with Chas in the fore-noon Towed three loads manure Sold butter 28 cents lb. Paid back Saul $10."*

"What?" exclaimed Tico. "What a boring life! No instant messaging or DVDs!"

"Totally predictable response, Tico," I said. "Every teenager in America would have said that."

"You're stereotyping teenagers, Tal," said Mira.

"Okay, every teenager in America except about five."

Then, trying to induce wonder and historical imagination, I said, "Think about it. This was the way life was. It was real, maybe more real that sitting face-to-face with your so-called friends on a computer."

"I have like ninety people in my e-mail address book," said Zoe.

"You don't have diddley squat, Zoe," I said.

We passed the diary around. The more we read, the more interesting it became—how much hard work was required, the importance of neighbors, the centrality of the weather, the price of products, and the necessity of getting a good price.

The kids observed that the brief entries told of a deep connection between the land and life, of a rare kind of simplicity and a purifying lack of contemporary complication. Others noticed that the journal was "simple," in that the grammar and spelling were not exemplary, and yet we marveled at the seriousness of what was written there. Tico noticed that the diary left out the farmer's intimate and personal thoughts, his feelings. Still, we surmised, he must have had an inner life, one we could only guess at. Our last thought brought us closer to the man and his time than I had thought possible when we first opened his diary.

"Do you think he would have ever imagined," I asked, "that one hundred and twenty-five years later a group of teenagers would be studying his journal at a little school in Ripton, or that his little journal would be a historical artifact?"

"Maybe someday people will be reading about us, how we started a school in Ripton," said Nick.

"Yeah, Tal," Tico added. "It's like we're making history."

Later, circled around the stove, we read Donald Hall's beautiful *Ox Cart Man*, the poem of a year in the life of a New Hampshire hill farmer. The patterns of work, the ways that work was so seamlessly a part of life and so literally one's "living"—these rhythms inspired the poem's rhythms. But the poem was more—there was the sublime unity of a family working together, isolated by neither distance, electronic devices, nor hectic schedules, as well as the circularity of the seasons and the pleasures that each brought; and finally, the farmer's strange willingness to surrender all of the products of his year's labor, to sell everything he made or built or grew, including his yoke and harness, his cart, and his beloved ox, which he kissed good-bye on the nose. Thus he began the year anew—clean and unburdened and grateful—as fresh as the wintergreen candies he bought for his family.

I hoped that we could keep the school in that same enviable position, that we could grow and yet remain small and self-sustaining, not ever burdened by needless bureaucracy, political mandates, or restrictive orthodoxy. It was necessary to begin each day and each year with an openness to the kids before me—their issues and thoughts and dreams—an openness to the community we were or hoped to become. I remembered how we had put up our woodpile, each kid bringing in what he or she could carry, some of us doing the stacking, others splitting, all of us working to build it into something useful and good for our collective future.

The woodpile was up. I bought the school three snow shovels at Martin's Hardware. Winter was here, and I hoped we were ready.

III.

winter

A serious house on serious earth it is . . .

Which, he once heard, was proper to grow wise in.

· PHILIP LARKIN, *"Church Going"*

I was mortified by the possibility that the school might fail. From the outside we certainly did not *look* like a school. The school projected no educational authority or institutional gravitas. It had no history or ingrained culture. We did not have any of the trappings or events that comprise the life of a conventional school. We did not have tradition, ritual, or established norms. We conducted no testing. The building itself was ragged and dark, cluttered with boots, posters, a potpourri of cast-off books, and a few beakers and glue sticks. I was fearful of rumors: *Oh yeah, that weird school, where all they do is talk about feelings. Isn't that a school for messed-up kids?*

Philip Larkin imagined a serious "house"—a place of sacramental pilgrimage where one might find oneself. Ours was most definitely not a serious house, and I was sure that none of the kids could clearly articulate why they had gravitated to it. All I could do was try to figure out ways we could transform the building—the gloomy rooms where our hungers and compulsions met—into a house where wisdom would flourish.

I was obsessively vigilant, searching for signs that the school was "working," but it was a difficult thing to measure. Like Santiago in *The Old Man and the Sea,* I kept my hand lightly on the line, sensing the direction and pressure, feeling my way forward by reading barely perceptible movements, turns, and rises.

I knew a school was working when the kids could make it beautiful, when the changes were their own. But I made up my own informal assessments: Did they remember the stories I told them—whether about Sun Ra or Hemingway or my old Plymouth Valiant, or why my mother did not participate in the American civil rights movement? I told them once about how, that morning, Henry had wakened me complaining, "Dad, I do not have a crumb of underwear!" Did they laugh? Did they laugh when I told them that all the public storage facilities on Route 7 were for holding my extra brainpower? Did they play along, or did they turn to other things? Could they write and speak openly of tender emotions and strange ideas? Did mistakes become a part of the discussion? Were they aware that *every day* the only thing of lasting value was what they created in the liminal zone between who they were and who they were becoming?

I waited, hungering and hopeful, to be able to say *yes* to these questions.

T he kids loved poetry class, and Steve seemed to love it the most. There was no possibility of a wrong answer in a poem, and for a boy who had failed virtually every class in his old middle school, this was liberating.

Steve had no organizational or even rudimentary study skills. His spelling was poor, his penmanship shoddy. His notebook was tattered, duct-taped, and covered with graffiti and stapled-on baseball cards. Dog-eared math sheets and three-month-old assignments spilled out, displaying a sort of half intention, half prayer that by holding on to them he might somehow one day do them. His responses to questions asked in class were terse, his motivation almost nonexistent. He had a hard time finding the words to express his ideas. He leaned back in his chair in a kind of dreamy torpor with his coat wrapped around his thin shoulders and his hood pulled over his brow, his eyes moving to whoever spoke. No matter the temperature, he walked two miles to school every day wearing a light New England Patriots coat and no hat or gloves, his hands pulled into the sleeves. The bottoms of his red silk sweatpants were always soaked from walking through the first wet snows. He had no boots. I had given him a bag of winter clothes, but he did not wear them.

"Steve, why the hell aren't you wearing your hat?" I asked, realizing as I said it that he would be embarrassed to wear clothes his teacher had given him.

"I don't get cold," he said nonchalantly.

"Tough guy, eh?"

"Oh, yeah, you know it."

Steve arrived before me every morning. No matter how assiduous I had been about locking up, he was always already inside the house. I knew why he came early: The school was a cleaner, warmer place than his home, a trailer in which there was no phone and where his father was almost always on the road driving trucks.

Most mornings he was in the school with the lights off, still wrapped in his jacket, playing games on the computer, doing a late homework assignment, or resting, still half asleep, on top of the science table. He occasionally answered early morning phone calls and left scrawled messages on my desk.

One morning in December I arrived to find Steve's footprints leading through the snow on the deck. I followed them around the building until I came to a window. Snow, leaves, and dead pine needles were ruffled where he had climbed in. I imagined him inside, dozing in the dark. I opened the front door, kicked the snow off my boots, and turned on the lights. He was pecking away on a computer with his hood pulled tight around his face, his eyes fixed on the glowing screen. He didn't turn around. I hoisted my backpack up onto my desk where I saw a torn sheet of composition notebook paper, placed perfectly in the center of my desk for me to see, signed *S.H.* Above the initials was a six-line poem, handwritten, the neatest handwriting he'd ever proffered.

Steve knew where I was and where I was going to be, and he had met me there. It was his offering, a tentative idea, a fragile gesture saying, "Look, will you look? I have something to say."

I held it in my hand and read it.

"If I could pick a day
To spread my wings and fly
I would never break a promise
Even to this day.
I wonder if I'll have to pay
To spread my wings and fly away."

It wasn't much of a poem, but it stood for something magnificent, a little prayer infused with hope and tragic longing, laced with an awareness, as well, of his relative impoverishment. His words expressed a sense of ordained limitation and his coexistence with dead ends. At the same time the poem was about the possibility of freedom. This boy, who'd never left the state of Vermont, who'd never seen the ocean or a big city, this boy was asking for flight, praying for it, worrying what it would cost, still believing that he had wings. Then it occurred to me: The student, not the schoolmaster, had arrived early to light the woodstove. Steve had kindled the classroom with the gift of a poem. When I stepped over the threshold, our school was already warm.

When I began class that morning, I told the story, a story that had never been told in our school, never had been told in the world, the story of a boy who hated school, who believed school hated him, who believed school was a place for failing, a boy whose most memorable moment in school—aside from having his head hammered into lockers—was his daily trip to the high school gym where, as he passed the Diesel Mechanics class at the Hannaford Career Center, he could catch a fleeting glimpse of his father working toward his GED. It was the story of a boy who had come to a new school and there resurrected his hope of becoming a student who could spread his wings and fly.

I told them I had found Steve's poem on my desk.

"Do you all realize what this means?" I asked, trying to engender some awestruck wonderment. "Do you see what is happening? Steve has written a poem. This fantastic youngster is a poet. This sorry, pants-sagging teenager has got the juice!"

"Way to go, Steve," said Annie, in dutiful support.

"Steve wrote a poem?" said Doug, as though we had been presented with a sonnet typed by a chimp.

"Yes, he did indeed."

"Well, can we hear it already?" asked Mira.

Ignoring her, I said, "Steve turned this in without it being an assignment. He's thinking, his heart is pumping, he's got a pulse, he's alive. He's not just sitting brain-dead in front of a computer playing Diablo Hell Avengers II. Well, he was this morning, but at least he wrote a poem before he did it. I'm proud of you, Steve."

I looked him in the eyes.

"Tal!" shouted Nick. "Can we hear it!"

"Of course we can hear it. But I have to get everyone all ginned up. This is a moment of great importance." And it was, because I wanted them all to feel and never forget what it meant for one of us to cross the threshold to become a maker.

"Okay, we're 'ginned up'! Or whatever you call it!" Nick clamored.

"But now we have to get our thing together, man," I said.

"What *thing*?" Najat said.

"Our thing, man. We got to get our thing together!"

"We have our thing together, man!" they shouted.

"All right, all right. You're ginned up and we got our thing together, man. But wait, hold on, let me tell you about the time Steve Hoyt presented me and the North Branch School with his first poem he ever wrote on his very own. One snowy morning I arrived in the dark classroom and it was sitting—"

"For God's sake already, read it!"

"Okay. Now hush. Here it is."

And I read the poem, as delicate as a gossamer thread—small in stature, monumental in its existence.

They were silent but looked over at Steve, who was blushing and dipping his head so that his greasy bangs hung over his face.

"I'm going to read it again," I said, and I did, according that slight poem every bit of dignity and loving attention I could.

"So, what do you think?"

They all raised their hands. There was no more wonderful sound and sight I knew than that class full of hands rising up because they had all been moved, that rustling, forward-leaning, smiling excitement of hearing and seeing as though for the first time.

"I think it was really great, Steve, that you wrote that and turned it in," said Annie.

"I'm proud of you, Steve," said Mira. "It shows a whole other side of you."

"It makes me want to go write a poem too," Nick added, smiling.

"We're waiting, Nick, we're waiting," I said.

"I like what it was about, how he talked about—" Janine began, halting, not quite sure of what she knew or felt. "That part about being willing to never break a promise."

"It's beautiful, isn't it?" I said.

"I have always thought of Steve as a grungy teen punk skateboarder," said Doug. "But obviously he has these other aspects to his personality. It makes me think that Steve is more of a student than he has shown so far. Sometimes it seems that he doesn't really care about school, or perhaps it's hard for him. But a poem. I'm impressed."

The praise and affirmation were real, expressing their growing awareness not of ideas or facts, but of each other. That poem was the beginning of a fountain of poems, from Steve and from all of them. That is how the lives of these kids, once separate and distant, began to be stitched together. That was how we began to ungovern our tongues.

Snow was falling fast. One day in December in the middle of class Nick looked out the window and shouted, "Look, it's a fisher cat!"

We ran to the window, straining to see the animal, which was clambering over the snowed-covered embankment, its bushy, sable tail disappearing into the woods.

"We saw one of those at our house once!"

"Can you see where it went?"

"Move, Tico, you freak, you're stepping on my foot!"

It was a complete distraction from our ostensible purpose, but somehow, when we were looking out the window like that, I didn't mind. We watched the snow pile up all afternoon, we remarked on it, we talked about how much snow might fall. None of these things were on any state standards or unit plans. By allowing them to happen, a different rhythm was conjured, one that these kids had not felt, that I had not felt, perhaps, since kindergarten.

One day I announced I was going to read them passages from Wallace Stevens's "Extracts From Addresses to the Academy of Fine Ideas."

"You're going to read that guy again?" moaned Tico.

"Yeah, I'm going to read that guy again. That guy happened to be a guy you loved. Remember? You loved 'Thirteen Ways of Looking at a Blackbird.'"

"Yeah, but he's weird."

"Yeah, but you're not yet intelligent. So you might learn something. So listen."

We turned off the lights. "What one believes is what matters," I read. "Ecstatic identities / Between one's self and the weather and the things / Of the weather are the belief in one's element, / The casual reunions, the long-pondered / Surrenders, the repeated sayings that / There is nothing more and that it is enough / To believe in the weather and in one's self, and part of that / And nothing more."

I looked up from my book.

"Sweet," said Nick.

"What one believes is what matters," I said.

"What are the long-pondered surrenders?" Annie asked.

"That's what we're trying to find," I said. "Ecstatic identities. Ponder long and surrender to something great."

I feared cabin fever as it got colder and darker. Cooped up in the house, facing only each other, it was bound to strike. Eric's and my prescription was to demand that we all had to go outside often, even if it was two degrees above zero. They needed to move, they wanted to move—it braced and brightened us.

"Okay everybody, get on your boots and coats! We're gonna run the nature trail!"

There were cries of glee, and there were cascades of moans.

"Oh, why do we have to? I don't have any boots. Taa-al!"

"How many times have we told you to bring your goddamn boots and be prepared?"

"You never told us."

"Yes, he did," said Doug, with emphatic disgust. "Like five hundred times."

"Tal, I can't run. My back hurts," said Janine, who seemed always to discover an ailment as we embarked on physical activity.

"Jesus Christ, Janine, then walk! Let's go."

We would dash out to the trail, with Nick, Tico, and Steve in the lead. They sprinted through the snow, leaping over stumps and boulders, tripping and stumbling and pushing each other. Sophie galloped gracefully along with Najat, while Annie might stop to inspect snow formations on a tree. Doug would be in the back taunting Zoe and Mira about their teen gossiping. Janine brought up the rear, exclaiming over and over that I was a *sac des poux*—bag of head lice—for making us walk in the cold. We came crashing down the hill toward the front door, panting, snow in our shoes, our cheeks burning red, and we would throw snowballs at each other until our hands were numb.

We came back into the warmth of the school, collapsing into wobbly chairs and crowding around the small gas stove in the kitchen. We hung wet mittens above the stove and tried to dry our shoes. There again, in the dark room, warm and close together, we turned back to whatever discussion we had broken off, waiting for whatever would come next.

Every day at break and lunch they raced to put on their boots and snowsuits. There was not a moment to spare—they wanted to take advantage of the time given them to play. At any other middle school they would not have been granted recess—they would have headed to the lunchroom with approximately eighteen minutes to eat and then back to class. Here, though, the essential, perhaps most memorable, part of elementary schooling—recess—continued. The sweet freedom of being able to play and construct activity without being told what to do was alive.

At lunch I watched them falling all over themselves, jumping off rocks, and stick fighting, running through the woods shouting like riotous Norse berserkers. When I rang the bell, they staggered into class, swinging the front door wildly against the piano, huffing and bellowing with snow in their hair and hats, shouting, "Tal, what are we gonna do?"

I remember looking out the window at Nick and Tico making a giant ramp out of snow. Nick, in particular, had the obsessive desire to pack and repack the snow to make the jump perfect for everyone else, which I liked to think of as an expression of his caretaking instinct. Then a sled loaded with Annie, Zoe, Mira, and Najat would come skittering down the hill, over the big rock ledge, and crash hard into the snow pile, or, barely catching the edge of it, dump all of them headlong into the deep snow. Janine shook her head at them and then at me. Nick jumped to repair the ramp. I watched them through the window shouting at each other and laughing, shaking my own head, thinking, *You are a headmaster, and this is your school.*

W e did not have dances or football games on Friday nights, or any sports at all. We did not have assemblies on school climate or the dangers of drugs or cyber bullying. We did not have secretaries, hall monitors, computers, or lockers. Nothing about us made us look like a conventional school except the rusting bell perched on top of a post on the snow-covered deck.

At times, my students, in the way only adolescents can, spat out, "This isn't a *real* school."

I cringed, but my disconsolate despair inspired a corollary feeling, a strange determination, something like rage and pride, anarchy and love, boiling in me and making me desperate to show someone, anyone, how brilliant adolescents could be. Most of all I wanted to show my students how brilliant *they* could be, how much they could love the place of their own making and love the making of it. School was more than enduring the clammy indeterminate darkness of adolescence, doing time, or watching clocks in wire cages.

Our schoolhouse had to become a place where torpor, emptiness, and apathy were obliterated, where my students could answer the hunger in themselves to be more serious, to feel and become great. We desperately needed a destiny toward which we could move, a process or ritual through which we could look at each other and say, *This is who we are. This is how we say who we are. This is who we want to be.*

Najat came to my desk one afternoon after school.

"Tal, someone stole ten dollars out of my cubby." She was frantic, about to cry.

"Are you sure? I mean, have you looked everywhere?"

"Yes, I'm positive. I checked at lunch and it was there, and I just checked everywhere and it's gone."

Nick was standing by.

"What?" he asked. "What happened, Najat?"

"Someone stole my money." Now she did begin to cry. "It was the money my mom gave me to go to the movie this weekend."

"No way," Nick said, with disgust in his voice. He moved toward her and put his hand on her back.

"All right, okay," I said. "Go look one more time. We'll figure it out."

Najat looked and no money turned up and we all went home. That night Marcia called.

"Tal, you need to find out who stole Najat's money. I don't want her in the school if this is going on. I'll pull her out in a red-hot second."

I could agree with Marcia on one point: I did not want to be running a school where there was stealing and rampant disregard for others. If students were afraid of stealing, they would be afraid of everything else—afraid of trying difficult tasks, of saying true feelings, of respecting or even loving each other. In a school of ten kids, that was a problem.

Her statement tapped into my nascent fear that the whole school could disintegrate at any moment, that any crisis might cause parents to withdraw their children—and Marcia was a founding parent of the school. I promised we would figure out what happened.

The next morning when I walked in there were two Butterfinger candy bars on my desk. A week or two before I had been holding forth on my favorite candies, and this was the payback.

"Butterfingers! Sweet! My favorite," I shouted into the preclass racket. "Who gave me these?"

"I did," Tico murmured. He smiled under the brim of his hat.

"That's what I'm talking about!" I shouted. "Thanks, Tico. You have a great memory, especially since it benefits me."

But as soon as math started, I began my inquisition, the operating theory of which was to create a situation of such tension that the truth would spill forth. Never mind the possibility that Najat actually might have lost the money and that there might not be a guilty one among us. I had to go after it as hard as I could. The kids were going to discover that there was no way out.

I stood halfway up the staircase. "Nick, get your ass up here, now!" All heads in the room jerked up from their math problems.

"What? Me?" he asked, wide-eyed.

"No, the other Nick. Come on." He pushed back from the table and trudged up the stairs behind me. I sat him down in a small dressing room. Above us in the ceiling was a skylight. His chair sat in the shaft of light beaming down.

"Tell me what you know. I mean, everything. I already know who took Najat's money, but I want to know everything you know. Don't leave out one detail. Not one, or your ass is grass, and I'm the lawn mower. And if you waste one second of my time, you're dead."

I was lying, but he didn't know that.

"Uh, all I know is what happened yesterday when you were talking to Najat. That was the first I heard of it. I swear."

"Nick, I said don't leave out a freaking speck of the truth. No bullshit!" My anger was both real and feigned. I was also pretty certain Nick didn't know anything, but I was working myself up and creating an electric fear simultaneously.

"Tal, I swear to God, I don't know."

"All right, Nick. Go back down and don't say a damn word. If you do, I'll kill you. You understand?"

He was shaking.

"Steve, get up here." Steve was already scared, having spent the last few minutes wondering what was going on. To tell the truth, I suspected it was Steve, and I hated the fact that I was suspicious.

"Okay, listen, Steve. I already know everything. I already know. The only thing that's going to save your ass is if you tell me every single thing *you* know. Don't leave out a freaking speck of truth. If you do, you're a goner, dead, finished at the old North Branch School."

"Uh, Tal," he stuttered, pale and skittish. "I swear I have no idea what you are talking about."

"Dammit, Steve! I said don't leave anything out."

"I swear to God. I don't have a clue to what this is about."

I double-checked and then I released him. "Steve, if you say one freaking word downstairs, you're dead."

One by one I brought them up and repeated the sequence—Sophie, Zoe, Janine, then Tico.

I sat him down in the shaft of sunlight.

"Tico, if you leave out one freaking detail, you're dead. Leave out one fact, you're—"

"Uh, Tal, I stole Najat's money," he said in a quiet voice, looking straight at me. I didn't blink or pause.

"Well, all righty, then. You saved your ass, Tico. I'm glad you were honest."

He didn't respond.

"Why?" I asked.

Now he was looking down and tears landed on the dirty carpet between his feet.

"I don't know. I didn't think it would matter."

"Did you use the money to buy me those Butterfingers?"

"Yeah."

"You thought you would do something good with the money?"

"Yeah."

"Tico, it's nice you did that. I understand what it means. I appreciate what you're saying to me, but it doesn't make the stealing go away. The stealing, that's a big mother of a problem."

He nodded.

"Tico, guess what? You've got to face the music. You have to go tell everyone. Friends, peers, and countrymen. Your neighbors and your old granny. You have to tell Najat you took her money. Right now. You've got to tell your mom. Tonight. You've got to take whatever punishment comes up. Whatever we all decide, okay?"

He nodded again. We went downstairs. Everyone in the room looked up at us from books and problem sets.

"Everyone up to the table. Now!" Without a word they pulled up, all of them looking at Tico.

"All right Tico, go ahead."

"What do I say?" He looked at me, and in his eyes was anguish.

"The truth. And why. Why is the most important."

"Najat, I took your ten dollars," he murmured. "I don't know why I did it. I bought two candy bars for Tal with it. I have the change. I can give that to you and pay you the rest."

I called on Najat.

"I'm mad that you stole it," she responded in quiet voice. "But I'm glad you told me."

There was silence in the room, as cold and still as it was outside. For once Tico was not moving.

"Uh, Tico, there is going to be more than just paying the money back," I said.

"I know, I know."

I asked all of them to say what the felt, in that moment, one by one, around the table. They were glad Tico had told, because his telling removed the feeling of mistrust and doubt that had begun to seep through us. They were glad for something closer to the truth, and now the truth might begin to come clear. They didn't understand why he had done it, and they were angry. Behind the anger they wanted to understand why.

"I came to this school because I didn't want to deal with this kind of stuff," said Doug. "Stealing is what happens at places where people don't care about each other. This is what I feared if I went to the middle school."

"I don't see why it's such a big deal that he stole," said Mira. "I mean, I know stealing is wrong. But it was only ten dollars. God. Why do we have to make such a big deal about it?"

"If we don't want it here, Mira, we *have* to make a big deal out of it," said Doug. "At the high school it's no big deal, yeah. That's why everyone does it. That's why they have locks on lockers."

"Here's what I think," I said. "If any one of us feels it's a big deal, it's a big deal. Najat cried, because she wanted to go to a movie on that ten dollars. That's a big deal. If Tico feels bad, then it's a big deal. If anyone has less trust than before, if anyone of us feels unsafe, it's a big deal. The amount of money is irrelevant. I couldn't give a shit if it was a goddamn nickel. But I sure as hell don't want to come to a school where I have to worry about my wallet or my backpack or that we don't care enough about each other to hold each other and each other's things sacred."

"It seems like this is the point of this school," Nick started. "I mean, most of the time when this stuff happens it just happens and there is nothing you can do about it."

"Yeah," Steve said. "People even bragged about stealing at the middle school."

"What'd you do about it?" I asked.

"I don't know. It pissed me off."

"But what'd you *do*?"

"Nothing. You couldn't do anything."

"You could fight."

"Yeah and you get suspended or killed. Tal, you couldn't fight."

"You could talk about it or discuss it to solve it."

Tico and Steve laughed.

"There was nowhere to talk about it," said Steve. "No one discussed things. It just happened. Teachers didn't deal with that kind of stuff. If you told on someone, you'd be a snitch and everyone would hate you."

"Everybody hates people who rat," said Nick.

"Everybody? You've got it ass-backward. Why don't you hate the person who hates the rat? Whoever hates the rat is just making it easier to be unethical. The rat is the only moral one."

"But anyone who tells is hated."

"Here's what I understand. Everyone hated it when we didn't know who stole. Nobody wants it. So that means that finding out who stole should be paramount. That means finding out is the most important thing. That means anyone who rats, which is a put-down for someone who doesn't want lying and wants the truth and is making everyone else face the truth, should be the goddamn hero. Do you understand?"

They stared, nodding faintly.

"Tico ratted on himself. Do all of you hate Tico?" I asked.

"Of course not," said Zoe, as though the thought was utterly ludicrous. "I really like Tico. He's sweet, he listens, and he's sensitive. Unlike some people in this school." She glared at Doug.

"Tico's awesome," said Nick. "I don't hate him, but I want to know why he did it, and I guess he should apologize."

"To Najat or all of us?" I asked.

"I think he needs to apologize to Najat and all of us," said Nick. "Because when you think about it, he did it to her and us too. From yesterday until now I felt, like, uneasy and less trustful around everyone. And I didn't really like being yelled at by you upstairs."

"Does everyone agree he needs to apologize to Najat and the class, and to figure out why he did it?" I asked.

"Yeah," they all said. "And also pay her back."

"Najat, would that do it for you? Would you feel okay and good, or better, about Tico after that?"

"Yep."

"Okay, then that's what we'll do. On Monday morning we'll have a conference. Tico, between now and Monday you have to figure out what you did and why. You have to write five pages telling what happened and what you were thinking. You have to tell your mom tonight and tell her to call me. If she doesn't call me, I'm going to kill you."

"Okay."

"A turbocharged John Deere lawn mower will mow your ass into the ground."

"Okay."

We moved on through the rest of the day, a little more slowly, a little more quiet, and a lot more serious.

That night I talked to Deb and she had already talked to Tico. She was grateful, above all, for the attention we were bringing to her child.

On Monday we gathered around the table.

"All righty, Tico," I said. "Give us the good stuff, big feller. Lay it on us, chief."

"I did it I think—"

"Just bring home the bacon! Give us the juice, chief. Don't hold back!"

He glared at me.

"I did it because I thought it was easy and it didn't matter," he began. "I didn't think about what it meant to everyone here. I didn't think that it would make Najat not trust me. I thought of it only as money, not as something that could hurt her. And as soon as I did it I wanted to do something good with it, so I bought the candy bars for Tal."

"So, you mean, like giving Tal a candy bar was a way to 'do good'?" asked Annie.

"Yeah. After I stole the money, I felt bad. But then when I gave the Butterfingers to Tal, I felt better. But I still felt bad."

"Tico, what were you feeling before you took it?" I asked.

"Um, I guess I feel bad a lot in school. I can't do what other kids can do. I can't read and I can't think up genius stuff like Doug or Annie. At my old school no one seemed like they cared for each other."

"Did you not feel connected to anyone here?"

"I guess. I mean, I'm sorta friends with Mira and Nick."

"Do you feel close to them?"

"I've never felt close to anyone in school."

"Having a hard time reading makes you feel what? Embarrassed, ashamed, separate?"

"All. It's easy for everyone else."

Tico had never directly spoken about not being able to read. The kids were aware enough to know that he struggled; they knew why he handed me his papers to read; they knew why he drew when they wrote. But they had never heard him say the words out loud.

Najat raised her hand. "Tico, I have trouble with lots of things like reading, writing, spelling, and math. Just about everything. I like, suck at school."

"Najat, you don't suck at school."

"I do!"

"Tico, do you think kids here think you're dumb?" I asked.

"I worry that they'll think that. All the time."

"Every day?"

"All the time. Every day."

"Do you guys think Tico is dumb?" I asked.

They all stared straight at me, shaking their heads as though I was crazy.

Mira's hand shot up. "I think Tico is incredible. He's like my best friend here. He understands things no one else does. I admire him. Everything we read of his is like the best writing in the class. His poem was incredible. There is a lot more to him. Not being able to read is just a part. I don't care about him based on whether he can read or not."

Rarely had Tico known the feeling of collegiality, of learning with peers in an intellectual community, of feeling like an equal. Never in school had he heard that his peers had affection for him. Maybe, now, he was telling us what he wanted to feel, deep and far under the backward hat, baggy jeans, and hyperkinetic motion.

"Maybe, Tico," I said, "you were stealing to find out what *would* happen. To see how it feels here, in a new school, with these kids. To see if it was the same as your old school, or different."

"I think I'm realizing that it's different," he said.

"Tico, you know what giving me the Butterfingers was about?" I asked.

"What do you mean?"

"I mean that it was a gesture of affection or caring or thanks."

"Thanks?"

"You were saying you care about what's happening here. You're saying thanks, showing me you were listening, regarding my thoughts."

"Okay," he said hesitantly.

"If you love a place, and you want to do something good, you have to let yourself do good all the way and love the place all the way. You can't go halfway or sabotage the thing you need. If you feel affection, you need to feel it all the way for everyone and everything."

"This is kind of weird," said Najat, "but I like Tico better now."

"I think this is the right way for us to deal with things," Annie said.

"Like there are no secrets. At my old school things would happen but no one would talk about it or even know about it so there was always a feeling of mistrust. If there was a problem it always got dealt with in the resource room. It seems like here we are trying to make it better for all of us and Tico can maybe learn something. It feels kind of good."

"I hate the frickin' resource room," said Steve.

At the end, we had doughnuts and cider, a breaking of bread that said, "Tico, you are still among us." He was not apart—he was *a part*. We were no longer carrying out an inquisition. As openly as we could, the whole school tried to mend a rupture. It didn't happen in isolation, but in the circle. In the open space of the classroom we established boundaries and an ethical law by which we could live. Those boundaries and laws, paradoxically, were also connective tissue, bonds that could not be imposed externally but had to arise from within the lived experience in the classroom.

Tico was learning that not being able to read did not place him on the outside: What he did mattered, and he mattered. We didn't have computers, lockers, clocks caged or uncaged, Friday night football games, or resource rooms. But we had each other.

Our school was becoming a serious house on serious Earth. And when it was not, we would make it so. After that we could only move forward.

Nick had recently gotten in trouble throwing apples at cars at a birthday party. I knew, because his mom had told me. She was hoping I could get to the bottom of it, or at least get something useful out of it for Nick. I gathered the class for a conference.

"Any of you been in trouble lately?" I asked.

"Like, what do you mean?" asked Steve.

"I mean, like, have any of you screwed up lately?"

No one raised a hand.

"How about you, Nick?"

"Me? Oh, me. No. Everything is cool with me."

"Really?"

"Really."

"Tal, why are you hassling him?" asked Tico.

"Because, Tico, it's my goddamn job. Nick, you sure nothing's wrong lately?"

"Yeah, I'm pretty sure."

"Pretty sure?"

"Well . . ." He paused. "I did get in some trouble last weekend."

"Oh. Well, tell what happened, Nick."

He described the afternoon. He was with older friends at an orchard. They started throwing apples. He wanted to play along with them.

"Why'd you throw apples if you knew it was wrong?" I asked.

"I was afraid if I didn't they'd call me a pussy."

"Would they call you a pussy?"

"Yeah."

"Are you a pussy?"

"No."

"So why were you afraid?"

"Well, Jamie, one of the boys, he had been throwing apples at this cat in the garage. The cat ran away. I guess I was afraid of him. Jamie, I mean. I didn't think he'd throw apples at me, but it was like, you kind of had to be all macho and stuff."

"Macho and stuff. Like throwing apples at barn cats?

"Yeah."

"So then you threw apples at cars?"

"Yeah. I wasn't a pussy. I was stupid."

"So then what?"

In our dark room, Nick started to cry.

"Well, I didn't want to do it anymore. So I left and hid in the garage. And when I was in there I found the cat. She was hiding behind some boards and junk and she was really scared. I got her to come out and I just sat in there holding her and patting her while they kept throwing apples at cars. I could hear them laughing by the road. Then we all got caught."

"When you got scared, when you wanted to get away, you went to the cat? Why?"

"Because I thought the cat felt like I did, and I wanted to make it feel better. I wanted to feel better."

"Nick, this is incredible. Are you getting this? Think about what you are telling yourself, Nick. Where are you most truly yourself? Kissing up to a bunch of older kids acting like jackasses, or tending to cats."

"Cats. I love cats."

"Why?"

"Because they're so soft. I sleep with mine every night. It purrs on top of my head."

"Cats are soft. Yes. That soft cat is who you are. Not some cruel show-off jackass. That's why you felt so awful and hid in the garage. You want to be soft and gentle."

"Yeah."

"Nick, when I asked if you were in trouble, I didn't care about the trouble part. I cared about this other part."

"I know, I know."

"Nick?"

"Yes?"

"You know what you have to write your story about?"

"What?"

"Being in that garage with that cat."

He raised his eyebrows and smiled.

"I think I can do that."

We approached our first holiday vacation. The school had been together for three and a half months. We were coming to know each other. I was finding ways to get them by the hand or head or heart and draw them out, to where and to what I mostly didn't know. But I had a hold on them.

The week before the holiday break I initiated my annual advertising campaign.

"Okay, listen up, you teenage cretins. Here at the North Branch School, we believe in the true meaning of Christmas, Hanukkah, and Kwanzaa. Probably Ramadan too. These are the holy days. So here's how it works. If you plan on giving your old teacher, Tal, a special holiday gift, let's make those gifts count, shall we?"

"What on Earth are you talking about?" asked Janine.

"I'm talking about proper gift ideas for your old teacher, Tal."

"Tal, you are a disgusting, pathetic old goat," said Zoe.

"Tal, I thought you cared about love and stuff," said Sophie.

"I care about love and stuff, but I care more about making those gifts count. So, if you give me a new special coffee mug with an inspirational quote I will lower your grade to a double F-plus."

"Tal, we don't have grades, there is no such thing as a double F-plus, and wouldn't it be pathetic and ungrateful to reject a nice new coffee mug?" suggested Annie.

"I don't *want* a coffee mug. But if you give me expensive electronics, that'll raise your grade. If you give me a gift certificate to a fine bookseller's shop, that'll raise your grade even higher. The possibilities are endless."

"And how do you raise your grade the highest, O teacher of no values?" asked Doug.

"Hard liquor will do just dandy. Or, perhaps, fine wines from Chile. That will give you an A-plus."

Zoe sneered. "You are getting a lump of coal and a sack of rocks, you sad little man."

"Zoe, that's a terrible strategy. Think about college, and how you'll need me to get into one. Keep your eyes on the prize. Think about expensive things you can buy. Think *high* grades. And don't forget, anything homemade with love, thought, care, and lots of tedious handwork, that's nice, but remember, the fine wines of Chile!"

"Tal, you are disgusting."

After class, I told Steve I had something for him.

"Will you be at your house on Christmas day?"

"Yeah, of course. I'll be waiting for Santa. Why?"

"'Cause I have something to give you."

"Me? Me?"

"No, the other Steve. Yeah, you."

"Okay," he said, looking at me as though he was certain I was going to commit some malfeasance.

W e sat around the stove at lunch just before Christmas. Snow piled up outside. Najat sat with her feet close to the flames and whined. "Tal, can we do something fun?"

She was chronically agitating for us to *have some fun*. "Let's do art," she would say, and in her voice I sensed the lament for a fast-disappearing childhood, for one last chance to play.

"Can we go sledding? Can we go somewhere? Can't we ever do something fun?"

Never mind that we had tossed eggs off the roof, built towers out of paper, and constructed bridges out of masking tape. Never mind that we were building a tree house, that we had biked up the Lincoln Road, played mud-soccer and played with clay. Never mind that we had drawn with Sharpie pens between our teeth, sledded on the hill outside the school every day at lunch, or had snowball fights between classes. Never mind that we sang songs like "Feelings" and "Ramblin' Man" regularly in class, practiced karate chops in the cold dark air to warm up in the morning, and sat in the woods drawing maple leaves. Never mind that we had traveled to see Monet paintings and English barns, or that we had limbo-'d under our broomsticks during cleanup, or hiked in the woods and to the tops of mountains.

Reality or a few demonstrable facts apparently did not stand in the way of an adolescent's assertions about what had happened.

"Like what, Najat?" I asked. "What would be a fun thing that we could do?"

"You know, I don't know, like, we could make little, um, little cars out of, like noodles or something." Her eyes were wide with hope.

"Noodle cars?" I asked.

"Yeah. It would be so fun!"

"You want us to make noodle cars?"

"Yes! Can we? Can we?"

"Well, all righty, then. We'll have a noodle car race. Najat, you hereby are recorded into North Branch history and lore as she whose idea inspired the first annual Holiday Pastamobile Race."

That night I drew up the plans: pastamobiles made substantially out of uncooked pasta, no engines allowed, rolled down a ramp, which we would illuminate with candles. Fire would be an enticement, along with awards for fastest, farthest, straightest, most artistic, most pasta used, best name, and most pathetic. Everyone would be rewarded.

"Don't tell anyone your plans," I told them. "I want everyone in a rabid, blackhearted, no-holds-barred quest for victory."

We were making history, such as it was, silly playful gestures that were, in truth, about placing small, necessary stones in a serious foundation. When I announced that Najat had come up with the idea, she beamed with pride and they all cheered. My students loved it when their words or actions had influence: *influence,* in which their ideas were recognized as an originating force, flowing, like light, from them.

I held fast to the faith that what impelled their actions, good and bad, was the desire to have a constructive, creative effect in a world they hoped to make their own.

I worked on my pasta car for days with Henry and Calder. We covered it with rainbow-colored fettuccini, ziti, linguini, and gobs of hot glue, crowned with a little Playmobil driver inside a roll cage holding a Playmobil fire extinguisher. The day before the race I brought the prototype to school so I could taunt the class and show them what I wanted them to do.

"Check this sick puppy out," I shouted, holding it aloft like a championship belt. "Check out the colors, the style, the 'multiflex chassis.' Check out the Tinkertoy wheels and the sleek design."

"Tal, that's not a puppy," said Tico. "That's a piece of crap," said Tico.

"It's a puppy, Tico, and you're jealous. Don't project your jealousy onto my creation." I spun the wheels for effect. "Check out that smooth running action!"

"You're going to race in the race too?" Annie asked in disbelief, as though all teachers everywhere were contractually barred from participating in activities with the students.

"Of course. My job is to school you, know what I mean?"

"Very funny, Tal," said Doug.

"No, Doug, my joke was very *punny*."

"Yeah right, Tal. Whatever. My car is going to smoke yours!" Tico boasted.

"Tico, my man, you don't even have a car yet."

"Whatever."

"But Tal, why are you violating your 'laws' of secrecy?" Sophie asked with a prim and witty investigator's query. "We might steal your ideas."

"No, no, Sophie. I know you can *try* to steal my ideas. I say *try*. But I do not fear you sad adolescents. For I am a man, complete in integrated wholeness. You are but members of the adolescent subspecies, half human, half beast, incapable of such greatness as I attain each waking moment."

"You are so full of it," shouted Nick.

"You are a false god!" Doug shouted. "No one will compete with my 'Confucius's Legacy'!"

"What the hell is Confucius's Legacy?" asked Tico.

"Confucius, great moral philosopher of China, birthplace of the noodle! My car is going to rock the house. Oh yeah!"

"Doug," said Mira, "your car is going to like, break in half."

"Check this out," I shouted. "Check out my patented flex chassis." I gently twisted the frame of my car and it snapped in half. This elicited great joy and delighted taunts.

On race day, cars arrived in carefully packed shoe boxes filled with wadded tissue paper. Cars were gently lifted out for display like works of art. Steve presented a fettuccini and duct-taped car with plastic wheels and a Santa Claus driver towing a wagon (with an elbow-noodle hitch) filled with miniature wrapped presents—the Christmas he dreamed to have. Janine's cappellini car had wheels frozen with hot glue—apparently she believed that the project should be a sculptural exercise rather than a competitive race. Sophie's featured strips of lasagna and bumpers made of kitchen sponges. Nick's was named "3.14159264." Zoe made the tiny, glitter-spangled "Z-armadillo," which did resemble an armadillo due to the single pasta shell with wobbling pasta pinwheels. Mira entered the multilingual "Chippewa Coche," meaning, according to Mira, "orphan coach," a poignant choice for a girl adopted from India. Najat entered "La Petite Fleur," decorated with plastic flowers with a Lego-man driver. Tico's linguini-mobile had battery-powered lights, toy motorcycle handlebars, and spare parts from a defunct remote-control car. Annie's pastamobile arrived in the form of a box full of shattered penne shells: "My brother sat on it in the car, okay?" she moaned. And finally, there was Doug's "Confucius's Legacy I."

In violation of every Vermont fire-safety code, we lit the candles lining the track, which extended through our classroom across uneven floorboards, past the woodstove, and into the kitchen. Cars bumped down the ramp, tipped over, or rolled sideways into walls. Wheels got stuck in dirt-filled cracks in the floor. The room was a cacophony of shouting, laughing, hissing, jeering, booing, bragging, and cheering. It was clear: My students still wanted to play, they still needed to play, and our school was not going to be guilty of killing that instinct.

Nick's car ran a straight line until it crashed into the first obstacle in its path, a stack of cardboard boxes. I graciously tried to clear the boxes, but one tumbled over, snapping his brittle car in half. Shouts of blame rang out, accusations of deliberate sabotage. My students chanted, "Cheater, cheater." I rushed to the pastamobile repair table and we hot-glued it back together.

For the finale we ran the still-intact cars down the ramp through a wall of fire, the holiday candles—which Annie named the "Rampa del Fuego." We crowded together for a picture, into the center of which we thrust our cars, our homemade offerings, our arms extended like spokes of a wheel.

Each car was a perfect microcosm of its maker, and that was what I wanted: a school where children made images of themselves, a continual process of self-definition, both important and silly. A rowdy esprit de corps of smiling antagonisms and gleeful shouts drew us toward each other and, in time, would give birth to greater affections and tenderness.

I had planned a ceremony afterward, to shift the tone from irreverence to accomplishment. I wanted to speak to what we had made together thus far, not just pasta cars, poems, or inquisitions, but our community. I spent the week prior sketching my students in words, as individuals first, as students second, my testimonial about who each was and was becoming. I reconstructed them with as much depth, honesty, and celebratory affection as I could muster—what they had said, done, made, thought; what they had revealed, hidden, or hinted at; what particular graces and artistry they had shown. The remarks were the antithesis of the perfunctory report card filled with tired, meaningless phrases like "meeting the standard." There was no standard here but the one we set together.

I addressed each one as a letter, printed, signed, and placed in envelopes to give to them—something solid to hold and to keep. I wanted to tell them, out loud in the public sphere, what they had not yet become—to say that there were glimmering forms just ahead toward which they were moving—beautiful shapes they might take. In those first few months we had made the outline, and I wanted them to believe, as I did, that there was so much more to fill in.

With a few of the candles still burning on the table, I read the descriptions. Some were funny. Others were chiding, reflective, encouraging, imploring. As I spoke, I gazed at them, trying to establish the invisible, mysterious, electric-synaptic connection between the teacher and the taught, in hope that they could not ever escape whatever it was I had to give them.

When I came to Tico, I simply reconstructed the best of what he had shown us. Yes, I said, reading and writing were difficult, if not impossible. But Tico also understood electronics, sound, perspective, graphics, patterns, the way one idea joined to another. He was familiar with the properties of materials, models, wires, batteries, computers, machines, and how shapes fit together. He had his own secret solutions and hidden paths for finding his way forward. He had once told me ten ways one could know if a car had recently been driven. He knew how to build with his hands, use tools, draw up designs, and to describe the invisible mind. He had an ecstatic identity, a self waiting for his embrace. I told him to not run from that self or the school. I told him to grab hold of what was growing in him that he did not yet value, that he did not yet know. I told him to remember what lived in him, despite the battles he fought or lost every day in school. I told him his mind was worthy of celebration.

I wanted his dread of school to die. I wanted him to feel some joy in the willingness to surrender to what he could do. As Seamus Heaney counseled for himself through the mouth of Joyce: "Let go, let fly, forget." Forget what you can't do, and build from what you can. I wanted that to sing in him, so I sang it to him. *You can, you can.*

And as I did I felt myself surrendering to something like love, a flowering devotion to my students in this dark house in the woods, in this place called school.

The first time I had met Steve he told me his favorite baseball team was the Atlanta Braves. I knew he didn't have cable, much less a TV, and I still wondered how he'd come to idolize Chipper Jones, the Atlanta third baseman, when he lived in the middle of Red Sox Nation, on a dirt road far away in the Green Mountains.

My brother had once worked at Ted Turner Field in Atlanta and had collected a batting-practice ball hit by Braves center fielder Andruw Jones. I asked him to send me the ball so I could give it to Steve.

On Christmas morning I drove over the frozen roads of Ripton, down to the bridge over the North Branch River, over steep roads under snow-laced firs to Steve's house. I pulled into the driveway, where his dog howled behind a cyclone fence. The house had not changed much, except now the woodpile, junk cars, old tricycles, and bags of garbage lay buried in snow. Pale blue vinyl siding peeled off the trailer. I climbed cinderblock steps onto a makeshift stoop, which was littered with cigarette butts and empty Pepsi bottles. A single strand of holiday lights hung over the bay window. The door, the screen torn, hung from a single hinge.

I knocked and Steve answered, standing in the open doorway in nothing but a pair of gargantuan red silk basketball shorts, his thin arms and chest bare to the cold morning air. His three-year-old brother, Matt, stood behind him holding a new Wolverine figure, staring up at me with wide eyes.

"Merry Christmas, Steve."

"Merry Christmas."

"Merry Christmas, Matt." Matt lifted the Wolverine figure up for me to see.

"So I brought you something, Steve. It's not perfect, but it's pretty damn good."

I pulled out the baseball from inside my coat.

"It's a foul ball hit by Andruw Jones in batting practice. My brother got it at Ted Turner. Sorry it's not a dinger hit by Chipper."

I handed it to him.

"Whoa, that's awesome." He rubbed his finger over the seams and raised it to his face to sniff the leather.

"How's it smell?"

"Like summer," he said.

"I guess you have a ways until summer."

"Yeah."

"Well, as the famous poet says, if winter comes, can spring be far behind?"

"I'll bet the famous poet didn't play baseball."

"But he could write poetry."

"Yep."

"Well, I just wanted to give you that. A little present from Santa in Atlanta."

"Cool. Thanks, Tal."

"Well, have a good vacation. See you in January."

He closed the door. I stepped off the stoop into the snow and headed home.

When we gathered after the New Year, I looked at them and asked, "What is love?"

They looked up. I was sure they had never been asked the question in a school setting. Maybe they had never been asked the question at all. They looked at me as though I was asking them to do something forbidden.

"What do you mean, like, what do we think it is, or a dictionary definition?" Nick asked.

"I don't mean collective 'you,'" I said. "I don't mean collective 'we' or 'humans.' The last thing I want is the dictionary definition. I mean you, only you, what *you,* Nick, think love is, in your own experience."

"Okay," said Janine. "Like, love is—"

"Don't think in terms of one thing. Think of many things. Think of thirteen things. Use your experience and what you've felt to make up your own terms and definitions. What do you know about love? How many things do you know about it? Where did that knowledge come from?"

I had never asked the question of any class. I had also never had so much open space in a classroom. I had no predetermined destination or endpoint, no unit to complete, no idea where it would go. I just had to react nimbly enough to steer and, simultaneously, generate velocity—a Socratic improvisation. The thing of it was—*I* wanted to know what love was.

"But how do you want us to define it?" said Najat. "It's, like, kind of a big topic."

This familiar stalling technique was frequently employed when they approached a task that might push them into the unknown.

"Najat, I'm not gonna tell you. What is the point of me defining something for you that only you can understand for yourself? Everybody got a writing implement? Get some parchment. Write everything you can think of about the topic. Any feeling, fragment, idea, glimmer, hint, suggestion, image, word, texture, memory. Don't think, just scribble like a maniac. Don't analyze. Try to find the words equal to the feeling."

They ripped paper out of binders and scuffled about looking for writing utensils.

"How much do you want us to write?"

"For God's sake, we're talking about love! It's infinite! You should not be able to ever stop. I'll time you for eight minutes. Just don't stop writing."

I glanced at my watch a few times to make them feel time moving. Love in eight minutes, infinity in an hour. They scribbled, looked up, crossed out, stared at the floor, wrote sideways up the margins until they ran out of space.

When time was up I sang out: "Stop! In the name of love, before I tear your heart into two parts and break it into little bits and pieces. . . ."

"Ah, Tal, no! Be quiet! We're still writing! God!"

They kept writing. Several of them pushed their papers up to me. They asked: *Read it. Will you read it?*

"Okay, everybody got something juicy?" I interrupted again.

"Hold on, I'm finishing up. . . . Jeez Louise," said Najat.

"Love is juicy," I said. "Juicy juicy juicy."

Zoe giggled. Najat glared. I granted them the privilege of feigning irritation in exchange for probing the unknown regions of their souls.

"Well, then, I guess some of you had a little to say about old love after all. Which of you nuts has got any guts? Who wants to read what you wrote?"

All hands went up. I couldn't stop them. The room was suddenly filled with all kinds of crazy and beautiful ideas about love. Little poems. Zen koans. Memories of waiting for the one they loved. Ghostlike images of the ones they loved. Questions: Where to find love? How is love known? What threatens it? What makes it grow? How do we show love? Why do we need it? Why is it withheld? What *isn't* love? What could love do? Why does love elude us, fade away, and disappear, or remain after time or anger? I asked them over and over: How did you come to know that? What experience taught you that?

A miraculous thing happened when we talked about love: They

became aware that they possessed powerful knowledge. Another miracle: They began to speak to each other and to the community they comprised.

Nick read: "When I worry about Steve, and if he is doing good in school. That's a kind of love."

Empathy, derived from the Greek root meaning "feeling together," was a powerful notion to them at this age precisely because they were all suffering together—suffering through puberty, enduring adolescence, together in a new place, not sure of where they were heading. When they discovered that they each had the same essential needs and desires, that they had all felt the sting of loneliness and existential emptiness; when they saw how beautifully expressive they each could be—that was when cliques and divisions melted away.

Sophie read: "Love. I like knowing what it is and giving it. I often say to myself: Is this love, or is it something else? If you have love, you don't need anything else. It's the dominant force."

"I think that if you really love someone then you'd never lie to him or her, or be false," read Zoe. "I might be making up fantasies and letting my imagination get carried away, but I think that truth is the key to love."

Janine raised her hand and read: "Knowing and understanding. Trust and everything good and sincere. The unconditional surrender of thoughts and feelings."

I could feel that surrender, all of their thoughts and feelings filling the space, spilling out over the table. It was the happiest class I had ever taught.

As they talked, it occurred to me why I had asked the question. Once, before the holiday break, I had walked into Calder's preschool class to pick him up. I liked to sneak into the room so I could watch him before he saw me. On this day Calder's teacher, Stefany, was sitting at a small table while a half dozen three-year-olds swirled their hands around in a large pan of gooey purple paste. The other children were outside; the room was quiet, with afternoon sun angling in over the heads of the children. Stefany quietly, almost absentmindedly spoke to them, asking questions with a slow, gentle voice.

"So what's it all about, you guys, what's it all about?"

Quietly, almost thoughtlessly, the group of preschoolers answered dreamily, "Love."

"Yeah, that's what I'm talking about," Stefany answered back, as though in a meditative trance. "Love is what it's all about."

As my class discussed their own ideas about love, I told them that story.

"That's awesome," said Nick.

"That's what it's all about, love. I've been looking for the answer and now I know," said Annie.

Pure stillness hovered over the room.

"Maybe it is that simple. Maybe we know that but then we forget it," said Doug.

"Little kids are so cool," said Mira. "Sometimes I wish I still was one."

"Maybe you still are," I offered. "Maybe the little girl in you still knows those things. You wouldn't have that sound of longing in your voice if you didn't."

"I don't know," she said, as though she was simultaneously enticed and repulsed.

"So, what's it all about?" I asked.

On cue, as if they had been waiting their whole lives, they shouted in a gleeful, single voice: "Love!"

Collectively my students were a frenetic life force, full of beautiful contradictions and imbalances, capable of soulful expression and the profundities borne from the discovery of their still-forming, fumbling sense of selves. Still very much children, but with intimations of the adults they would become, they were hormonal pods, zinging and darting both physically and in their thoughts and feelings.

They could be tracked by the wreckage they left behind, the messes they made, the incomplete projects and half-realized initiatives, their banal judgments, the absurdist logic they mastered, the monuments to procrastination they engineered. They were noisy and off-kilter, impulsive and sedentary, mentally sluggish and spectacularly intuitive. Yet when we discussed love, noble passions were stirred, and, miraculously, all of them were ancient Greek scholars.

I constantly suppressed the impulse to regulate and order them, to direct and manage. It was a wild, unpredictable process, a ragged map with an indefinite destination. Sometimes our school seemed to me very much like a lot of two-year-olds experimenting with color and texture in finger painting, or a three-year-old singing dreamily about love. Yes, I wanted them to let go, fly, forget, but when we let go and forgot, we left a dripping mess. Nothing was tidy, and a day's painting might be a muddled brown.

One Monday morning after the first winter holiday, I arrived to find our toilet backed up and, having sat in such a state all weekend, reeking pungently. I looked around for a plunger—none to be found.

The kids hollered and moaned in complaint.

"It like, stinks in here!"

"Don't worry, you weenies, I'll like, have it fixed in a jiffy."

I had to fix it by 9:30 that morning because our first-ever prospective parents were visiting the school. They were coming to see the school in action and we had to impress, lest we start our second year with diminishing enrollment. I called Mia and she said Freeman, Sophie's dad, would bring a plunger down. The school day started—phone calls, math, conversations, assignments, handing back papers—and I forgot all about the toilet.

At 9:15 I looked out the window to see an unfamiliar Honda pull up. Our first prospective parents were here and they were early. As they waited in the driveway, I suddenly remembered the toilet. In a panic, my mind whirled. It would be one thing for them to have reservations about the school, our philosophy, our methodology. But I would be damned if they went away thinking, *That poor school doesn't even have working plumbing. It stunk like the Union 76 on Highway 41.* Otherwise it would be only a matter of days before the State of Vermont came to close us down.

I leaped for the phone. "Mia, where's the plunger?"

"Freeman's coming. He's on his way."

"Okay, Jesus, all right, bye!"

At that moment Freeman walked in, smiling, with the plunger and a couple of towels.

I ran for the bathroom. I plunged madly. Toilet water sucked and surged, then exploded upward, onto the ceiling and my face, cheeks, and eyelashes. I flushed and swabbed the floors. I was superhuman: admissions director, mail opener, poetry teacher, secretary, headmaster, coach, custodian, and plumber. There was nothing I couldn't do.

I rushed out of the bathroom. The front door opened. My eyes met those of Barbara Cunningham and Jim Burns. I was about to reach out and greet and welcome them to the North Branch School. I looked down at my wet hands holding soggy towels and a dripping plunger. I smiled.

"Just a second," I said. I threw the towels under my desk and stashed the plunger behind the copier.

"Please come in and have a seat," I said. "Welcome to the school."

We sat down at my desk.

"So Tucker is interested in North Branch?" I began.

"Yes. We have heard so many great things about the school," Barbara said.

My heart was pounding, sweat was running down my back, my cheeks were still wet. I heard again, *Great things.* Inside, I was glowing, I was laughing. *Great things.*

Nowhere in America was a teacher having an experience like this. We were so deep in it, so close to the making. And strangely, that was something I couldn't help but love.

Sometimes, in the mornings driving to school, I imagined the school was an old Vermont homestead, the students were my family, and we were barely making it. Our food stores were running low and spring was far, far away. It was cold and it was lonely. During the holiday I had developed an avid interest in candles and evergreen as symbols of faith and hope that spring might come. But a few twinkling candles and a couple of sprigs of balsam against the long Vermont winter was shabby equipment when quartered for most of whole dark days with ten adolescents. We could huddle around the stove, we could throw snowballs, we could chase each other. We could talk about feelings and the heroic exploits of R. P. McMurphy in *One Flew Over the Cuckoo's Nest.* But the windows iced over and the sun's arc never rose above the hemlocks behind the school.

Below the surface inevitable tension was mounting. New kids, seventh graders. Older kids, ninth graders. An imbalance of social power had to occur. Mira and Zoe—looking cooler, in style, more knowing, making a secret language of friendship, a code of looks, glances, references, inside lines—the fulcrum over which the school tilted.

I knew this, but I continued on, waiting for something to happen. Any attempt to root it out before it surfaced would be altering the true course, like manipulating an experiment. I had to let it come, let them bring it forth, let us feel what happened, and let the school learn to mend or correct itself.

I watched Sophie watch Mira and Zoe. She stood quietly, half smiling at a joke between Mira and Zoe, without knowing what they were talking about. I watched Najat try to fit awkward comments into conversations that closed her out. I listened to Tico laughing at the bicycle Steve rode to school, a knockoff brand with no brakes and rusted rims. I heard Nick exaggerating his skiing exploits to impress Tico. I watched Doug and Annie playing in the woods by themselves, staying away from Nick, Mira, and Tico. I watched Sophie standing awkwardly alone, not five feet from Janine, who also stood awkwardly and alone, both of them silent. I watched Mira roll her eyes if Zoe and Sophie shared a joke, and I watched Najat roll her eyes when Mira rolled hers. I watched Mira install Steve as her boyfriend, and I watched her scowl when he spent lunch jumping off the deck with Nick. I watched Najat recede into a wordless gloom, wanting the new fashions from Hot Topic that Mira had. I saw phony hugs between girls who were afraid of each other. I saw boys resort to the vocabulary of *sick* and *that's so retarded* and *you suck*.

I watched walls going up, walls of fear and uncertainty.

All of this was going on while we discussed old-growth forests, plutonic intrusions, Big Rock Candy Mountain, and symbolic thinking. This occurred while Eric taught about stream systems, algae blooms, and photosynthesis, or when the kids labored over linear equations. All of this had a visceral, subterranean life, because these were adolescents, each trying to find a place, each trying to forge an identity. The immutable law: Whatever was in them would come out in some form or fashion, with the question *Who is my friend?* decisively gaining the upper hand over everything else.

Lately Najat was ever more desperate to work her way in with Zoe and Mira. I saw the bewilderment on her face when she listened to Zoe and Mira recount the dialogue of "How the Emperor Got His Groove Back." It was not that Najat wanted to know the lines—she knew them by heart. But she wanted to have a place to share it. She wanted to laugh the same way Mira and Zoe did, laugh at their jokes, know the timing, and so feel integral. Sometimes they let her in, sometimes they kept her out. Some days Najat's face carried an ebullient smile. Other days she walked home sullen and defeated, her eyes pegged to her feet, kicking clumps of snow down the driveway.

One afternoon after lunch we gathered around the table.

"Tal, what are we gonna do?"

"First we're gonna get our thing together, man. Then we're gonna talk."

"What thing?"

"Our thing, man."

"Whatever. What are we going to talk about?"

"About you. *I want to talk about you.* That's a song by Coltrane."

"What *about*?"

"You. I said you." My humor evaporated and my voice carried a sharp edge. "Here's what I am wondering: What the hell is going on here? What's happening right now in this school?"

No one raised a hand. They stared at me and looked around at each other.

"Is everything hunky-dory? Everyone loving everything here at the old alma mater? Everyone feeling groovy at the old North Branch School?"

"Well, yeah, North Branch is cool," said Steve.

"Yeah, Tal, I guess everything is fine," chimed Nick.

"How about you, Najat? Are you lovin' it? Is it finger-snapping time? Is everything like a Doritos commercial with parties popping out of bags?"

"What?"

"I mean, are you happy, Najat? Do you feel great, secure, content? Do you feel like you can say anything, be anything, do anything, express your ideas, be free to imagine the world in your own image? Or do you feel not so great?"

"Um, like, are you asking me if I am happy all the time?"

"Um, like, yeah."

"Well, I feel happy like, about ninety-eight percent of the time."

"Tell me about the two percent."

"The not-good two percent?"

"Yeah, those two percent."

And then her voice cracked and tears began dripping down her cheeks.

"Don't hold it in. Let it go. If you let it go you'll feel better."

"Um, I feel like I want to be friends with Mira and Zoe but they don't want me to be. Sometimes I feel good around them, sometimes I don't. Sometimes it seems like they hate me."

Mira shot back, "I don't *hate* you, Najat."

"Well, it seems like it. Every time I try to talk to you, Zoe and you just leave me behind."

"What are you talking about?" asked Mira.

"You know what I mean. You guys will be talking and when I walk up it's like you just stop and don't say anything."

"Well, Najat," I said. "Why are you trying to be their friend if they don't want you? If they are being exclusive jerks, why would you want them as friends? And what about the people you turn your back on when they turn toward you? If you want friends, it seems like you picked the wrong ones. If they're mean, pick someone nice."

She didn't answer.

"Why are you not trying to be friends with Sophie? Janine? Or Annie? Or Doug? Why do you choose the two so-called glamorous ones who don't always accept you, who are sometimes mean? That's choosing to inflict pain on yourself and that's a bad choice. That should make you ask yourself why."

"What do you mean?"

"Well. If they're cool and glamorous, and that's what you seek, what does that tell you about you? Who are you? What do you want to be? What do you value?"

"Why should you be afraid of me, Najat?" Mira spat. "It's not like it should be painful to be my friend."

"Because you can be mean sometimes, Mira," Doug said, interrupting with ferocity.

Mira rolled her eyes.

"You're mean and people are afraid of you," Doug said. "Maybe that's why they try to be your friend."

"It's true," said Najat. Now her voice came out of the dark, seeming to arise from another place. "I just feel so ugly. I'm dumb. People are mean. I never know who my friends are. Sometimes I feel close to Sophie, but other times it's like she doesn't want to be my friend. I am sometimes friends with Mira. I mean we laugh. I hang out with Sophie. But other times I just feel lost and forgotten. Sometimes I go home, my mom's asleep, and I just cry."

"Did you hear that, Sophie?"

She nodded.

"Tell the truth, Najat. Are you sucking up to Mira and Zoe?"

"I don't know. Probably. I just want to feel like I have a best friend in the world. I've never had that."

"How do you feel about that, Sophie?"

"Well," Sophie began, "sometimes I am not sure if you like me or if you just want to hang out with Mira and Zoe. It seems like you care more about them than the times when we are together. And I am never mean to you. And sometimes I want to be alone."

Tears dropped out of her eyes and pooled on the gray table.

"And here we have Najat, a girl adopted from Morocco," I said. "Basically an only child. And her mom works a lot. And, man, she is *wanting*. Do you see that, Mira? She's not trying to take something from you."

Mira stared down, penciling a word darkly onto a torn paper.

"I'm not sure who I should be with," said Zoe. She brushed a strand of hair away from her eyes. "I want to be friends with Mira, but I want to be friends with everyone."

I looked at Mira. Her mouth was set tight, her eyes narrowed.

"Do you feel like Mira will let you be friends with other people?"

"Sometimes." Her voice was almost a whisper.

"I want to have real friends," Mira said. "I don't want people sucking up to me. I don't want people to be afraid of me."

As gently as I could I said, "Maybe they suck up to you because they are afraid of you."

"I don't want them to be afraid of me."

"Maybe you act in ways that scare them."

She didn't respond.

"You know, maybe you're scared, so you keep them scared and at a distance. You're mean so they won't get too close. You've been alone too. You don't want to be alone, so you'll do any damn thing to keep people close, even driving them away."

"Maybe."

"Mira, when you're around little kids, how do you feel?"

"I love little kids," she said. "I have so much fun with them. It's easy around them. They make me laugh. They're so funny and innocent." In her voice there was a subtle brightening and a half smile—a kind of revelation.

"And safe? Never judging?"

"Yeah."

"Are you a better person around them than you are around kids your age? Truly."

"Yeah."

"Think about why that is."

I looked around the dark room. There was not one rustle or extraneous movement.

"Is this only a girl thing, or does everyone feel it? I don't only mean sucking up, I mean feeling fear about who is your friend? Does this fear run through the boys, or are you all badass tough guys? How many of you feel fear on a daily basis? I mean, every day, worry about how you look, what you wear, if you're cool, who your friends are? I'm talking about every day."

Every hand in the room went up.

"I've never had any friends in school," said Janine. "This is the first time I have ever had *any* friends. This is the only place I have ever felt safe. Well, except for being in the barn with my goats."

Laughter erupted, lighthearted relief, a glimmer of adolescent catharsis in the dark in the woods. Even Mira was smiling.

I said, "Hell, anybody with any sense at all would rather be friends with smelly old goats than you shit buckets."

"We're not shit buckets."

"Yeah, you are. All of you are shit muffins stuck in a shit bucket. I mean seriously, isn't it more enlightening to be in a barn with the contented animals than to be hanging out with a bunch of socially desperate teens?"

"Yeah, whatever, Tal."

"I bet not even goats would hang out with you, Tal," said Tico.

"I don't need goats. I've got my kids and my chickens."

"No chicken would be your friend," said Tico.

"My chickens are my friends. We like, hang out and we do stuff."

"That's only 'cause you feed them and keep them in a prison."

"Very funny, Tico. But look. Here's what I see. You're all growing up. You've been with your family most of your life, where it's mostly safe. But now you're twelve, thirteen, fourteen. You're heading out into the world where it matters what you are to your peers. But you don't have any special path you know that brings you into this new world, and now you're thinking about what your peers think, constantly. You can't stop thinking about what others think. You are aware of your *awareness*. Sometimes your only thought is what *their* thoughts might be. Or you're criticizing your own thoughts, or you're questioning yourself. You're afraid because it's like walking into a wilderness. You're alone for the first time, alone with new ideas, hyperconscious of everyone and everything, so you protect yourself by lining up with someone, anyone, who seems powerful or cool. Or you cower in the corner, not knowing what to say, what you're supposed to do, who to bind with, or how to connect."

"It seems like we do all the wrong things when we are afraid," said Annie.

Najat spoke up. "I know I am less myself, trying to be liked, saying I like some movie when I don't, when I am worrying about if I am cool."

"I should just be some nerdy girl," said Annie.

"You are some nerdy girl. Why do you worry that you're some nerdy girl?"

"Everyone hates nerdy grade-A students. That's kind of what I am, I guess."

"Do you want to be that?"

"Yeah, I think so."

"Then be it. All the way. With joy and no regret. And the world will love you truly."

"I constantly fear who I am, or if I'm a nobody," said Najat.

"So what can you do with that fear? How do you make yourself know you are somebody? How do you make the fear go away?"

Mira began to cry, finally. Everyone turned to her.

"I want to make it go away," she said. "But I don't know how to."

"Fear of what?"

"The fear of being nice."

"You're afraid of being nice?"

"Yeah."

"You guys," I said, looking at all of them around the table. "How can she make the fear go away?"

Zoe answered. "I love it when you are sweet, Mira, when you talk in little voices, or when you were worried about Steve, or when you read your poem. That's the Mira that I love and never feel scared around."

"Sweet?" I asked. "What is this sweet? What does that mean?"

"Loving and tender," said Steve.

"Giving and pure," said Janine.

"Soft," said Tico.

"You hear that, Mira? If you want people to be closer to you, you have to be softer."

Mira nodded with her face in her hands.

"Like a cat, like a little kid."

She nodded.

"We have to be loving and tender, giving and pure," I said.

"Look at us," said Annie. "We're all in the wilderness."

"And what are your choices?" I asked.

"We can hold on to each other," said Doug. "Or we can line up against each other."

"Would you hold on even to Zoe?"

"Even Zoe."

"Would you hold on to chickens?"

"Even chickens."

"Goats?"

"Goats too."

"That's love, you guys."

"Besides my family, I would rather be holding on to these people more than anyone else," said Annie.

"Right on, sister," I said. "So what do we have now?"

Mira raised her hand. "I think if you go a long time without being treated well or right you become mean. You close yourself because you don't want to be hurt again."

I didn't answer but let the words hang in the room.

When we walked out of the classroom onto the deck, it was a quarter to five. A dozen parents stared at us with mouths hanging open.

The following morning I asked them what had happened in the conference.

"We counted it up on the way to school," Annie said gleefully. "Seven of us cried. That's a North Branch record."

"Uh-oh, there're some wimps among us," I said. "Let's get after them."

"Who are the pansies who didn't cry?" demanded Tico, with his eyes narrowed.

"Hey, you didn't cry," said Nick.

"I already cried another time, butt munch."

"Enough about that. Tell me what happened. Actually, don't tell me. Write it down, then we'll read it."

We sat in quiet for five minutes. Nobody had trouble starting—they had all been there, alive and close to what had happened.

"Okay, Sophie, start us up."

She read: " 'Every one of us has had a shock of truth, or will have a shock of truth. If you look harder you will see the little waves of thought that erupt the silent still pond in the mind.' "

"Sweet. Nice. That's great, Sophie."

"Can I read what I wrote?" asked Steve.

"Yeah, bro, fire it up."

"It's kinda from *Star Wars,* but Doug and I added some stuff. Here it is: 'Fear leads to anger, anger leads to hate. Hate leads to the dark side. Realization and vision leads to courage, courage leads to understanding, understanding leads to happiness, happiness leads to love, love leads to light.' "

"I hate *Star Wars,*" said Doug, "but that's pretty good. Now can I read mine?"

"All right, go."

" 'The conference wasn't a mask shouting the truth, it was just there, glowing like an iridium flare for all to see.' "

"An iridium flare? What the hell is that?"

"It's an immensely bright flare you can see for tens of thousands of miles."

"What's the difference between a mask shouting the truth and the iridium flare of truth?"

"The flare is not trying to be something. It is pure and makes us see and you can't miss it."

"So what was pure yesterday?"

"The tears, Tal."

"Great. I got it. Annie, you wanna read yours?"

"'A conversation? NO, it was not a conversation: it was a fight for peace, balance, and the truth. We grow closer together as a group when we fight for what we believe in.'"

"Damn, Annie, that's great. We grow closer when we fight together. That's a paradox. This all makes me think of something that my old friend Rūmī said."

"I thought you said you didn't have any friends," said Annie.

"I don't, but I have Rūmī."

"Who's Rūmī? Is he a chicken?" asked Tico.

"Not a chicken. Jalāl ad-Dīn Rūmī of Balkh. A thirteenth-century Sufi mystic, a wicked cool Islamic poet and philosopher. He traveled around saying poems, drinking wine, and spinning around."

"Tal," said Tico. "If he was from the thirteenth century he could not be your friend and he probably wouldn't want to be."

"Very astute, Tico. But Rūmī and I are tight."

"Very funny, Tal."

"Here's what he said: 'We are the mirror as well as the face in it. / We are tasting the taste this minute / of eternity. We are pain / and what cures pain, both. We are / the sweet cold water and the jar that pours.'"

"Sweet," said Nick.

"What is tasting eternity?" asked Zoe "Is eternity a flavor, like ice cream?"

"Zoe, you wing nut, think about it."

"I get it," said Steve. "We are the ones who must face and fix our-selves."

"Yes," I said. "What is important is happening now and happening forever."

"Yes."

"It doesn't lie outside of us, it's within us."

"Yes."

"We must be the cure of ourselves and others."

"Yes."

"We can solve our problems."

"Yes. And you know what else?" I asked.

"What?"

"We are mystics. All of us. We have the inner light and the eye of the heart. We are great souls. We are the sweet cold water. Our minds and hearts are whirling like the dervish. But we have to listen."

"We're listening, Tal, we're listening."

From the outset, the board of the school and I planned to invite local artists to conduct workshops with the kids. After the winter holiday I invited in John Housekeeper, a local artist and sculptor, and a jolly rattle-bag of quirky ideas. I thought he would liven up the dark days of January. We had been invited to exhibit sculptures made from found materials for the Re-Use Showcase at a local gallery for an art show that featured works made only from recycled materials, something I imagined the kids would relish.

I went to visit John one snowy Sunday morning to discuss what we would do. John's "studio" was a defunct dairy barn, the upper floor of which was filled with dusty sports cars and obsolete farm equipment. John's sculpture studio was below, cluttered with arc welders, engine hoists, and bundles of iron rebar. His sculptures consisted of I-beam frames with boulders suspended from thick chains.

"Let's go look at what stuff I have," he said. Room after room, stall after stall, was piled to the cobwebbed ceilings with boxes of electronics, plastic toys, scraps of aluminum and wood, window shades, bike parts, old engines, motors, exhaust pipes, fabric, carpet remnants, curtain rods, cyclone fencing, cardboard tubes, and a dusty mannequin. His barn was like Tico's room, all grown up.

For a school with almost no money, making art out of junk was the best we could do. I communicated to parents the need for additional "materials." I did not anticipate that our school would become the de facto junk depot for ten households. The school was soon filled with dozens of cardboard boxes of unimaginably useless items: garden hoses, chicken wire, foam rubber, Styrofoam, rats' nests of wires, telephones, copper pipes, computer innards, figurines from kiddy meals, pie tins, broken ski bindings, bicycle wheels, old jewelry, lace collars, and high-heeled shoes.

When John came to class the next week, he brought a "sandwich" he'd made out of scrap material.

"I made this in my barn this morning," he offered. The sandwich was composed of bread slices made of foam padding, linoleum meat, and Astroturf for lettuce.

"Awesome," said Steve. "It's looks so real."

Our idea was to build something gargantuan, in the radical style of Claes Oldenburg's building-sized clothespins, flashlights, hamburgers, and dessert spoons. We bandied about ideas: a giant animal? a two-story cake?

"We could make like, a huge ski boot!" suggested Nick.

"How about a giant tube of lipstick?" said Zoe.

Najat peered into boxes and pulled out some large hoop earrings and a pair of mildewed patent leather pumps.

"Hey! I know, let's build a giant woman. Like, totally huge! Wouldn't that be funny?" She was jumping up and down.

"Yeah, yeah. That's a great idea," said John, who seemed to be willing to try anything.

In order to get the proportions right, we needed to scale up a human figure. The kids chose me and commanded me to lie on the big table. Ten kids commenced to measure my fingers, ankles, feet, head, neck, and arms by pressing lengths of tape measure and rulers against me. I was a patient on a plastic table, defenseless at the hands of decidedly unprofessional physicians. With John directing, my students clambered over me like hyperactive Lilliputians over Gulliver.

"Make sure you get accurate measurements of my gigantic muscles," I said. "They are hard to measure because they ripple so much."

"Yeah, right," said Nick.

"Don't move!" said Annie, who was used to such operations due to her experience as a surgeon in local Revolutionary War reenactments. "Don't move or I'll stab you with a . . . plastic ruler."

I had no idea exactly what we were trying to accomplish. *A sculpture of a giant woman made out of useless crap?* And I, the head teacher, had assumed a position of complete submission. Through me and through such ostensibly purposeful activity something great, something like learning, was supposed to emerge? Yet I also felt a vague sense of elation. We had achieved some kind of healthy intimacy, a constructive silliness, where my students used me to map out their ideas. I was the springboard and their starting point, and I was entirely in their hands.

Each length of me was duly recorded by Annie and Doug, who, as the designated class geeks, were charged with figuring out enlargement ratios. I was lengthened to a height of ten feet. This included adding, to their great delight, an enormous bosom.

"Oh, yeah, give him—or her—huge boobs!" said Najat. "That way I won't have the biggest boobs in the class anymore, thank God."

"Najat!" Annie said in almost feigned shock.

"What? It's not gross, it's the truth. I'm sick of always having the biggest boobs."

"I wish mine were bigger," said Zoe.

"I don't think I have to worry about that too much," Sophie said matter-of-factly, shrugging her thin shoulders.

"Is it a him or is it a her?" asked Janine.

"Whatever it is, it's going to have huge boobs," said Najat.

We brought in drills, jigsaws, and circular saws, and Fridays became a chaotic workshop. The dozens of boxes were ripped open as we scavenged among the spilled contents for choice materials and parts. Kids were either building on Big Woman, as she was now known, or they were working on their individual junk sculptures.

Disregarding rational judgment and the "reasonable person" standard, I relished the idea of handing power tools to my students as part of their learning. It seemed right that we actually carried through the notion that learning was about constructing something—even a sculpture of a buxom woman. Like small children, using "grown-up" tools gave them the feeling of self-importance and being trusted.

I peered out the door one afternoon. Nick and Tico were giving Zoe a lesson on using the jigsaw to cut lengths of strapping for Big Woman's armature. The sweet smell of sawdust, the whirring drills, the three of them standing out under the porch amid a tangle of power cords, with the snow melting off the roof and the sun reflecting off the blinding snow—I loved the picture they made.

"You punks be careful," I said. "If a digit falls off, come get me."

"Don't worry, Tal, my dad's a carpenter," said Nick, with boastful confidence.

"I know, Nick, but that doesn't mean you are a carpenter, know what I mean?"

"We'll be safe, trust me."

"Okay, Nick. Just be careful that Tico doesn't try to saw the school down."

"Yeah, right, Tal," said Tico, holding out his hand in the shape of an upside-down gun, gangster style.

"Hey, Tico, how come you always hold your gun upside down when you point it?"

"It helps me aim," he said, without blinking.

"Whoa, a real tough guy, eh. Old Clint Eastwood."

"Watch it, Tal."

Janine scurried about supplying other kids with screws, tape measures, and duct tape, chattering about whatever legal catastrophes loomed just over our horizon. She gave me a schoolmarmish shake of her finger.

"Tal, someone is going to chop their hand off. I'm warning you. Blood everywhere. The State of Vermont will arrest you and close the school and all your sad students will have no North Branch anymore."

Through an ungainly process, Big Woman grew to thrillingly large proportions, boobs and all. Each class, my head whirled with questions and requests to hold this or that, replace drill bits, telling Nick and Tico to stop shooting each other with squirt guns, helping Najat make plaster of paris, maintaining the momentum. We were drilling legs onto Big Woman, wiring her head to her wobbly neck, wrapping her in a polyester dress, hanging lightbulbs from her ears, and stuffing her blouse with newspaper. She wore delicate lace gloves, thick sprouts of foam rubber arising from her red vinyl head, her arms bangled with telephone cords, her nose a faded Transformer action figure.

The day before the Re-Use Showcase we all gathered around Big Woman and took a picture of her towering over us against the gray clapboards of the schoolhouse. We transported her to the show in the back of my old truck, with her jeweled arms protruding over the windshield like great lace claws. She was installed at the entrance of the gallery. For a month, icicles dripped onto her head, her newspaper bosom soaked and sagging, testament to the artistry of the North Branch School.

We experienced moments of increased velocity and triumph, like making a giant woman out of trash. But sometimes the room was filled with apathy and we walked along the edge of total failure. If my students didn't like North Branch they could go somewhere else, leaving nothing behind but our rootless wisp of a school. I had nothing to make them stay, no power to hold them. There was no demerit, law, rod, switch, or dunce corner, not even the school's eminent reputation, that I could use to control or govern them. No power of compulsion was available to me except hope and faith, and sometimes anger.

We planned to make a quilt for our first fund-raiser. In science they were studying the animals of the woodland forest. I decided to have them draw woodland birds on fabric, which would be stitched into a quilt and raffled off.

I explained the project one dark afternoon.

"That sounds kinda corny," said Mira.

"Mira, it's a damn fund-raiser, okay. We're trying to raise money for scholarships so everyone can be here and we don't turn into some kind of snooty club."

I laid the fabric on the floor. "Okay guys. Let's cut this into squares."

They stared at me dumbly.

"Come on, let's go."

Mira rolled her eyes. No one reached for scissors. Janine lifted herself slowly out of a chair.

Najat moaned, "Can't we have a little more lunch?"

"Lunch is over. Let's get a move on. This is an art project. Time for class."

"Do we have to?" asked Tico.

"Listen, goddammit!" I stared around at all of them. "We can do this or we can read a fucking textbook. If you want to sit around being jerks and jackasses I'll get the textbooks and we'll write a goddamn book report. Yes, you have to."

They stared at me, unmoving.

"What the hell is the matter with you? This is important. Or maybe you just want to stand around whining."

My panic arose from disgust for their laconic apathy. I had told myself that all children had an innate desire to build and create. But on this day these children were not inspired. Whose fault was it? The distance between success and failure was paper-thin. My anger was only partly an act; it was also the last tool of compulsion I possessed.

Slowly, without talking, and then only in quiet voices, they knelt to the floor, picked up the scissors, and measured out their squares.

Later we taped the fabric to the windows. The afternoon light in the windows illuminated the cut fabric as we traced our birds in pencil over enlarged photocopies.

I watched them laughing as they sketched—Doug drawing a thin-legged killdeer, Tico a sharp-shinned hawk, and Mira, with her face inches from her hand, sketching the delicate lines of a black-capped chickadee against cold glass and the low, white February sun.

I constantly wondered if what we were doing constituted school by anybody's definition. With ten students, it took only two absences for it to feel unquestionably *not* like school. Sometimes our school seemed only one step from disintegrating. So when the phone rang one morning and I heard that a girl named Emma was interested in the school, I felt a surge of hope. In my ears rang the words: *interested in the school.* The constant worry that no one was interested at all, that no one believed, that no one understood, or cared about, ten teens holed up in the woods—for a brief moment that worry lifted.

"Can we visit tomorrow?" asked Gloria, Emma's mother.

"Well, my mother is going to be here doing art all morning," I said.

"It'll be a kind of a crazy day to visit." My mother, an art teacher in Atlanta, had made several sojourns north to help me teach art.

"Oh, that sounds perfect. Is it all right if I stay for the morning too?"

"I suppose so. But these are adolescents. It's kind of crazy sometimes. I can't tell you exactly how it will go."

"We're okay with that."

The next morning Emma and her mother showed up for class. My mother had brought fresh daffodils from Atlanta. The classroom was pungent with the sweet, light yellow-green perfume of spring, even with snow still up to our windowsills.

I didn't have much time to worry about whether Emma was having a useful school visitation experience. I introduced her and her mother to the class and then we started with our daffodil drawings. There were shouts for paper, brushes, paint. We crumpled tissue paper, mixed colors, and set up different lighting arrangements. The usual cacophony: voices and bustling, gathering and sharing supplies, spilled jars of water. And the usual complaints.

"Oh, mine is so sucky."

"That's not sucky. Yours is good. Mine is the suckiest."

"Why does my daffodil look like a spastic pine tree?"

"Oh, I have cool shadows. Tal, what color is this shadow?"

"Try to see it as it is," I said, trying to get my own shadows right. "Usually there are about five colors or tones in a shadow. Purple, blue, black, green, whatever you see."

Emma had her head down and she was flying through the project, bringing a bouquet of southern daffodils to life as they were meant to live.

Her mother called that night. "She wants to come. When can she start?"

"How about tomorrow?"

Like that, our enrollment grew by ten percent.

I did not know much about Emma except that she was young, still in sixth grade, and that she was a refugee from a miserable school experience, apparently unwilling even to go any longer, precipitating her switch to North Branch. We were one hundred pages into *One Flew Over the Cuckoo's Nest,* and I gave her a copy and told her to try to catch up. I worried it was too hard for her. The day after I gave it to her I found her reading on the derelict stained couch in the big room. She was curled up with her legs under her and completely rapt, oblivious to the sounds of the algebra class at the table in front of her.

"How far have you made it into the book? Did you get past the first scene?"

She looked up. "Oh, I'm caught up already."

"Caught up already? All the way?"

"Yep."

"And you follow what is happening? That Chief can—"

"That he can hear and talk but he's afraid to talk because he's stopped up like a dam and that McMurphy is sorta like Jesus?" she asked.

"Uh, yeah, I guess you're caught up."

So she was sharp and more than able. What, then, had been interfering with her ability and desire to be in school? To have her at North Branch was perhaps to see what might make our school different or effective, to see if we could make happen that which the system had not been able to make happen.

A week later I got another call, from Eileen Daniels. Her daughter was being homeschooled, and she thought it best that Debbie begin schooling with her peers.

"But her last experience in school was quite terrible," Eileen said. "Children can be very cruel. And Debbie's quite shy."

Bill, Eileen, and Debbie Daniels came to visit the next day. Bill was the minister at the Federated Church of Rochester. Surely, now, I would be exposed as the Antichrist of education, a shouter of obscenities, a raving anarchist with a barely legitimate operation, an inept blasphemer. Surely they would see the adolescent torpor; surely their eyes would catch the profanities in the stories the kids had written and decide that home was, after all, the safest place for their daughter.

Debbie walked behind her parents, nearly a shadow. Her hair was long and straight, strawberry blond, and she was pale and petrified. I talked with them for an hour while Eric conducted science class. They looked at our plywood bookshelves and hand-me-down encyclopedias, our walls covered with tattered posters and tree drawings, our coats and mud boots and dirty brooms jumbled in a dark corner. They observed the expanse of our student body: Nick in his ratty, untied skateboard sneakers, Mira and Zoe with lip gloss glistening, Steve with his baseball cap tilted sideways.

I was sure I would never hear from Bill and Eileen Daniels again.

That night the phone rang and it was Eileen. "Debbie loved it. How do we apply?"

"Well, to tell you the truth, I don't think there is any need to apply. We'd love to have her start immediately."

"Oh, that's wonderful. And when can she start?"

"How about tomorrow? We can offer financial aid if you would like to request it."

"Oh, that's wonderful. I'll tell Debbie. She'll be so excited."

Debbie started that Friday. In two weeks our enrollment had grown to twelve, the number Chairman Mao said was ideal for proper instruction.

P eople were coming to us. The students never said it, but I suspected that having new students join them made them slightly more secure about spending their early adolescence in a strange little school in the woods. I felt a glimmer of hope. There was more life, a slightly more complex ensemble, a new arrangement of voices and interaction.

We read Jacques Lusseyran's memoir, *And There Was Light,* his story of leading a movement of students in the French Underground during the Nazi occupation of Paris in World War II. Most remarkably, Lusseyran was blind. The governing theme of the book concerned his ability to see morally, to operate in the dark and yet retain his sense of righteousness. Darkness and evil occluded his civilization, but he lived in a world of uncommon moral clarity.

Mira could not believe that someone, seventeen years old like Lusseyran, could be so pure, angelic, and courageous.

"I don't frickin' get this. It's not believable. How could this guy, what's his name—"

"Jacques Lusseyran."

"—do this? Nobody is this good."

Hers was an objection not to literary reality but to *her* reality. If it was possible for Lusseyran, or any teenager, to be so good, then why was she *not* so good? What did it mean that she or any of us were *not* Lusseyran? And what could she say she was doing on this earth, with the blessings of a mother and father, a school, freedom, and her eyesight?

"Mira, does it matter if is true or not? I mean, it's a story. Isn't the purpose of us reading it to see if we can pull something valuable out of it that is true for us? To look for something we can use to see ourselves?"

"But if it is not believable, then what good can it tell us?"

"Maybe it's true, maybe it's not," said Doug. "We are supposed to think about the story he gives us, not criticize him. If you focus on whether it is true, then you can't take in what he says."

"Mira," I said, "you don't believe that it is possible to be this good?"

"No frickin' way."

"But that comes from your own experience. His experience is not your experience."

"But how could he organize all those people? How could he 'sense' who was good or bad in the room if he didn't know them or see them?"

"Isn't that what we're supposed to consider? That maybe there is something inside of us that knows more than we can see. That we are supposed to be listening and feeling, rather than being governed by fear or negative emotions. He's definitely exceptional. Of course, if everyone were like him, there wouldn't have been a Holocaust or World War II."

"I guess. But it just pisses me off."

"Mira," Doug said, "that's ridiculous. How can an inspiring story of someone who fought the Nazis, who you did your presentation about, piss you off? The problem is not the book, it's your reaction to the book."

"Look," I said, "let's just say it is completely untrue. Let's assume for argument that Lusseyran made it all up. What then can we gain? Does the story have anything to tell us? What would impel him to make up such a story? If this is the myth, what does the myth tell us that we need to understand?"

"Well, maybe he's telling us that a character like this, or courage like this, is a light in the world," said Zoe.

"That's right, Zoe Life Light."

"Or that there was some kind of light somewhere in the middle of the war," said Emma. "That not everything is total darkness."

"And yet we know for a fact that there was a French Underground, it was led by students, it's true that Jacques Lusseyran was the leader, and he was captured, and his fellow resistance members died or got arrested."

"Ugh, I know. Just forget it," said Mira.

"But we can't forget it. This is worth remembering. Your question is important."

"It doesn't matter anyway."

I could see the irritation on the face of Emma, who could not abide any kind of hopelessness or submission. From the way Emma wrote about the text, Lusseyran was her god for the way he had kept his soul together in the middle of unfathomable darkness.

"I just think it's inspiring," she said. "If he can do this, or if he only did half of this, it tells me that we should always be doing more."

"Doing more? Mira?" I asked.

"Whatever."

Immovable, she had run herself out. Yet her intransigence gave me a pivot around which to move the class. She was provocative, unyielding, feisty, and outspoken. I thought of what Wallace Stevens wrote: "What self, for example, did he contain that had not yet been loosed, / Snarling in him for discovery as his attentions spread . . ." The school had to be safe enough for my students to locate that self, to loose what was snarling and alive inside of them. Then the school could become a true reflection of their minds as *they* discovered it, as though for the first time in the history of the world. The class had to be safe for anything, including disharmony. Harmony in a classroom could be utterly numbing—dissonance and dissent, atonality and cacophony were, to my mind, the greater provocateur for learning.

Mira's voice was a perfect foil against which the class could assemble its own moral, literary, or historical philosophy. The energy with which she pushed the book away forced me to teach harder, working to make the book come alive for those who wanted to take it in. And yet I could not say Mira was *not* taking it in. She grappled with ideas, she read with a fighting heart and an unforgiving, hypercritical eye. Through her, the whole class was coming to see more.

I decided that we would take a crack at writing a constitution for ourselves—a statement of purpose, a manifesto of our ideals.

A few well-placed posters asserting that the school was "A community of respect" would not make them feel or believe anything, and would certainly not inspire art or beautiful ideas. If such platitudes were foisted upon them the students would know they were a sham perpetrated by well-meaning adults unwilling to trust that the kids could create such a place from and through themselves.

A collective document on the evolving philosophy of learning at the North Branch School was a difficult proposition. I loathed the whole concept of school mission statements, as if the infinitely complex organism of a school could be boiled down to mere bullet points. On the other hand, if the students wrote it, perhaps such a document could be authentically reflective of the direction and philosophy of the school.

"So what do you guys think?" I asked.

"What would be the purpose?" asked Nick. "I mean, what's it supposed to say?"

"We could write down how we organize the school," said Annie. "How we have all our classes in one room, and we call you by your first name, and how we do our own cleanup."

"I was thinking of something a little more lofty," I said.

"But who would read it?" asked Sophie.

"Hell, I don't know," I said. "Maybe we would send it to the president."

"Oh, that would be so cool," said Tico. "We should like, *so* do that."

"But I mean, why do we need to say what we do?" asked Nick. "Can't we already do whatever we want?"

"If we tell anyone what we're doing, you'll get arrested, Tal," said Sophie.

"Sophie, I am not afraid of being hunted down. As long as you all promise to defend me in a court of law when I get charged with many crimes and felonies. No, listen. The main reason to write it would be to say what we've figured out what works for us, *here*. If someone wants to read it, great. If not, who gives a rat's ass?"

Then I lied: "Actually, to tell you the honest-to-God truth, we have no choice. The state of Vermont is making us do this. They are requiring a mission statement. I can give them some crap I already wrote, but I think you should write it yourselves. Then we can send them that."

"You mean we would describe our school to the state?" Zoe asked incredulously.

"Um, Tal, they will definitely come and arrest you," said Mira.

"Like what if someone did read it and other people wanted to start a school like this one?" said Janine.

"Yes!" I shouted. "Our empire will spread."

"Yeah, right," said Mira. "Who would want to make a school like this one with a bunch of weirdos and a redneck teacher who drove a Plymouth Valiant?"

"I'm not a redneck, Mira. I am a poet."

"Yeah, a redneck poet," said Annie, "who drove a Plymouth Valiant with no muffler."

"Very hilarious again, Annie. Our constitution could say what we value. It could describe the ideas that we have been talking about. Our law."

"But that's kind of stupid," said Mira. "It seems like the reason the school is here is because we don't want law. We want to be free to have a school that's different. If we write it down, we'll be just like everyone else."

"But it doesn't have to be laws, and it doesn't have to be like everyone else, Mira," said Doug. "It would be a way for us to say what *should* be and what *is* different. It could be guidelines or principles that we try to follow."

"Well, what's the point of guidelines if we don't have to follow them, if there is nothing forcing us to?"

"Yeah," said Sophie. "If we want it to do anything, then it has to be a list of laws."

"So would that mean we have to have punishments and courts?" asked Annie.

208 a **room** for learning

"It could be like a reminder to ourselves," said Nick, who was himself in constant need of reminding—whether about his coat, his homework, or his highest ethical values. "Because when you say what you believe," he continued, "it's more likely that you'll follow what you believe."

"I think we should have a law that we have to fly the American flag," Janine suggested, as she swung her hair back.

"Great, Janine, but I was thinking we'd try something a little more complex and creative. However, as benevolent dictator I say bring in a flag and we'll proudly fly it here."

"Can't the school buy one?"

"Janine, we can barely afford pencils."

"I think we should have a law that we say the Pledge of Allegiance every day," she persisted.

"Uh, Janine, I'm not sure anyone here actually knows all the words," said Tico.

"I do. Do you want me to recite it?"

"Oh, for Christ's sake, we're not talking about the laws someone else made, or pledges. We're talking about the things *we've* made."

"But we haven't made anything yet," said Janine.

"Janine, for God's sake, that's why we're talking about writing down things we all believe."

"But is it possible to get twelve people to believe the same things?" she asked.

"Why don't we do, you know, majorities rule? What's that thingy?" said Najat.

"You mean *majority rule,* Najat?" asked Doug, with a barely suppressed sneer.

"Yeah, yeah, that's what I meant."

"That's a basic tenet of democracy, Najat," I said. "A small number does not overpower the larger number. But here we can do even better.

We can have a direct democracy. That means every person in the democracy gets a direct say and vote in the government and the decisions. You don't have to vote for someone to represent you, because you're directly involved."

"I don't think it makes sense to write any of this unless we all agree to it," said Doug.

"You mean complete consensus?" I asked.

"Yeah, I mean *totally*. Anything we say or write everyone has to agree together. That way everyone will feel like whatever we write is exactly all of our feelings. Because it seems wrong to have anyone here be required to live under a document that has portions they disagree with. No one should feel like they have been overpowered. If we all agree, that is the best chance we have for all getting along."

Doug was articulating an astonishingly complex ideal: unanimous, harmonious consent, in a class of opinionated and not always well-informed or logical adolescents.

"So nothing goes into the document without there being hundred percent agreement?"

The class boiled up into argument, voices climbing over other voices.

"We can't even agree to this!" said Mira.

"Hey, shut up!" I boomed. "Listen!"

They quieted, but I could feel acrimony seeping into the room. Maybe I had unleashed something not worth unleashing, a year's worth of irritations, insecurities, and petty grievances.

"If we follow Doug's plan," said Nick, "that means whatever we say will have everyone's belief behind it. That way anything we write will mean more to all of us."

"Yes, exactly," said Doug. "We have to proceed that way. It is the only way we can have absolute good."

"Absolute good? You think that should be our goal?"

"Yes."

"Doug, why do we all need to agree and get along?" Mira asked.

"What else should we choose? That's the only thing we should choose," he answered.

"There's a small problem though, Doug," I said.

"What?"

"Well, if one person does not agree to a part of the document, or in the document itself, then you have given that one person the power to overrule the entire rest of the class. In that sense, one person has the power of a king."

Mira raised her hand again. "Exactly. What's the point of it? I mean, if we all know what we believe and agree, then what's the point of writing it down?"

I tried again. "Mira, that would mean that the only value in writing a thing down is in what the thing ends up *doing,* not in the fact of writing it down. Maybe there's use in the act of writing it down. The Bill of Rights was a list of what the power or state or government could *not* do to the people. Maybe we could write it as a listing of what should *never* happen here."

"I don't get this," she stated.

"Maybe it's not useful to tell people what to do, but you could at least list what you *don't* want them to do. The Declaration of Independence stated all the crimes the king had committed against the people— that is, they wrote down what was wrong in the world, which they sought to banish. Ours could do something like that."

"Yeah, like a North Branch Declaration of Independence," said Janine brightly. "All of our feelings declared."

"But it shouldn't be laws. That would take forever," said Sophie. "You can't make feelings law."

"If you think of laws as a reverse expression of your fears," I offered, "then feelings are part of laws."

"I think we should at least try it. It'd be something to do in school," said Emma. "It's a lot better than some dumb project."

Zoe raised her hand tentatively. "But I mean, with only twelve of us, can't we take care of what happens? What's a piece of paper going to do? When Tico stole we didn't have laws."

I wasn't sure if Zoe believed what she was saying or if she was kissing up to Mira.

"Tico, would a law have kept you from doing that?"

"It might have, but I doubt it," said Tico. "I did break the law, and that sort of made it more wrong or something. If there was no law, how would I feel it was wrong? But if there was something we had written, I don't think that would have changed how I was feeling."

"But we could write basic guidelines of how we should treat each other," Doug said. "It would protect us by saying what we don't want to happen. If we all agree, it can't hurt us."

"Yes, we know, Doug," said Mira. "You already said that!"

I wasn't sure where it was leading. Between the extremes of Doug's idealism and Mira's cynicism I wondered if they were capable of writing a collaborative document without killing each other. It could easily descend into a *Lord of the Flies* scenario, where all best intentions were subverted by instinctual fear, blindness, irritation, or apathy. Yet it was vital to let them try. They were talking about ideal forms of configuring themselves and the nature of ethical relationships. Reason and feeling, hope and fear—these had full scope to come toward each other and, perhaps, become a fragile unity.

"Okay, here's what I propose, just to see what happens. I want each of you to write down what you feel to be the most basic ideas or ideals we have come up with. What you believe this school believes. Or should stand for. It's not law, just ideas, okay, Mira?"

"I guess."

"But in order to add anything to the list, in order to convince us why a thing has to be on the list, you have to explain the experience that led to it. Your idea has to have a concrete source, an actual experience behind it. It has to be real. Write either what we should always do here, or what should never be done here. Bring those tomorrow and let's see if we have anything that's worth keeping."

The next day we compiled the list. *Always be respectful of each other and teachers. Everyone should try their hardest. People should feel safe saying their feelings. Be honest. No one should steal from anyone. Everyone should make an effort to understand what another person is saying.*

The list was not too different from kindergarteners or elementary students writing down school rules for a year on a sheet of butcher paper and signing it with painted handprints. Their list was full of expressions of the highest good. But they were adolescents, and they still wanted to argue about every possibility of failure of their proposed document. They wanted to split hairs over the definitions of terms and procedural motions. They wanted to debate fairness, usefulness, and necessity. They wanted to ferret out every potential loophole, structural flaw, and moral inconsistency.

"You may think it is important to try your hardest, but what is trying your hardest? Isn't that, like, too vague?" asked Steve.

"What if different people have different feelings about that?" asked Nick.

"Of course we know we shouldn't steal from each other. Isn't that like, obvious?" said Mira.

"Because it's a reminder, a statement of what we want," Doug said. "Remember, Moses had ten commandments engraved in stone. Maybe it's good to have it written down so that we can look at it."

"I heard Moses had a third tablet that he dropped and smashed," offered Nick.

"Nick," I asked, "how exactly does that well-documented historical tidbit help us here?"

"I don't know. But if it was true, I wonder what the other commandments were."

"Nick, *hello!* Stay on task," said Emma.

"No, I'm serious. What would they have been?"

"Well, here's your chance to write them," I said.

"It's still too perfect to be possible," said Mira. "Twelve people will never agree exactly on one thing. I mean, isn't it possible that someone will only say they agree because they are scared to go against the other eleven?"

"Yeah, but at least they have freedom to vote what they believe," said Tico. "It's still their choice."

"Everyone has to decide in their own minds," offered Emma. "If they make a choice, we have to believe that's what they believe."

"So what are we supposed to do with these?" asked Sophie.

"We keep them as a reflection of our best selves," I said.

The process took a month. Amendments were added to and subtracted from the list, which we called a Statement of Ideals and Principles. We spent hours on wording and punctuation. Each night I retyped the document and each morning I read the revisions back to them.

"Hey, that sounds good," said Janine.

"Not too bad," said Doug.

"Um, Tal, I think it should say 'the' before 'NBS,'" offered Sophie.

"Okay." I penciled in the change.

"Wait," said Nick. "I thought we were going to put in that thing Tal was talking about, the elastic principle thingy, the thing that says this document can always be changed."

"Yeah," said Doug. "As long as we can change it, it's flexible to our needs. As long as we all agree to the changes, none of us will ever feel like it has been forced on us."

They saw the process of their thoughts taking shape. The document grew more complex—a pure, polished reflection of their most serious ideas.

We, the students of the North Branch School (henceforth referred to as the "NBS"), in order to create a lawful and safe learning environment, have established guidelines for our behavior. These principles and ideals are designed to ensure the protection of our personal rights and the rights of our teachers, and to shape a healthy and fun school for all persons involved. We solemnly agree that we will not become strangers to our good ethics, and we stand by them as students and human beings.

We hold that these principles are not laws but rather ideals that we aim to achieve. We have created this document, not to restrain or limit those to whom it applies, but to guarantee that they will be protected as much as possible; not to force our values onto future members of the class, but, rather, to state the values of our generation.

To not become strangers to our good ethics: Those words were Mira's—a powerful notion, containing the awareness that she and all of them, as adolescents, were in the midst of momentous physical, ethical, psychological, and intellectual transformation. By agreeing to include those words, the class showed a sense of themselves as *originators*—as a founding generation—with an eye to the future that would follow.

We approached the time of ratification. They all had to write a full essay describing why they supported or opposed ratification, with personal experience as the substance of their argument. No lofty abstraction permitted without a true story behind it.

We spent two weeks perfecting the essays, which were read in the rarefied atmosphere of our own North Branch Constitutional Convention. Every speech argued strenuously in support of ratification. They believed, it appeared, that they had written something valuable and worth keeping. We had aimed for unanimous consensus, and it appeared that consensus had been achieved.

Then we voted. I counted the twelve scraps of paper at my desk. Ten votes supported ratification. Two were against. After six weeks of effort, ratification had failed.

It was a sunny, cool day. Piles of snow lay at the edge of the woods in the deep shadow, littered with amber needles. We sat in a ring on the deck on chairs we had brought from inside.

I announced the verdict to the class. Ten votes for ratification, two against.

"What!" shouted Nick in disbelief. "Who voted against it? Everyone's speech was for it."

His voice registered as much disappointment as shock. I, too, was disappointed, if only because I had worked as hard as they, and I was proud of them for what they had made.

"After all that," said Emma, "and after everyone said they wanted it, who changed their mind?"

Annie raised her hand tentatively. "I voted against as an experiment. I wanted to see if we really would hold true on our belief that it should only pass with everyone agreeing. I was curious about what everyone's reaction would be. I thought I would be the only one. I was planning on changing my vote. I mean, I am voting for it."

"Then who was the other person?" asked Nick.

"Easy, Nick," I said. "We voted confidentially, so I don't think that person should have to say why they voted against. Otherwise they'd expose themselves to an inquisition. I'm not sure we can require somebody to undergo that if it's supposed to be democratic."

Mira raised her hand. "I voted against it."

"What? Why?" came several voices.

"All that work and now you just shot it down," said Doug. "Why would you do that?" The feeling of having been betrayed was palpable.

"Because I don't see why we need it. We can deal with anything that we face. That's what we've already done and there are only twelve of us. I don't see why we have to make it like a law."

"But Mira, we went over this so many times," said Doug. "You know it's not law. And if we don't like it we can change it. That's in the last law, the elastic principle."

There was despair in Doug's voice. He'd argued so passionately for a document of unity, for this expression of harmony, and he had risked his work on the principle of unanimous approval. Now it was all shot, by one vote, one voice.

I could understand Doug's feeling. And yet I also understood Mira's position. Fearful of being limited, wanting to expand, grow wings, gain mastery—all desires of adolescents—somehow these impulses were clipped by a list of laws. Maybe it *was* too much like a list of playground rules.

Her vote brought anger to the surface. Either her speech or her vote was a lie, Emma asserted. How could she say she was for it and then vote against it? And what about the principle of one person's position having power over eleven others? How could we give one person that much power?

This made me wonder whether perhaps her vote *was* a play for power. The class seemed to be circling Mira with what bordered on hatred. It felt like defeat—for them, me, and the North Branch School.

"But this is like you are against the school and everything it stands for," said Doug. "The document doesn't hurt you, yet by voting against it makes it seem like we are on two sides."

"I have freedom to vote how I want. That's what we said we were doing. I don't think we need it. A written document isn't going to change how any of us act."

"Well, then it seems like all our work has been wasted," said Nick.

"Has it?" I asked. I felt the same way, but I had to salvage from the experience whatever was useful. The school would not always take the course I hoped or expected.

"Is everything we did gone? All the conversations, the whole process, the work we did, it still exists. We have a document that represents a lot of the feelings of the class, something that represents what the school is."

"But everything we wrote means nothing because now it's gone," said Tico.

"You tried to articulate what you value and what you share, the protection each of you deserves, and what you hope the school is. You said what you hoped for and you said what you wanted to be rid of. You wrote down how and why we came to believe what we believed."

They looked at me.

"Doug, are you now not free to believe what you wrote? Do you still believe it?"

"Of course."

"Do you now know better your feelings about what constitutes real harmony?"

"Yes."

"Did we get those ideas across and think long and hard about what we believe?"

"Yes, but—"

"We worked together and each of you held to your principles, even if there is not a final piece of paper as the result."

They sat looking at me, at Mira, in exasperation. It still felt like failure.

"What else can you do? You gave it everything you have. Is that a waste? I don't know. What we did together is what we're after. The learning is in the conversations we had, the speeches, the arguments, even this argument. Trying to understand Mira's determination and her will to hold her ground. Trying to accept it, trying to understand what it means, what our work means, which mystifies even me. That's what learning is. It's not about a product."

We sat on the porch in the sun, looking at each other. Whatever was of value would live on inside of them. What else was there to say?

The school, and what we created in it, was not a stale reflection of something someone else had handed to us. It was our own original, stumbling search for our voices in the woods, the attempt to find what we were and what we were becoming. I drew them up to the mirror as close as I could, so they could see reflections of each other as collaborators in a difficult experiment. We were face-to-face with the complexity of ourselves. So it dissolved in the end. I had asked them to say whether they *believed*. They all did, including Mira, who believed in taking a stand, even if it put her at odds with her community. Taking a stand—that was something we could learn from.

IV.
spring

I've known rivers:

Ancient, dusky rivers.

My soul has grown deep like the rivers.

· LANGSTON HUGHES, *"The Negro Speaks of Rivers"*

In spring I sent out a letter: Who was coming back? I got replies. Every one of them was coming back. *Every one.* Some even sent in checks as a down payment for next year's tuition. That was money we could use.

We were spending the second four months of the year studying the civil rights movement. I continued to listen to John Coltrane on my drive up the mountain to Ripton, to listen deeply and ponder the endless tessellations of his artistic, spiritual development. Coltrane's musical career paralleled the civil rights movement. As I drove I thought about what I would teach that day; I thought about Montgomery, Little Rock, Oxford, Albany, and Selma. I let Coltrane's music sift into my thoughts. It was a conversation I needed to have. No rambunctious teenagers, no demands, no crises, no conflicts to defuse, no failure, no hyperactive stick fighters, no noise, messes, mediocrity, or apathy. Coltrane was a gift I gave myself.

When I listened I was relieved from giving and making. I was the receiver—of sound, movement, change, tempo, rhythm. In a meditative trance, passing dairy farms and trailers, I contemplated the arc of

Coltrane's music, the scope of what he said without using words, meanings that opened up. Coltrane let himself go toward lovely, blessed chaos. He embraced dissonance and the unknown, and he always found lyrical resolution. I wanted to understand and cross that distance between chaos and lyrical resolution.

Every morning that spring I listened to one of the five versions of Coltrane's "Spiritual," recorded in 1961. I knew that "Spiritual" was a swinging blues. Below that, in a deeper vein, the song was a religious meditation. It was a cosmos in itself, propulsive unfolding, doubling back, probing, always reaching and expanding. When Coltrane played his saxophone like it was on fire, or Eric Dolphy squealed out unworldly bending notes, or McCoy Tyner made rhythmic block chords and Elvin Jones pounded on the drums sounding like five wild men at once, I saw beauty unfolding. Every day I heard sounds and combinations I had not heard before.

I read analyses of Coltrane's artistic dream. One book examined the making of "Kind of Blue." Another dissected "A Love Supreme" phrase by phrase, note by note.

In one biography I found Coltrane's description of his quest:

> There is never any end. There are always new sounds to imagine, new feelings to get at. And always, there is a need to keep purifying these feelings and sounds so that we can really see what we discovered in its pure state. So we can more clearly see what we are. In that way we can give to those who listen the essence, the best of what we are. But to do that at each stage, we have to keep cleaning the mirror.

Inside the rooms of the song, the maker said to himself, *I can go farther. I can push into another place. There is never any end.* Coltrane refused to accept the idea of stasis or limitation. I pondered that going and coming.

I went on a reckless buying spree, tracking down bootleg radio recordings like *Miles Davis Quintet w/John Coltrane Live at Café Bohemia* or new releases from the Impulse vaults. *One Down, One Up, Live at the Blue Note,* anything I could get my hands on.

I told the kids about my spending and collecting.

"Thirty-six CDs?! Are you crazy?!"

"No, I am wicked hip."

"How many John Coltrane recordings are there?"

"It's hard to say with all the bootlegs. Probably about, like, you know, three hundred."

"What?!" they shouted.

"Don't you ever get sick of it?"

"No, never. I listen to how he got where he is. You go inside of his horn, into his throat, down into his heart."

Najat crinkled her nose. "Oh, that's gross."

"How can they all be different?" Steve asked.

"If you know how to listen, you knuckleheads, you hear beautiful changes all the time. 'The beautiful changes.' It's a quote from our former poet laureate. I thought I'd throw that in there."

"Great, Tal."

"And a hell of a lot better than the crapola you guys listen to."

If they never listened to one note of his music, at least they could say they once had a crackpot teacher who loved John Coltrane.

I had a chronic fear of institutional calcification, where school became a finished place and was no longer a growing creation. Coltrane countered that. *Never any end. Always new feelings to get at. We have to keep cleaning the mirror.* How could I keep the school at that edge, never ending, always unfolding, where questions gave birth to listening and reflection, where answers were not defined or bounded but were articulations of purification and essence?

As I drove to school past the old farms of the Champlain Valley, up the mountains where snow still lay in the woods, I thought that the school year should not ever end at some predetermined point in early June, at the end of the textbook, at the end of the unit, at the end of the section. A school should not leave students staring out blankly over a landscape of a year, a year of doing time; they should all arrive at that point where they believed there was always more to find, that we *had* to come back. If they still hungered, if they were thrilled to be still looking, then school was a desirable thing, true and alive, for the teachers and the taught.

One day I read the Coltrane quote to them.

"Who do you think wrote that?" I asked.

"You?"

"Nope."

"Gandhi?"

"Nope."

"It sounds like North Branch," said Nick.

"Well," I said, "maybe it should be. That's John Coltrane, my little friends. From *Ascension: Coltrane and His Quest.*"

"Sweet," said Nick.

"He sounds like a pretty intense dude," said Steve.

We discussed the quote and then listened to "Alabama," Coltrane's haunting song about events unfolding in the South in 1963. We had watched Spike Lee's documentary *Four Little Girls,* about the tragic Birmingham church bombing. Now we heard the same story in six minutes of wordless, fragmentary song, a brief shudder of drums and brushing cymbals, a piano fading to silence, the silence asking questions.

I told the kids to write responses to the quote and the music. Perhaps I was deluding myself, requiring my students to make paeans to my idols, but I felt that they might understand something of what Coltrane was saying, if not in perfectly articulate words, then in symbolic representation, translating it into their own ideas. I told them to type out their responses carefully and then to decorate their responses as wildly as possible.

The words they came up with were good, but I loved even more the ways they defaced those words, covered them up, enhanced them, drew over them. There were rainbows arching through their paragraphs, metallic gold speckles, Pollock-like spatters, frilly borders, and rays of sun on curled papers. I put all responses on the wall and it looked like a true flowering, our attempt to see ourselves in the mirror of the school.

Coltrane once said, "My goal is to live the truly religious life and express it in my music." He sought transcendence and the mind of God through a saxophone. I was coming to believe that a school could strive in the same way. Our burden and our liberation was that constant search.

I had once told my students that North Branch was a religious school. As was often the case, I had no idea what I was saying. Somehow, though, we continued in what felt, at times, to be a religious vein. This is not to say that the school became orthodox in any conventional sense. I mean to say that we sometimes pursued our learning with religious intensity and attempted to "take the moral law and make a nave of it," as Wallace Stevens wrote.

We were reading the poetry of Langston Hughes. Our discussion for the day centered on "The Negro Speaks of Rivers."

"It's like the North Branch River," said Janine.

"We are speaking of the rivers in the poem, you wing nuts," I said. "The Negro is speaking of rivers. He wants you to listen. Are you listening?"

"Yes, Tal."

"He's asking us to think about the meaning of rivers. What is the meaning of rivers?"

"Rivers are always moving. Always flowing," said Nick.

"Rivers are like time?" Janine offered.

"Nice cliché. Keep going."

"The end is connected to the beginning," someone threw out.

"Good. Beautiful."

"Rivers are a cycle? All the water circles up and comes back."

"Like history?" I asked.

"Uh, well, yeah, sort of."

Zoe chimed in. "He's talking about the rivers turning all golden in the sunset. Before they were brown and muddy. Like before there was slavery, now there is freedom."

"Good, Zo-Zo. But you guys, he uses the word *bosom*!" I said, squeezing my face into an expression of squeamish pain.

"Oh, God, you are so immature, Tal!" they shouted. Apparently I was interfering with their acquisition of mystical knowledge.

Doug explained. "When he uses the word *bosom,* Tal, he means 'close to the heart.' Something *essential* to him."

"Oh, okay, now I get it. Thanks, guys. So learningwise, soulwise, what's it mean?" I asked again.

"Tal, two seconds ago you're talking about bosoms," said Tico. "Why do you always have to get so metaphorical and junk?"

"Do you want the answer to that in poetic terms, or pedagogical terms?" I asked.

"Peda-*what*?" they shouted.

"Listen," I said, "you guys are half children, half adult. That means you are larvae: The definition of *larvae* is immature, wingless, and often wormlike."

"Very funny, Tal. You've said that before."

"You have feet in both worlds," I continued. "You are in that stage where you can see signs, physical things, concrete materials of the world. You are crossing over to where you can interpret these signs, make abstractions, assign meaning to things. I am training your minds to do this. It's called higher-order thinking."

"Uh, Tal, that sounds like higher-*odor* thinking."

"Very funny, Annie. But so very true. There are higher odors in here, adolescent odors. That's why I use Teen Spirit deodorant, so I can be hip with you teenyboppers and not smell like an old goat."

"Oh, for God's sake, Tal! We are talking about a poem by Langston Hughes, and you're talking about goats and deodorant."

"Perhaps you all should stop changing the subject."

"What!?"

"Quiet! Listen. The Negro speaks of rivers. We're listening. Okay, my question: We see something muddy turning golden. It's beautiful, isn't it?"

"Yeah," exclaimed Nick. Then, with a sudden awakening of revelation: "It reminds me of the late afternoon in winter when the sun shines on the tops of the trees, and they go from being black and gray to glowing, sort of all gold. The whole mountain behind our house becomes almost, like, golden white with light."

"Oh, yeah, that is so awesome!" said Tico. "At my house sometimes all the silos turn from silver to golden. Right when the sun comes under the clouds before it sets. Even the fields shine."

"Right!" I shouted. "So what's it mean? I mean, what is this image about? Light shining over, coming out of dark things. Light suddenly penetrating, everything coated in gold. The long history of man, of slavery, depths, growing and deepening. The inheritance of time, suffering, devotion, work?"

"Oh, so it could mean the light is what being deep means?" asked Annie. "The poem is saying that to have a deep soul is to have a golden thing? He has it because he's connected to his past. Like all the rivers are connected. He feels the flow of his ancestors in his blood."

"Yes, Annie, right on, sister."

"And before, when he was a slave, or his ancestors were, he helped create the gold of wealth for other people," added Sophie. "But he has a better kind of gold in him."

"A better kind of gold—that's great, Sophie."

"He has all of human history inside him, so it makes him like a god," said Janine.

"And he is the one who made history," said Doug. "He built the civilizations, either as a king or a slave."

There was a pause in the pace of observations.

Najat raised her hand. "It seems like he *feels* beautiful," she said. "When he says, 'My soul has grown deep like the rivers,' it's like he's proud and happy. Like he has something that no one can ever take from him. Like he lasted forever. He built the world, the pyramids. He was a slave, and now he is like a king. He's gone where no one else has gone. That's what makes him deep like the rivers, like he's a god," she finished.

Mira's voice rose up. "I think *he* is beautiful. He's beautiful because of what he knows."

For a moment we lingered there, with no more words, only the sound of the poem, this man, these rivers. For the moment, we understood something approaching the divine—having beautiful depths, absorbing the vastness of history, transforming suffering into a muscular, golden, flowing soul.

I loved these conversations. I hoped for them every day. Sometimes we got to them, sometimes we didn't. Sometimes the trees remained dark, sometimes they lit up. And when they did, we made a discovery: testing, five-paragraph essays, research papers, and diagramming sentences were not a part of the soul's code. In the hearts of these adolescents was a hunger for religious epiphany. They wanted to clean the mirror and know, as deeply as the Negro knew, how deep their souls were.

One day in the spring, in the course of a discussion about how to be a good student, I mentioned my own desultory and undistinguished college career.

"I was not a scholar, you guys. I was kind of a bum. I was a crap student. Crappers-town for the Big T. Practically the only thing I remember from Art History 101 was Caravaggio's painting *The Calling of St. Matthew.*"

"Who's Caravaggio?" asked Nick.

"A great Italian painter from the sixteen hundreds."

"What made him so great?" Nick asked.

"He was able to tell the story he wanted to tell with light and facial expressions. He could paint the light of God in earthly terms."

"Why do you remember that painting?" asked Annie.

"Because he was able to capture a moment when a man recognized what his purpose was, who he was to become. He felt the light on him and in him. In the painting, Matthew sees Jesus enter the room, and the light shines over Jesus' head, and shines in the face of Matthew. That's illumination."

"Is that like what you mean when you say 'epiphany'?" asked Janine.

"Yeah. Illumination, epiphany, revelation, recognition, awakening. All of those."

"Can we see it?"

"I think so." I rummaged around on the bookshelf and found my Janson's *History of Art,* which contained a small black-and-white picture of Caravaggio's painting.

"Come in here close," I said. They crowded up on the table around the open book.

I showed them the composition, the way the light arrowed in on the tax collectors over Christ's shoulder.

"What do you see here? What's happening?"

"Uh, there's the light shining down into the room."

"The divine light. Do you know who these guys are?" I asked. "These are the tax collectors, but they stand for all the superficial, godless ones. They're decked out in the latest fashions but they are fools. They're the unawakened souls. See, these guys are you guys."

"And I suppose you're supposed to be that guy?" Annie said, smiling and pointing to Christ.

"I never thought of it that way, but now that you mention it—"

"They're all dressed up in such fancy clothes," said Sophie.

"Exactly. You see how Christ is barefoot? He's the real deal, he's earthly and godlike at the same time, with dirt on his feet. He is directly connected to Earth, but he's also divine. These other guys are asleep in their hearts. They only care about money. They look good but they're lost, they're in the dark. Only one of them recognizes what's happening and the light shines only on him. Only one of them can read what is being spoken into the room. That's Matthew."

"That's him there?" asked Tico.

"I think his expression definitely says, 'Oh, jeez, there's God!' " said Mira. "It looks like he's saying, 'He wants me. I better get up and do something, ASAP!' "

"Yeah," said Doug. "If God came in and caught me hanging out with a pack of drunken fools, I'd jump up too."

"Yeah," burst out Tico. "If Jesus said, 'Jump,' I'd say, 'How high?' "

There was much laughter.

I kept on. "Caravaggio was painting this for people who knew the story. They could read this painting like a book. He was reminding them of how light filled the room, how it filled Matthew—only the elect few could perceive it, but it was available to everyone. God could come calling at any time. Caravaggio wanted to paint a reminder of that moment."

Nick was awed. "How does he paint the light like that?"

"I don't know. I've never seen the painting live and in person."

We continued to look. Where was the light coming from? See how it put the others in shadow. What was the nature of this unearthly light? At first I didn't know what made me want to talk about Caravaggio. But then I knew. The light in the picture said everything about learning and teaching, about self-recognition. I wanted to fill my class-room with the same kind of light. I wanted all of them to look up and point to their hearts and say, *"Me,"* to be stunned from complacency and indifference, to be awakened, to believe that there were always more sounds to imagine, new feelings to get at. We could spend an hour looking at a reproduction of a Baroque painting. We could gaze into the rose window, we could talk about the light burning in the tops of trees at dusk, we could come to know rivers, our own rivers or the ancient, dusky ones. It didn't matter who or where we were: My students were believers. Any way we did it, it was often close to wondrous.

The next morning I came into the kitchen, with the sound of the gas stove whispering. On my desk was a computer-printed color copy of *The Calling of St. Matthew.* There was a note from Annie—my calling.

"I thought you might want this to have with you next time you teach your students about Caravaggio."

With early adolescents, it was always a matter of rico-cheting between the sublime and the absurd. My students were in the middle, caught in strange crosscurrents always pushing them one way, then another, with no clear sense of direction. They wept often—for things they lost, their mistakes, the difficulty of choices, their uncertainty about the future. But they laughed as often, and laughter was the counterbalance to tears. Just as I wanted them asking unending, unanswerable questions, just as I wanted the tears to flow, I also wanted them whipping from themselves, as Stevens wrote, "a jovial hullabaloo among the spheres." Whatever made us laugh was what we talked about in the mornings, or in class, or at break or lunch, no matter who stood in the circle. Laughter was the liberating lingua franca of our activity, our shared knowledge of what was unique among us. Laughter leavened our long discussions and bound us to each other. Tears and laughter—both as necessary as books and pencils—were the currency of my students' souls.

Unbridled, expressive, fully alive—"unfenced existence," to use Philip Larkin's words. If we were going to defuse the fear circulating in the classroom, we would stay until 4:30 to do it. Just as important, if we were going to have a snowball fight, I demanded that we all play and we all play hard and laugh all the way through, even if it took time from class. If we were going to tell stories, we told the beginning, middle, and end, because if we excised one part of the story, if we excised the laughter or the tears, we excised the heart.

I gave them the opportunity to write our "crimes" in the school newsletter. We did not have any serious crimes, but we had a multitude of silly ones. We decided we should include an "NBS Blotter" in every issue.

"But Tal, what if someone reads this and thinks we are crazy?"

"Good."

"Good?"

"If they don't like us for this, they'll never like us. Why would you want people in your club who despise or don't understand you?"

In the subsequent issue of *The Current,* the numerous crimes of the North Branch School were exposed to the reading and donating public.

> Doug Woos was charged with slander when he called teacher Tal Birdsey a "Cro-Magnon." As Woos was being taken away by the authorities he was alleged to have said, "It's not slander! It's true!!" Later Mr. Woos allegedly attacked Mr. Birdsey with a serrated cracker. He is being investigated for aggravated assault.

The humor, the absurdity, and the unabashed celebration of who they were—silly and profound, childlike and wise—was ligament that united us.

Emma hung around my desk, never straying far. She was wary, furtive, almost distrustful of the other kids. She seemed to look upon them as younger siblings obsessed with irritating, narrow concerns. At lunch she loitered, leaning against the copier table and watching me at my desk bantering with Tico. Her face was pale, her arms folded across her chest. She wore a huge hooded Rochester Rockets sweatshirt that seemed to enfold her. Her brown hair hung in her eyes. It was impossible to make her smile.

Annie and Doug sat by the stove trying to recite pi up to the twentieth decimal; Zoe and Mira whispered about high school boys in Bristol. Steve walked around my desk pounding a baseball into his glove asking when we could go out and play pepper.

"Tal, when are you going to bring your glove? Tal, Tal, see, I brought my glove," he said, with his eyes wide open.

"Great, Steve, now if you could only remember to bring your homework."

Janine carried on about our unpatriotic ways and the fact that we did not have a flagpole or say the Pledge of Allegiance. We were under assault by the terrorists, in case I didn't know.

"My only allegiance is to education, my little friend. I don't give a rat's ass about the Pledge of Allegiance."

"You are a terrible man," she said with a smile. "It is educational to have love for your country, you unpatriotic old goat."

"Janine, it is also educational to have your own thoughts, to learn to love that which your heart compels you to love. I am not going to use our valuable time reciting a pledge that someone else wrote when we could be creating our own thoughts and our own allegiances."

"You should love your country."

"I love my country. I don't have to demonstrate it every day by reciting someone else's words about living under God."

"Huumph."

Fun was at the center with meaning creeping around at the edges. It was easy enough to move from an argument about patriotism to prying her about why she hadn't turned in her story, or about why she was compelled to fight with her mother every day because her mother would not let her wear eye shadow like Mira and Zoe.

Emma, however, was not about fun. She was seriously consumed with serious feelings.

Shortly after she came to the school, Emma's mother, Gloria, had told me that Emma had been sexually molested by her ex-stepfather over a substantial period of months. Two months before coming to North Branch, Emma had given her mother a diary that told her what was happening. Emma then stopped going to school and left sixth grade at Rochester. Court proceedings were currently under way.

When Emma asked me what the topic of her story should be, I debated about whether I should suggest that she write about what had happened. It was surely too much too soon, stirring up too many raw emotions. On the other hand, she was an extraordinary student, far beyond her years. She was at this school, I assumed, because the elementary school in her hometown was filled with doors that did not lead her to where she needed to go. She had come here looking for the one right window. I decided I would push gently and let her decide how far she could go to begin sorting it out, getting clear, just speaking back to what had happened.

"Well, you could write about the business."

She glanced up. "You mean, um, what my mom told you?"

"Yeah, about him, the uh . . ."

"Son of a bitch?"

"Yeah, that one. That weasel son of a bitch. The lousy son of a bitch whose name shall not be spoken."

She smiled.

"The goddamn son of a bitch!" I said a little louder. Mira and Zoe looked over at me.

Emma was smiling broadly. Her eyes lifted again in something like relief, the relief of finding herself in a protective embrace.

"So you mean write about what happened?"

"If you feel like it. Any feeling you want. Or you don't have to say anything. But I am giving you absolute free rein to say whatever you are feeling. You have permission. Right or wrong. Just get it out, scream on the paper. The scream inside you."

"So what should I do?"

"Silly willy, you can write about what you are feeling. About what happened, yeah, if you can. Write whatever comes up. Any damn thing. Call him a son of a bitch for twenty pages, for Christ's sake, I don't care. Anything you can say that might make you feel different or better."

I screamed out into the school: *"Scum bag! Son of a bitch! Mother fucking bastard asshole son of a bitch!"*

Everyone looked up from open lunches. Tico's head popped around the corner. Blood was pounding in my temples. I was not an expert, and I didn't know what I was doing. I was rolling the dice. The whole thing could go up in smoke. They could shut us down, or the parents could decide this wasn't education.

Or we could say this school was a sanctuary and the kids were, truly, free.

"Emma, you are allowed to say whatever you want to say. I don't give two shits about what anyone says. You've got that right."

She smiled again.

"Until it comes out you'll be scared and slinking around my desk until hell freezes over."

"Ha-ha," she said, smiling.

All I knew was that I was going to make it safe for whatever she needed, for her to say whatever she needed. I could ask my students to make something true out of their lives, whether their lives were torn and frayed or blessed Edens. I could throw curses into the wind, and she could go home and sift through the wreckage and try to say how she wanted to live again. At least I would have gone all the way down the road to let one eleven-year-old girl climb her way out of her darkness. That was what I could do.

"So you're saying—"

"Goddamm it, what I said. Yes! Go home and write whatever feeling comes up first. Follow the feeling. Let the feeling exhaust itself. Rage. Disgust. Self-hatred. Anger at Mom. Him. The shit world. Confusion. Whatever. Spit on the computer. Cry on the keyboard, throw things, rip your curtains down. When you can't write anymore, bring in what you have and we'll look at it."

She was looking at her shoes.

"Emma, look at me. You haven't committed a crime. There's no right or wrong in what you say. You have free license to say or feel whatever you want to say or feel. Okay? If it's too much, forget about it. If it's too much, stop and go out to the barn and comb your horse. Sit in the barn, smell the horse smells, and come in when you feel good."

"Okay."

When she walked away from my desk, she was smiling another smile all to herself.

Emma wrote. Pages and pages, every day two or three more pages, dense, typed paragraphs, impeccably edited, fastened with pink and brass paper clips.

I told her not to bother with narrative structure or chronological order. It was all hacking through jungles of undergrowth. Surges and currents, rants and collisions, broken thoughts, ruptures, rivulets of tears. Her words were disembodied from concrete reality, a dreamscape, sinking into black feelings, rising again. She was clawing and tearing at a disordered haze of events to force them into the shape of sense. It was all shadows and forces bearing down on her. Dark bodies, pressure, slamming doors, deep snow, locks, running.

Each day I chose one sentence out of her pages. I read it to her and then suggested how she could use it as the starting point for the next night. *I could feel the shadow. Wracking pain. Thunder in the darkness. Mommy. Mommy! Running down the road. Running through the snow. I balled up on my bed. I heard the door close.*

I didn't comment. I didn't editorialize, criticize, or analyze. Her experience was beyond me.

"Emma, take this feeling and go inside it," I said. "I don't know this feeling. I haven't been there. You have, you know it. So go back into it, and I promise you, you'll come back out and we'll all still be here. See where it leads, okay?"

Every day, this encouragement. Every day, her standing by my desk, waiting for me to read what she had written. Waiting to be primed, another resuscitation, another push or stroke of loving faith. Waiting for me to say. *Yes, you are okay. You are still okay, and you must keep going until there is no more. Wring it all out. Writing it out will destroy the bad. What will be left is the good. What will be left is the you that could not ever be destroyed or taken.*

Renoir said, "Pain passes, but the beauty remains." I didn't know if I believed it, but I had to believe it.

The narrative led toward her speaking, telling, breaking her silence. She wrote about her diary, one with a lock and key, which was the only place she would speak. Everything was locked inside. For months she had spoken to no one, but she had written. She screamed at her mother. She had tantrums. She was like a caged animal. She hugged her pillow and listened for sounds in the house. She locked her door and wouldn't come out, curled up on the corner of her bed. Her mother sat outside the door and pleaded, asking for her to talk and say what was the matter.

The words were in me and they were screaming. No, I won't open the door. No No No.

Yes. I will open the door. I have the key. I will unlock the book. I will open the pages. I will give the diary to you, Mommy.

On Christmas I left the book for my mommy. I can't say the words. I will unlock the book and the words will come out.

And this is how she told her mother, her act of courage. He whose name would not be spoken was evicted from her home and life and then prosecuted. She stopped going to Rochester Elementary, and then she came to our school.

Through her words she was clawing back against a nearly unspeakable violation against her body and soul. The story was her way of saying, *I am still here.* She unfolded herself from her hunched-over, protected ball and reassembled herself. In the dim, cramped space of our school, words had the power to do something; here was a sanctuary where she could come back into the light.

What made our school be a place where that could happen? What was *here*? What distinguished it from the rest of the world Emma knew. Wisława Szymborska, the Polish poet, defined utopia as an "island where all becomes clear." Our school was not utopia. But perhaps the school *was* an island in the lives of these kids. One where they could look to the next horizon, where the face looking into the mirror could be studied, spoken to, even loved. North Branch was an island in the middle of the woods, a stopping point, a place for sifting and making, an island where meaning was scoured and remade, where bits of gold were lifted from the muck.

Emma had arrived in our school, slid into the dark map room of herself, and asked my permission to see what good still remained. She asked my permission to place her finger on that map and trace backward and forward. I was simply there to hold the map in place, keeping it from being ripped away by the wind, offering words of sympathy mixed with guiding love. I was the creator of the environment where she was permitted to chart the course. We—my students and I—were saying such motions could take place, that such permissions should be granted.

North Branch wasn't only an island. So long as the kids knew I held the map and kept it safe and dry, they were willing to look and to journey. They were coming to know that their lives depended on being courageous: Here their courage would be recognized. Here they learned to look at the past and the present. Here they could find clarity and then launch.

Against the odds, Emma had figured this all out. She was walking out on the edges of what a school could be, along an old stone wall in the woods, leading us into another secret field.

One morning she handed me the finished draft. Emma had written herself back into the world. Forty-two pages of one girl's life, a girl who loved to ride horses, galloping on the trails and all sound crushed out of the world except for the wind in her ears. Forty-two pages leading to unlocking the book and ungoverning her tongue.

I held the story in my hands—clean, heavy, and thick. I read it while the kids were in science and I finished it at lunch. I had tears in the corners of my eyes, which I wiped away. I called her over to my desk.

"Did you read it?"

"Emma, what do you think? Do I look like I have been playing Tiddlywinks?"

"No. But is it okay? What do you think?"

"What do I think? Is it okay? Is it *okay*? Do you know what this is, Emma?"

"No, what is it?"

I held the story up between us. "This is everything. This is you, this is life, this is what could not be taken. One comma in this story has more guts in it than the son of a bitch could ever dream of in a hundred lifetimes."

"Um, okay."

"What I'm saying is *god damn*!"

"Okay."

"Emma, this is incredible."

She looked at me, holding her smile just inside, chewing on her lip. I looked outside at the kids frolicking on the hill.

"Hey everyone, get your asses in here! Hurry up. Let's go!"

Everyone came in holding their sandwiches and apples and stick swords, out of breath from running around, warm from the early spring sun. Steve was pounding a ball into his baseball glove.

"What's going on, Tal? Is it time for class already? Didn't we just start lunch?"

"Yeah, you just started lunch. Lunch is not important. Sit down. Hurry up. Get a chair."

They all crowded around my desk.

I held up the story. "Do you all see this? You see this story?"

"Yes, Tal we see the story."

"Look at this story."

"We see the story, Tal. Whose story is it?"

"Emma's. Forty-two pages. Forty-two pages of kicking ass now and taking names later."

"What's it about?"

"It's about how to live. It's about courage. It's about how to fight. It's about how to go into the blackness and come out with the light." I paused.

"That's a poem, you weenies."

"Uh, Tal," said Sophie, "what are you talking about?"

"What I'm talking about, you weenies, is Emma has written the story of the year, the story of the century."

They looked at me like I had lost my mind. But they were intrigued. Something had happened. Perhaps it pertained to them.

"Here's what I think," I continued. "I think that Emma has blown the roof off the damn school and everything else. She's the champ. She's gone and done it. So give her a big hand."

A year's worth of training had prepared them. They clapped and cheered with moderate gusto.

"But Tal, what are we clapping about? What's the story about?"

"The story is about how great Emma is. It's about how great you all are. It's about the rotten world and how to beat it. It's about art. It's about the invincibility of a girl's soul."

"But are you going to tell us what the story is *about*?" asked Annie. "Or are you going to keep going with these oh-so-suspenseful movie trailer pronouncements?"

"Ah, Annie, I have many tricks that I learned in the army, and this is one of them. I will not tell you what the story is about. You'll find out when I read it."

"And when exactly will that be?"

"At the chosen and appropriate time."

At least eight eyeballs rolled.

"Okay, Tal. We get it."

"Hey, everybody, give Emma another huge frickin' hand!"

Again, they clapped. "Now go out and play before we start class."

They tramped out of the room. I gave Emma a little high-five. She smiled again.

"So when will you read it?" she asked.

"Just wait, my little friend," I said. "You just wait."

In early May, on Green Up Day in Vermont, we walked up the road to do yard work for an elderly couple. Nick carried Emma on his back and Steve chunked rocks into the woods. The sun shone between gray clouds. We raked out dead, matted, ice-clotted leaves and cleared beds of irises and day lilies. We stacked wet firewood and dragged fallen limbs into a ditch. Suddenly the clouds closed, the sky darkened, and the wind picked up. For ten minutes a snow squall passed over, icy snowflakes blowing sideways against our bare arms. We shouted, "What in the Sam Hill happened to spring!"

We conducted a photography workshop and the students were given Polaroid cameras and told to take portraits of each other. As the kids wandered in the woods looking for subjects, I patrolled the school, watching them. I walked through the front door and found Annie, Sophie, and Emma standing Debbie up on a chair by the woodstove. They had draped her in a shimmering green curtain they had found upstairs, and they had piled Debbie's long strawberry blond hair on top of her head in a disheveled bun.

"Look, Tal, we turned Debbie into a Greek goddess!" shouted Annie. Debbie shook with uncontrollable laughter as they posed her like a living doll.

"Isn't she just smashingly gorgeous?" shouted Zoe. "Look at that hair!"

Annie gleefully commanded, "Stop moving, Debbie. You have to hold the pose so we can take your picture and put you on the Parthenon."

For weeks after Mira, Zoe, Sophie, and Emma gathered around Debbie to comb her hair. Each day at lunch they took turns drawing it out from either side, running their fingers down the straight lengths while Debbie blushed proudly. I don't think she had ever had such intimacy with friends.

In class the kids presented their projects on African-American history. We crowded under the table, shoulder to shoulder, to try to understand the feeling of what it would be like to be human cargo on the *Amistad*. We ate hardtack and tried to jump as far as Jesse Owens had at the 1936 Berlin Olympics. We enacted a lunch counter sit-in, watched the entire "I Have a Dream" speech, and studied "A Letter from Birmingham Jail." We listened to Hendrix's "Hear My Train a-Comin'," Billie Holiday's "Strange Fruit," and Mahalia Jackson's exhilarating "I Will Move on Up a Little Higher." I told the story of attending a Ku Klux Klan rally in Atlanta. They didn't believe me when I described how the Klan had to be protected from a seething anti-Klan mob by a hundred mounted Georgia State Police.

Huckleberry Finn believed the only thing you could do to ruin food was cook everything by itself. But, he said, "in a barrel of odds and ends it is different; things get mixed up, and the juice kind of swaps around, and the things go better." Maybe it was my Southern upbringing, but I sided with Huck. I thought school should be more of a gumbo, where we threw in everything we had. I mixed up all the disciplines and hoped that something good came out. We studied many things over the year—Vermont history, African-American history, forests, self-government, photography, land use, poetry, and ourselves—but I never tried to separate the topics from each other.

When we looked at photographs for photography class we discussed Ansel Adams, who had also been a subject in our Wilderness Ethics class. I read the class the children's book *Henry Hikes to Fitchburg,* based on Henry David Thoreau, who was featured in our study of nature writers. In the book we saw Henry's dedication to the study and documentation of the plants and animals around him, something we had been doing all year. We were shown the history of the settlement of Vermont by a local logger while we stood in the wet woods and strolled down mountain slopes that, one hundred years ago, had been clearcut. His careful work gave counterbalance to the view of maniacal and environmentally insensitive loggers whom we heard about from time to time. Our Addison County forester and state representative visited, bringing their deep knowledge to provide us with new perspectives in their debate on forest management, forest succession, and local government.

In science the kids had studied animals of the Northern hardwood forest; Steve wrote a "wish poem" about flying like a bird. In literature, we discussed the symbolism and imagery of birds as they related to freedom in *One Flew Over the Cuckoo's Nest.* Later, while discussing the religious imagery of *Cuckoo's Nest,* we discussed a question raised earlier in the year: What does it mean to find the god within you? Some of the kids thought that McMurphy had found the god within him. Others said that to find the god within meant sacrificing something in oneself for a cause beyond oneself. Doug quoted Martin Luther King, whose words—"A man who hasn't discovered something he will die for isn't fit to live"—we had examined earlier in the year. I asked the kids to read that quote to their parents and see what responses they got. At school we discussed their parents' ideas, which, to my students' amazement, were similar to their own. Someone said King's pronouncement was so intense it was scary. Someone else pointed out that rebels are often feared, which brought us full circle to the black history projects: Malcolm X, Nat Turner, Jesse Owens, and Cinque.

At the beginning of the year we had looked at the Ten Commandments as a way of understanding the Bill of Rights, and how neither of those documents had eliminated hierarchies among humans. Our Independent Declaration of Principles and Ideals, with a preamble modeled on the preamble to the U.S. Constitution, was an attempt to make a purely egalitarian community. Someone noticed that the social hierarchies of adolescents mirror those of the characters in *One Flew Over the Cuckoo's Nest.* "That's just like us," said Tico. "Like McMurphy says, a chicken-peckin' party." Someone else noticed that the same hierarchy was visible in the way that whites treated blacks, and blacks treated each other, in the film *Glory.* As we watched the story of the Massachussets Fifty-fourth, we noticed the music, which was sung by the Harlem Boys Choir. The kids were attuned, maybe even enraptured, since we had been listening to samples of African-American music all year long. We came upon an article about Jacob Lawrence, the African-

American painter who happened to be a focus of Mira's history project on the Harlem Renaissance. Then we read another Langston Hughes poem, "I, Too," a vision of egalitarian democracy, which brought us circling back to our own Independent Declaration of Principles and Ideals. When one of them exclaimed, "Hey, that's like when we were talking about—!" then I knew we had done it right.

Frost wrote that nature's first green was gold. That spring I discovered that in the mountains, nature's first green was, physically speaking, red. The first buds on the trees emerged as a light red dusting over the gray and brown trees. The wet snow still lay heaped in the shade. Each morning heading up the mountain listening to Coltrane, I watched the red-tinted slopes give way to the lightest wisps of pale green, a subtle mist brushing up through the branches.

When the sun warmed and the sap buckets hung from the sugar maples, we bet quarters on what day the last of the snow under the eaves would finally melt. From those patches of old snow emerged soggy, faded handouts, lone mittens, a snow shovel, and all the pine needles that had drifted down on our heads in the first warm days of September. The life of our institution, brief as it was and though not carved in stone, now had a geologic history.

The feeling of having survived together, of bonds forged through enduring the long winter, was resonant. I felt that pleasure playing catch or Wiffle Ball in the driveway, when Steve drove the ball against the side of the school or ripped a grand slam over the chimney and we all cheered. I felt it when I struck out and they cheered louder. Zoe and Mira sat on the big rock on the hill. Emma chased Steve. Nick and Tico rode bikes in the driveway. Debbie chased Doug, who stole her lunch box every day. Annie climbed trees and Sophie ran laps on the nature trail. Janine stood under the porch watching, smiling, and occasionally reminding me that we had not had even one grammar class.

Coming out of our winter entombment, those first warm days when the sun rose above the trees on the fern-covered hill were soft, lyrical, a gift. Tossing baseballs, eating lunch, jumping bikes off the deck, and Sophie strutting around at lunch listening to *Chicago* on Mira's iPod.

Tico shouted, "Sophie is becoming a teenager. She's shutting out the world. Tal, look. She's addicted to technology!"

In defense Sophie pleaded, "But I'm listening to a Broadway musical! I'm not a teenager, I'm sophisticated."

"You're a teenager, Sophie. You're cursed and there's nothing you can do about it."

We sat on the big rock, taste-testing to see who had made the best bowl of ramen noodles. Nick was trying to earn ramen master chef status, an honor I bestowed grudgingly.

A grasshopper landed in Nick's steaming bowl of broth.

Debbie shrieked, "I hate bugs! I hate them all. I hate spiders most. Make it go away."

Nick lifted the grasshopper out and released it. "Debbie, it's a freaking grasshopper, not a spider."

She was hysterical. "I don't care. Spiders like, freak me out. I hate spiders! Ohmygod, and I saw one last night in my room when I was reading my lit assignment. I attacked it and I killed it!" There was a near psychotic growl in her throat. These were the most words I had ever heard her say at once.

"You *attacked* it?" I asked. "A spider? You're a shy girl from Rochester. You can't attack spiders. You're supposed to run from them."

"I killed it with a book!" Her eyes were wild with rage.

"You crushed one of God's creatures?" I burst out.

"I killed it with my Bible I got for confirmation!"

"Your Bible!?"

"The one I got for confirmation!"

"What!" I burst out. "What would your father say? He's a man of

God? The minister of the Federated Church. You killed a spider with your Bible!"

Nick shouted, "Debbie! That will make you like a witch or something. You might go to hell!"

"I don't care if I am a witch or if I go to hell. It was crawling on the ceiling. I had to."

"Debbie, I am truly disturbed, shocked, and dismayed. I thought you were a gentle, mild-mannered girl."

"It needed to die!"

"Debbie killed a spider with her Bible!" Nick chanted. "Debbie killed a spider with a Bible!"

"Your dad's going to, like, excommunicate you. God will strike you down!"

"I don't care about God when it comes to spiders."

I knew that Debbie loved talking. She was laughing, we were all laughing, and she was at the center of the conversation. The rumor spread around school by the end of lunch: Debbie was a spider killer and an infidel to boot. She basked proudly in her fame.

We read *Fahrenheit 451*. Montag, having fled his burning city, arrives at an encampment of book-loving hoboes. He discovers that each of those men possesses in his memory entire books and oeuvres. And from each of these men who can speak volumes of Whitman and Cicero, Montag draws warmth and hope.

It was not only the fire that was different. It was the silence. Montag moved toward this special silence that was concerned with all of the world.

And then the voices began and they were talking, and he could hear nothing of what the voices said, but the sound rose and fell quietly and the voices were turning the world over and looking at it; the voices knew the land and the trees and the city which lay down the track by the river. The voices talked of everything, there was nothing they could not talk about, he knew, from the very cadence and motion and continual stir of curiosity and wonder in them.

We were making our own place by the river, our own cadence and motion, where we could turn the world over and look at it. Making a warm place by the fire was only the beginning. A conversation about all the world was what we needed. I hoped that there was nothing we couldn't talk about, and I kept pressing for the conversation to deepen.

I stopped at the passage in which Montag tries to keep from going numb as advertisements for Denham's Dentifrice are piped into the subway train loudspeakers. In desperation he counters the racket by recalling the words from the Gospel of Luke, his gasping revolt, the last strains of purity raging against the meaningless prattle of a soulless world. "Consider the lilies of the field, shut up, shut up," he says. Against the onslaught of a culture gone mad he protects the last sanctuary, his interior mind. With his gaze on lilies that lived only in a hazy memory of words, he repeats, "Consider the lilies, the lilies, the lilies."

"What is all this about?" I asked the class. "Is he going mad? Why is he fighting a toothpaste advertisement with this phrase, 'Consider the lilies of the field'? Where is this coming from?"

"It seems like he is trying to resist something," said Nick.

"But it's just an advertisement. What's the big whoop?"

"If that advertisement fills him," said Annie, "he becomes unreal, like his wife and her four walls of television."

"Do any of you ever feel like your own thoughts can't get through because other thoughts are being pumped into you? That's how I feel when I hear 'Gillette, the best a man can get' over and over. I feel the need to resist."

"What's Gillette?"

"Gil-lette! The best a man can get," I sang.

"Okay, that's enough, we get it," they shouted.

"That's the beautiful truth I found out from a shaving cream company. It's the best I can get."

"How can you get the beautiful truth from a shaving cream company?" asked Nick.

"That's what I want to know. Telling me that Gillette is the best I can get makes me feel homicidal right this very instant."

We digressed about the Gillette advertisement until I called them back.

"But Nick, does hearing that make you think you are losing your mind? Would you care if that's all you heard? Would you scream in public places for the noise to *Shut up*? Or would you let it settle into your heart and soul? Montag is losing his mind here."

"It seems like in order to survive, he has got to keep the superficial stuff out of his mind," said Steve.

"Everyone else on the train is mouthing the words and they don't even know it," said Mira. "It's like they're already gone. They're completely oblivious, total fricking idiots."

"So repeating the words about the lilies is his own inner war?" suggested Zoe.

"Is it real?" I asked, "this madness that Montag feels?"

"It's kind of like when I was at the middle school," said Steve. "Everyone was talking stupid shit all the time and acting macho and calling everybody a fag. No one could say anything real."

"Sure you could. Why didn't you say, 'Hey, goddammit, consider the lilies of the field, you mother fucking homophobic punks!'"

"Because you would be called a fag."

Nick chimed in. "Anytime you say anything, people say, God, you *fag*."

"They would think like, you were out of your mind," said Steve.

"Ah, like Montag. Montag is out of his mind. Do you think he's a fag?"

"No, he's a hero," said Mira. "He freaking burned Captain Beatty."

"Montag kicked ass," said Tico.

"Okay, okay, you guys. We know, or we think, Captain Beatty was evil. But here Montag is not burning up things. He's talking about considering lilies. What's it mean *here*? I mean, can we, here at the old North Branch School, consider the lilies of the field? Or are we just saying and hearing the same old Denham's Dentifrice crapola, metaphorically I mean?"

"That's what we have been trying to do all year," said Doug. "That's what the school is about." There was a shaking in his voice.

"Go on."

"Why else would we bother to come up here into this moldy mole hole where it's so dark, wet, and cold that our hands shrivel up like prunes if we weren't trying to do something different? The analogy makes sense. The regular world is Denham's Dentifrice, we are Montag, trying to hear something else, trying to shut out the noise."

"Yeah, the stuff like, *you fag*," said Nick.

"Trying to listen to what is real, or find it," said Sophie.

Annie looked contemplative, perplexed, and almost sad. Always, her face seemed to contain many feelings at once, her hair pressed down under her blue bandana.

"Sometimes I have thought that this school is like the only place where the lilies are considered at all," she said.

Here was a girl who once could think only about the germs on doorknobs and the dirt on mud boots. Her story, the one she had written and the one she was living, was about trying to overcome her obsessive-compulsive disorder. In *Fahrenheit 451*, Montag was trying to keep the filth away, and Annie—all of them—seemed to understand his struggle.

This was our subject: How could we keep the beautiful things

before us, at the center of our gaze? How could we create our own conception of meaning and beauty, and kneel before it in a state of devotion? How did one countenance the struggle, like Montag, and keep
from going numb, even as our old childhood selves died away and the
new adult body was born?

"Can we look up the quote in the Bible?" asked Nick.

I knew it was from the New Testament but I wasn't sure where. So,
as we sat in class, I picked up the phone and called my dad, who happened to be at home.

"I think it's in Luke," he said. He left the phone to consult the King
James Bible.

"You're calling your dad? In literature class?" Annie asked, wide-
eyed, as we waited.

"It's called the pursuit of knowledge, Annie," I replied.

My father found the quote in the Gospel of Luke, read it to me, and
then I read the quote to them.

"Here it is: 'Consider the lilies how they grow: they toil not, they
spin not; and yet I say unto you, that Solomon in all his glory was not
arrayed like one of these.' That's from the New Testament, Luke, chap-
ter twelve, verse twenty-seven. What do you think of that? If you were
to say what the lilies are in some other terms, what would you say?"

"The lilies are stand-ins for love or purity," said Annie. "The thing
not stained. Montag is losing everything that matters and he's afraid."

"Solomon has glory but not ultimate beauty," said Nick. "If that's
true, then the quote is saying that the lily is the true thing, and simple
and pure is the most beautiful."

"But here, in Montag's world, all the books, all the poetry, all that is
dying or being extingushed. Montag is trying to keep the last pure
thing alive, the image of the lilies. He's trying to ignite the truth. And
he's doing it by trying to hold on to a half-remembered phrase in a
book. A message he has to remember in order to live."

"The lily is the one symbol of meaning that we should keep in the center of our minds," declared Zoe. "When I was little, it was the apple tree in our yard. That was my lily. I would go climb it whenever I wanted, if I was happy or sad."

"What would you do up there?"

"Just look around at everything. The leaves and the limbs and the grass and my parents' garden."

"Chickadees are my favorite," said Mira. "When I think of them that's what purity is."

"I would say it's the pond near our house where I go with my mom and look at the cattails," said Tico.

"That's great, Tico. Sometimes I think a red-winged blackbird sitting on a cattail is the most beautiful thing in the world. Or the sharp chirping of a chickadee."

"So the lilies are our best thoughts," said Sophie, "the part of us that was beautiful."

"Why do you say 'was'?" I asked.

"Well, you know in that poem you read us by that ugly guy, what's his name, Charles Butkowska—"

"Bukowski."

"Oh, God, he was some butt-ugly," exclaimed Najat, who remembered the picture I had showed them of Bukowski's craggy, pocked face.

"Yeah, him," said Sophie. "He talked about how no matter how ugly his life was, he kept his memory of the bluebirds. Or the bluebird in him. But sometimes the bluebirds get covered over. Maybe the lilies are the bluebirds in our souls that we have to keep alive."

"So you mean to say that we all have little lilies or bluebirds in us, like Mira's little chickadee," I said, trying to pull together their ideas. "The song of the bird or the sight of the lily is spare and fragile. All the impurities of the world have a tendency, to take over. We all lose sight of the bluebird or the lily or whatever is the sacred voice."

Annie spoke. "So, like, when you force yourself to consider the lily, or hear the song of the little bird, you are connected to the real world and not the stain of toothpaste commercials?"

"Montag will not let himself be blind or deaf to what he knows is real," said Steve.

"But think about it," I said. "We ourselves know the slogans of products better than we know the words of Luke or Shakespeare. For instance, if I say, 'UPS,' you say . . ."

The reply arose in mindless unison: "What can Brown do for you!"

"If I say McDonald's, you say . . ."

"I'm lovin' it."

"If I say, Keats's 'Ode to a Nightingale,' you say . . ."

"Uh, what?"

"See what I mean? How can we be living if the songs in our heads are sales pitches or the images in our eyes are products? How can we know who we are if the only identity we have is what brand is printed on our shirts? If that's all we have, then we're just like old Mildred with her sleeping pills and four-wall television room."

Nick raised his hand. "When we were in fourth grade, Doug and I would play imaginative games. We made everything up. We had all these code words and secret symbols, like when he was Captain Rover, and when we would try to solve mysteries. It was so much fun. Those times were the lilies for me. I didn't give a damn what anyone thought about what I was doing. I have to consider those times because now I'm . . . I don't know . . ."

"Turning into a teenager? Growing up? Turning toward material things? Your next pair of new skis? Worshiping Porsches and Maseratis and sweet sound systems?"

"Yeah, I mean, I like those things, and they're not bad things, but I also need to remember what I used to be like, like when I was, I don't know, uncorrupted or something."

"The lilies connect you back to a time of innocence, a time before the fall?" I asked.

"When you were free enough to follow Captain Rover," said Doug.

Nick looked down and fingered the corner of his paper. "Yeah. I should not forget that."

Bluebirds and daffodils. Nightingales and lilies. Red-wings among the cattails. That was our song of spring, our mountain spiritual.

We ended the year reading the poems of Langston Hughes, his first collection, *The Dream Keeper*. Who was the dream keeper? I asked. Why was the dream keeper a poet and not a historian?

"Historians keep the facts of what happened. The poet feels the meaning of the facts, I guess," said Zoe.

Sophie raised her hand. "Maybe the historian keeps track of what is happening in the world. The poet keeps track of what is happening on the inside."

I suddenly had a flashing thought of the cave painters of Lascaux.

"Forty thousand years ago these people painted deep in the earth on the inside of walls by torchlight or in the dark. They painted animals and the spears of their hunts. Beautiful, graceful drawings of bison that have not been improved since. Were they dream keepers?"

"In those pictures they maybe were painting their dreams of what they wanted to happen," said Nick.

"Or," said Sophie, "it's like they were the inside of a person writing the dreams of that person so they would stay there."

"What? Explain that."

"You know, like being in the cave was like being in the stomach. They were inside, writing down the dreams."

"You mean," I asked, "they went into the deepest place to inscribe the dreams so the dreams would remain and be indelible? Anywhere else they would be washed away?"

"Oh, that's really freaky," said Annie.

"So why is it necessary? I mean, why do poets, or artists, or historians go to all the trouble to record what happened, what is happening inside of them, or what they want to happen? Why do people go down into the cave to write it all down?"

"It's the only way to find what is important," said Steve.

"Poets are the 'necessary angels of earth,'" I offered. "That's what Wallace Stevens said."

"It's like the poem 'The Dream Keeper,'" said Janine, "where he says 'bring me all of your heart melodies.'"

"Read it to us," I said.

She read Hughes's words.

"Bring me all of your dreams,
 You dreamers,
 Bring me all of your
 Heart melodies
 That I may wrap them
 In a blue cloud-cloth
 Away from the too-rough fingers
 Of the world."

"What's the blue cloud-cloth, you guys?"

Steve answered. "Something soft, like a baby blanket. Something sacred."

"But to whom is the poem addressed?"

"Well," said Doug, "wouldn't he have been speaking to other African Americans?"

"Probably, yes," I said.

"But it's also addressed to us," said Nick. "He's saying we are the dreamers and he'll protect our dreams if we bring them to him."

"To the poet?"

"Yeah, but he almost sounds like a god, up in the clouds," said Steve.

"What kind of god?" I asked.

"Or goddess," Zoe corrected.

"Or goddess," I said.

"A kind god, a loving god, like a parent," said Nick.

"Your parents are like gods?"

"Yeah, I guess so, even if I always say they are annoying."

"Tender, careful, wise," said Annie.

"Listent to this: If we want to be gods, or godlike, then couldn't we learn our shape from the dream keeper? Couldn't we shape ourselves to become kind and loving, wise, tender, and careful?"

"That would be a good god to be," said Najat. "Maybe we could be both—dreamers and dream keepers? Couldn't we?"

We took a field trip to the Rokeby Museum, a historic farmstead of an eminent Quaker family dating back to the 1760s that had been a destination on the Underground Railroad. Among the treasures there were copies of the abolitionist newspapers the *North Star* and the *Liberator* and letters from early women's rights advocates. The Rokeby stood as a monument to Vermont's history as a socially progressive state. It provided a place to resolve our year of studying Vermont history and the civil rights movement. Since Frederick Douglass had stayed there, we were in the footsteps of history.

Our guide asked if any of us had a rough guess about how many sheep per capita there were in Vermont in 1850.

Mira snapped off the answer. "Twelve."

The guide was wide-eyed. "That's exactly right! Wow! Do you know how much of Vermont was forested in 1900?"

"Eighty percent had been clear-cut for sheep grazing and timber, and twenty percent was forested," said Doug.

"Which diminished habitat for native species," added Nick.

"Exactly!"

"Now it's the other way around," said Annie. "Twenty percent clear, eighty percent forested."

My twelve students turned to see my reaction.

I silently pumped my fist and mouthed, "Oh, yeah."

I gave Mira a high-five on the sly as we moved to the next room.

We wandered among the barns and outbuildings and saw the same tools we had used in September in the English barn at Shelburne.

Nick pointed out the joinery of a post-and-beam shed. "That's what my father does," he said, with pride in his voice.

We came out from the dark kitchen of the main house and ate lunch under ancient, giant blooming lilacs in the dooryard. *With many a pointed blossom rising delicate, with the perfume strong I love, / With every leaf a miracle.*

I felt like we were alive inside Whitman's words.

We took an end-of-the-year field trip to the Mashantucket Pequot Museum in Connecticut. Steve had never been to Connecticut; for Janine, it was her first visit to a museum larger than a historic site. The kids were excited by the exhibits, but the joy was traveling together, eating at every Brickfords we passed, playing Wiffle Ball behind the motel, trying to keep track of room keys, running in and out of rooms and slamming doors, staying up late. Annie had written a poem in response to Hughes's poem, called "Dream Variations," and she galloped between motel rooms shouting her version.

Blurting, yelling, singing
not euphonious, but harmonious
with all other things
free and unrestricted
in the open air and sky.

Surging free of the confines of her anxieties, she embraced a larger world—our school, at the very least—without fear of dirt or disgrace.

We set up a chessboard under a tree in the late afternoon after returning from the museum. I sat with Doug, who one day was likely headed to an Ivy League school, and Steve, who had failed virtually every class he took in seventh grade and who lived in a trailer on a dirt road in the mountains. Doug attended astronomy conventions on the weekends, while Steve helped his father split wood, which they sold around Ripton. Doug played the violin, and Steve hunted deer. Now Steve was putting Doug in checkmate in a motel parking lot off I-95 in Connecticut.

We had come a hell of a long way.

We were trying to finish the last presentations, projects, and stories. In science the class was studying energy, and Eric had them building solar concentrators, which were inverted cardboard domes lined with sheets of chrome Mylar. The intent was to reflect the sun's rays to a specific point inside the concentrator and so increase the heat until water boiled. Most of the concentrators were lopsided and misshapen cones, like Mira and Zoe's "Queen Witchie." Doug and Annie, whose concentrator was named the "Death Ray," used the parabolic equation $y = \frac{x^2}{4p}$ to design a perfectly arced "radar dish." While testing the device on the deck at school, the Death Ray heated an empty Budweiser bottle to the point that it cracked and exploded.

Doug hoisted the shattered fragments and shouted, "Oh yeah, who's good? Who's good? We will dominate Earth with the Death Ray!" He danced a little jig on the deck.

We didn't have a trophy case, but we placed fragments of the bottle in a place of honor—wedged in a ceiling brace in the corner of the kitchen.

On a sunny morning the last week of school, we loaded the solar concentrators into the back of Eric's truck. At the Ripton Community

House we arrayed them facing the sun and proceeded to see who could boil water and bake a tray of cookie dough the fastest.

"Ours is so going to rock," shouted Doug, co-opting macho teen slang for the cause of nerddom.

"Eric, Tal, the temperature is going up," shouted Janine.

"Hey, this cookie dough is barely cooking. It's oozing," said Tico.

"Who cares?" said Nick. "If it gets warm, I'm eating it."

It took only thirty minutes for them to transform the sun's power into gooey chocolate chip cookies and steaming water.

Queen Witchie boiled water first. Zoe galloped around, bragging to Doug. I couldn't help but to think of the first day: *Life-Light,* Zoe's name.

"Who's good, who's good?" she called out, cackling toward the sky.

We had studied many poems—"Thirteen Ways of Looking at a Blackbird," "Song of Myself," "Jabberwocky," poems from schoolchildren in Swaziland and from children in the Bronx, Countee Cullen, Charles Bukowski, Wallace Stevens, Robert Frost, William Carlos Williams, and James Weldon Johnson. We had written beautiful stream-of-consciousness poems and we had mimicked the poetry of the Beats.

We madly pulled together our year's worth of poems. The table was piled with papers, photocopies, our journals, gel pens, paper clips, and staplers. We discussed possible titles of our volume-to-be.

"We should name it after one of the poems."

"We should name it 'Lunatics with Pens,'" said Doug.

"Yeah, yeah!" came a clamor of assent.

"You guys, that's dumb," said Emma. "People will think that we're a bunch of mentally ill teenagers who can't cut it in a real school."

"We *are* a bunch of mentally ill teenagers, sad to say," said Janine.

"Yeah, thanks, Tal, nice job," said Tico.

"Who would want to cut it in a regular school anyway?" said Annie.

"What about Zoe's poem?" suggested Sophie. "We could name it that."

"Which one?"

"You know, the one where we pasted together words from magazines."

From a pile of papers Sophie read Zoe's words. "'From every effect and angle / Lights and trauma. Stop necessary reply mail. / Mix truth with shimmer. / Now imagine essences illuminating experience.'"

She looked up. "Maybe we could call it 'Truth and Shimmer'?"

"That's like totally cheesy," said Mira.

"But it kind of gets everything," said Annie. "You know, like we are phony and shiny, like lip gloss, but we are still trying to find the truth and it's all mixed up."

"It's sort of like a recipe!" said Janine.

"Okay, how about 'Truth and Shimmer: Lunatics with Pens,'" Doug offered, still working for consensus.

"Okay," I said. "Let's vote."

As Najat said, majorities rule, and Doug's compromise was accepted. I asked the kids to write a brief description of what the year of poetry class had made them feel or think.

"At the bottom of my binder," Zoe wrote, "there's a wrinkled piece of paper, with two corners missing. From the bottom of backpacks and corners of cubbies pieces of paper unfold. Some of us say, 'Uh-oh' or 'Thank God, here it is,' or whisper, 'I did it at lunch.' Others wonder what's the brown mold growing on it and, if the mood is right, should I eat it? But we all hand in our poems wrinkled and unread, saying, 'Oh, my God, I hate it!' But the class coaxes it out into words. 'Come on, it sounds great.' And it does."

Emma wrote: "I believe if you let yourself, you could tell your whole life's story in a poem or millions of poems."

Steve wrote: "Sparkling imaginations stroll about, the young adolescent minds are being put to the test." Steve's verb was key: *stroll*. He did not write *drag, slouch, creep, slump,* or *slither*. His word connoted playfulness, openness, and contentment—a rare state of being for thirteen- and fourteen-year-olds. If there had been any test, it was a test of courage—to ask, simply, as I had asked them, to give the truths they knew and then to apply those truths to the illuminated material of the world.

In one poem Steve had written: "I wish I could fly / To catch air in my hair, to play tag with a cloud. / What's better than soaring with a bird, Or playing peek-a-boo with the sun?" Amid the noise, hormonal chaos, social intrigue, and spilling forth of emotions came the light glow of a kid happy to be in school. Steve's discovery: Here was a place where he could play peekaboo with the sun. There was high seriousness in what we studied, in how we went about it, in the standards of quality and our work ethic. But tag and peekaboo still had a place.

In the course of the year my students had begun to unearth the great hidden stories of their lives, stories waiting like seeds in cracks, stories of first memories, thresholds, glints of light reflecting and stitching the past to the present. The present took root in the past when Annie remembered climbing in trees, or when she told us that the fabric of imagination paid off. Janine brought the past to the present when she remembered riding on her father's back on a hot day in summer, walking through a field along a fence, kicking him in the side as his warm hand rested on her ankle. Mira had written the poem of waiting to be taken into the United States, sitting on a counter at immigration, her hands pressed together, waiting for the woman coming toward her. Steve wrote the story of helping his father deliver newspapers, of hearing Casella's garbage trucks firing up in the cold and the snowmobiles screaming across the windswept fields—a remembrance of freedom and no worry, thinking it was always going to be like this. When Tico described a coil of orange wire, his poem became his gaze, how he entered the places between the coils where, he said, "I think of empty space. Like me sometimes." Sophie's story was walking through a pasture of dandelions in spring, among those uncountable yellow suns of the grass. Annie, who once perched like a scared bird on the stairs and gazed down on our fumbling class, told the story of her wish to blunder about in a sea of innocence. Mira believed she was just braving time and asked plaintively: "Why is my spirit always in peril?" Janine wrote a story of sitting with her horses, sitting by herself in the barnyard, sitting with the person she longed to be: "Here I am on a fence watching the sun fall into the earth. On a fence between then and now and looking to tomorrow. Here I am watching the end of one day, waiting for the new world to begin."

They recovered these fragments and released them into the room and to each other, release that carried feeling, words that intensified perception, phrases that wandered, echoed, hovered, words that called us back, made us look up or in, stories that pulled time together, words that told the story of how we had pulled together.

I read and remembered Doug's message, enclosed in a found poem: "We want you to let *us* teach you." These were the essences illuminating experience. That was the formula for a school—that was something we had taught each other.

I placed the stamp of what we had become on the last page of the book—Annie's final poem, one that contained the story of a year, the treasure we had gotten. It was titled "Consider the Lilies of the Field."

> *Quirks are the things,*
> *The lilies will sing.*
> *Solomon rots in hell.*
> *Take it all in.*
> *Numbness is sin.*
> *The lilies sing in the dell.*

So often, I knew, so easily in schools kids went numb or the lives of children were stifled. But for Annie, experience was now to be consumed passionately. The world could be utterly beautiful, washing over her, filling her with a present of wishes, dreams, and possibilities. Imaginations could stroll about, quirks *were* the things, and there was time to drink it all in.

My students told me things I had never known, words as good as any I had ever read, singing like flowers in a dell. We considered the architecture of a flower, and it was more important than an upcoming battery of tests and assessments. On the cover of our book we drew a circle, divided up into equal portions. Each of us decorated a portion, which we reassembled into one mandala, a book made of the mind and heart, a book made from all of us. My dream of what I wanted them to learn did not come back to me regurgitated on a test or other conventional achievements. It was creation out of nothing, creation out of them, meaning wrested from the simplest, most complex materials: books, a box of pencils, two tables, and twelve kids and their teachers looking for something great inside each other.

Our last day and closing ceremony was a week away. I decided we should have a paddleboat race to celebrate our year—homemade boats, toy boats we would launch on the small pond up the road, a pond in the shape of a heart surrounded by a grassy embankment, spring fed and cold. We had walked by it many times on hikes to the woods.

The rules of the race were simple.

"All boats must float and go," I said, "and all should be propelled by rubber-band-powered paddles."

"Hey, Tal," said Nick, "can I use rocket engines?" His eyebrows were jumping.

"Of course, Nick, that would be very fair and very safe. What do you think, you nimrod?"

The day of the race Annie showed up wearing a yachtsman's cap, white knickers, rubber boots, and a navy blazer. A sailor's pipe jutted out of her mouth.

"If we are going to go boating, I wanted to be ready. I'm Annie the Sailorman."

"Not sailorwoman?"

"Sailorman."

We loaded our boats, lunches, and towels into the defunct and rotting garden cart, which had two flat tires, and walked up the gravel road.

I called for all hands on deck. The boats were introduced. Boats called *Blood of My Enemy* and *The Annihilator* and the *Happy Little Boat*. Boats made of plastic soda bottles, balsa, and jigsawed boards. Boats with fins, keels, and sails, Playmobil fishermen standing on deck, and Playmobil figures reclining with tropical drinks. Mira's boat was made from a cardboard cereal bowl. Eric's looked like a launch from the Victorian era, with a copper roof covered with solar panels. As long as the sun shone, it would motor all day. Doug entered a slab of blue insulation with a stained dish towel duct-taped to a twig mast. Tico's boat was suspended between two four-foot pontoons, driven by a half-horsepower circular saw motor hitched to a drooping bicycle tire tube, lashed together with an extension cord. It looked like something Rauschenberg might have built when he was thirteen.

"Tal," shouted Zoe, "here it is. I worked with my daddy for three days. It has a remote-control car engine. See! I can make it go backward and forward. And it steers! See?" She flipped the switch and motors whirred.

"That's a work of art, Zoe. I am deeply impressed. Truly, I am."

"Yay! You wanna see it go?"

"I do indeed. Now let's race!"

The boats tipped, puttered, spun, and petered out. They churned, sank, and nosed into the green weeds. We laughed and jeered and nobody won or lost.

"Tal, can we go in?" Nick asked.

"Of course. Go for it."

"With our clothes on?"

"It's the only option."

Mira slipped in from the bank, then Nick slung Zoe in. Then everyone, except Annie, who sat with her legs crossed in the grass, pointing her pipe at us, shouting, "Avast, ye swabs."

Eric's boat circled out in the middle of the pond, the metal fins on the wheel spinning and dripping in the sunlight. Around and around it went, as waves from our frolicking lifted and carried it.

Enough time had passed and I could see my students growing up. I had come to know them, their siblings and parents, their dogs, their cats, their secret hideouts, their fears, and their dreams. I thought of Zoe, who, when she first stepped into the North Branch School, was scared, shy, and scattered, her uniqueness buried under layers of self-consciousness and superficial fretting and cheap eyeliner. Now she blossomed wildly.

In a year she had done so much. She had made the first sign for the school driveway. She had befriended the strange geeks and oddballs like Steve and Doug who had elected to attend our zygote of a school. She was responsible for bringing in Molly May to write poetry with us. She had come up with the title of our poetry magazine, *Truth and Shimmer*. She had run in the woods on the nature trail even as she claimed that she did not have an athletic cell in her body. She had helped build a ten-foot sculpture of a woman with an enormous bosom from chicken wire, newspaper, and lightbulbs. She had made a six-foot-tall conical solar concentrator named Queen Witchie that boiled water and cooked cookies faster than anybody else's. Zoe's DNA, her joie de vivre, was encoded in the school.

Once we were in the woods cutting up and stacking firewood for community service. As we walked back in the snow carrying chain saws and with wood chips in our hair, Zoe bounded up to my side and said, "Tal, O headmaster, can you make this school go on forever?"

It was not so important that she wanted her schooling at North Branch to go on eternally. She had discovered that *school* was infinitely important. The love of learning and the love of community went hand in hand, and she didn't want to let go.

I remembered the stories she had written, especially the one about overcoming her propensity to kiss up to Mira. It had been satisfactory, but had been too easy. She had not penetrated to any kind of deep, mysterious place of beauty. I had told her that her story was crap and that she had to write a new one. I had told her she had to rewrite it by looking into the mirror to see herself truly and see who she wanted to become. She had cried, argued, and cursed me.

When she finally wrote *the* story, I thought, *My God, look what she has done.*

I read it to the class, a story called "The Day I Met Myself." The premise of the story was that she was talking to herself as she gazed into the mirror and the many images of herself, trying to merge and integrate them. In the end she wrote:

> I was looking at the girl on the other side of the mirror. Look, I said, I'm flying. See, I don't cry as much. Sing with me? I'm singing—it might sound prettier if we sang together—I'd like that, you know. I'm almost ready; I know something big could happen at any moment. Do you hear that music? It's beautiful. Emily Dickinson once wrote: "I'm nobody, who are you? Are you nobody, too? Well that makes two of us, you know." And I am nobody and I am somebody and I *am*. Look at me! Do I look like I am flying? I feel it; it's the wind and sunflowers and purple, lots of purple. You're on the other side! I can see you, are you ready? I think it's time. I stood in front of the

mirror and looked up. She looked back at me. I closed my eyes because I wanted to make a picture of her in my memory and when I looked again, the person staring me in the face was my own blue/green eyes, my own nose, and cheeks. She wasn't on the other side any more, but I knew I'd be okay. I was stronger now. I was me. She was me. We were me. It probably doesn't make much sense. But I have my own hips, my own breasts, my own lips, and hair and toes. They're all a part of me. Part of us. Whether I wear pants that cover my every feature or show everything I have, I will always be what I am. I am flying now.

I love dancing although I usually do it alone in my room. I enjoy every kind of art that I know of, fine art being at the top. I could sketch and paint for years. My favorite stuffed animal is a brown monkey named Chee-Chee. I love winds coming from the south and as little as I like to admit this, I love the movies my science teacher shows in class because they're extremely fascinating. I simply cannot help but to learn about tornadoes, lightning, and Antarctica while watching beautiful pictures flash across the screen. I get caught up in each one as it spins through the facts, flashing warnings and moving us all to a place where we know a bit more. There are many things I don't know about me, but I am sure that over the years I'll find out. And that's me, Zoe. It's nice to meet you.

That was what she did at our school. She became herself, in full. Her two words: *I am.* Against all the shifting unsteadiness of adolescence, against depths of self-loathing, insecurity, glibness, or boredom, she could say with electric joy that she was *here,* and this was where she wanted to be.

That was a feeling she could take with her forever.

Mira's mother hired a photographer to take pictures of us before the last day of school. It was raining, but we wanted to be photographed outside. We found an unopened box of translucent vinyl ponchos and donned them. I thought of them as our graduation gowns and threatened anyone who would not wear one.

"Do we have to?" whined Mira.

"Yes. Do you think you will get out of here alive without posing with your peers in this wicked cool poncho that's as durable as a plastic grocery bag? Put it on, you weenie."

We posed on the hill, on a big rock, among the ferns and wet grass, the founders of the North Branch School.

For the last day of school I had saved two stories. The first was Tico's "How NBS Saved Me." Dictated to his mother, it described his journey through elementary school. It included a description of him in the "special room"—the resource room—with another kid who was on his level. Tico understood this to be the lowest level. He described giving up, shoving assignments and "some of my feelings" into his desk and under the baseboard in his room. He described throwing out the papers he didn't do, hoping that the feelings of failure went with the papers into the trash. He described his growing recognition that he lacked some of the skills his peers acquired naturally.

By third grade things started to change. In the second week of school, the teacher assigned us a book report. I figured I could read a book about five pages long. But the teacher said we needed to read a long book. Since I knew I couldn't read a long book, I decided to pick out a book in my collection that my mom had already read to me. I chose one about *The Atocha*—a sunken Spanish ship. So I got around the reading problem, but I still had to write a book report. I sat at the kitchen counter so my mom could help me with spelling, and I started writing. I filled a few lines with letters, like *tssstiii*. After a while my mom asked me to read her what I had written. That was a big mistake. Of course, I couldn't read it. So I got mad. I gouged the paper and the counter with my pencil. I banged my chubby fists on the counter and started yelling. Then I started crying. Then I stormed off, knocked over the kitchen stool, stubbed my toe, and went screaming up to my room and slammed the door.

Then I realized that I really didn't get this writing thing. To me, reading was just looking at a page with a jumble of letters that meant nothing. So here I was putting down a jumble of letters on a page. People who knew how to read told me that my jumble of letters meant nothing. That was no surprise to me, but it seemed to be a surprise for them. They seemed to think that the letters should actually tell them something about *The Atocha*. I didn't have any idea how to arrange the letters so that they would tell people something about *The Atocha*.

Tico's story was not about *The Atocha;* it was about the distance between *tssstiii* and *Atocha,* an impossibly vast distance as great, to him, as the Atlantic Ocean. Why wouldn't he give up, swim for another shore, or let the current take him where it would? Certainly Tico had something useful to say about *The Atocha,* but there was deeper meaning that needed to be articulated—a yearning to succeed that as yet found expression only in gouges on his paper.

Throughout elementary school, Tico got away with not being able to read or, more precisely—and more important to him—he got by without people noticing. He described wearing low hats and wraparound shades, trying to hide, playing the role of a badass. He stole, he vandalized, he burned candles in a meadow. He graduated from elementary school, getting an award for art. "I didn't think I deserved the awards because I knew other kids that were better than I was," he wrote. "I just thought the teachers felt sorry for me."

He described his beginning at NBS as "pretty rough. I was afraid people would make fun of me because I couldn't read, so I pulled my hat down over my eyes and pretended I didn't care. I was trying to be cool, but I wasn't making too many friends. Maybe I didn't care about school, but I did care about friends. Not having friends made me feel even worse than not being able to read." He stole Najat's ten dollars. After that, he said, "It was almost like NBS wasn't for me."

In time, though, in the dark small rooms in the beginnings of the North Branch School, Tico made a few friends and those friends knew he couldn't read, and they didn't care. Or they did care, because they cared for him. And at North Branch he didn't get sent to the resource room. He had the class all around him, and when he told us that the origami cranes were like a prayer we could see, we heard him. "I wasn't quite sure where that thought came from and I was afraid it was too short. My mom thought it was awesome and Tal thought it was okay and he printed it out on a sheet of paper that was handed to the people who learned about why we made the cranes. I wasn't quite sure if I deserved the attention, but I felt good."

In poetry class, he began to feel something different. In poetry class, his ideas were as good as anyone's, even Wallace Stevens's.

> When we started poetry class I wrote a poem about ten differ-
> ent ways of looking at a mind. I had a hard time thinking it up,
> and I was afraid it would be terrible. My mom was amazed that
> this came out of me since the one year before I could only talk
> about the latest movie or what I wanted for Christmas—even in
> summer. I felt really good about writing it, and I was proud that
> it was published in the NBS first-ever literary journal.

Tal was always making us write things. Like character sketches and place descriptions. I was doing okay. Sometimes my writing (or should I say my dictation) was even excellent. I was beginning to feel like I wanted to go farther and I wanted to succeed. I had never felt that way before. Even my classmates sometimes thought my writing was okay and sometimes even good. It made me feel like there was something inside of my head that was working; it made me feel like I could go somewhere if I wanted to go.

I don't mean to say that it was perfect. There were definitely bad days. I could get very frustrated with myself for not doing well enough. I would forget assignments and lose papers every week.

I don't want you to think that miraculously I could suddenly read and write. No, my mom was still my reader and scribe. But the difference was that I suddenly had insights and ideas that were okay. And that made me feel like I wanted to actually do something. I had never felt like that in school before. I used to only hide and get through the day. But now, knowing that my thoughts were okay and people might want to hear them, I wanted the school day to slow down. It was fun and interesting. Everyone pretty much noticed I was happy—even my dogs. They wagged their tails every time they saw me, instead of keeping their distance when I got home from school. If my dogs noticed a difference, I knew the difference was real.

When I made friends with Mira, my idea of friendship changed. It wasn't just about hanging out and doing cool things together—it was also about really getting to know people and caring about them. That friendship made me stronger. It made me want to be on many tracks, to see everyone's path.

School work definitely isn't easy. But I have learned that I have to work—both in school and in life. I might not be ready to face it, but I know I have to. In the long run I think the work is worth it. I used to run, run, hide. It's now walk, stop, look around, and give it a try. And some of the things I thought would be hard or bad have actually turned out to be fun.

And I know that it's okay to put myself out there, even though I might fail. I still don't like to fail. But, it's a lot better to try than to go running into the resource room to get away from the hard stuff. So I've stopped running.

This was a novel written by a thirteen-year-old who, it seemed, was now able to stand still high above the landscape of his life and understand, accept, even embrace who he was becoming. His story mattered, and he mattered. The class erupted in cheers at the story's end. They looked not at Tico's mask, not at his fear, but into the soul of a boy they had come to love. They were cheering, as well, for their own part in the story—that they had made the school where Tico could become a student even if he did not always have the prescribed answer or the conventional skills. They celebrated the inescapable fact that Tico's story was *the* subject, a victory of movement and transformation. He had instructed us all that learning was not about what one *knew* but about how one discovered and negotiated new forms of being. Tico's story was great, and Tico was great.

I sent the class outside to play in the sun. We still had the afternoon ahead. Mira came and sat in a chair next to me at the head of the table.

"I don't get this."

"Don't get what?"

"Why everyone is so frickin' happy."

"Mira, they're happy because it's the end of the year and they're celebrating what Tico wrote. They're proud of him."

"Whatever." She held her head between her hands, as though she was trying to squeeze something out of it.

"Mira, what's the matter with you? You don't feel those feelings?"

At that she began to sob, her chest heaving, hyperventilating. I couldn't understand what she was saying. All words muffled into her hands, which were tangled with her hair and tears streaming down her cheeks.

"What is the matter, Mira? Tell me what is the matter."

"I'm going to have no friends. When I leave everyone will hate me. No one will care about me. I'm going to be totally fucking alone."

"You mean at the high school?"

"Yes. They all hate me. Will hate me. They're all frickin' gossiping assholes."

"Mira, you're not leaving yet. You still have another year here."

Her eyes were bloodshot, mascara ran down her nose, mixing with phlegm and tears.

"Mira, you have a lot of work to do, and you have a lot inside that you're going to have to keep alive. You have what we learned here. You have Tico's story. You have a little bird in you and you have to know it's there and you've got to let it sing. No one else will know it is there and you know you can suffocate it and cage it when you're afraid."

"I'm so afraid. I am so afraid."

I looked at her, folded in on herself, hunched in a chair on the last day of school. But she was afraid, and when she was afraid she raised a fortress and protected herself with ornery, rabid fierceness. I wished this catharsis had happened four months before, not on the last day of school. I had taught her for a whole year. I had given my heart trying to embrace her, hold her, build her up, to give her a place to say the beautiful things she held inside.

"Mira, look. You're beautiful, you're smart as hell. You're tough as nails and you can fight and claw and you know what's right. You've got to have the courage to bring all that out. You're stronger than a brick shithouse. That's all I can tell you now. You will be alone sometimes, yes. But you have yourself, and you can't let that self disappear. You understand?"

She nodded, her shoulders small and shaking. The sounds of joy, shouts, glee, and excitement bubbled all around her.

I gave the last hours of the year to Emma's story. It was the afternoon, and the room was dark, as always, though the front door was wide open.

"Guys, if anyone asks you what this year was about, it's this. This is Emma's story, but you all helped her make it. She couldn't have written it if we hadn't all been here, trying to write things that matter. If anyone asks you why writing matters, if it has value in the world, you can say, 'Read the story my friend Emma wrote.'"

They stared at me, waiting, as close as twelve kids and a teacher could be, with two plastic tables between us, a few scattered papers, an empty spritzer can, a three-hole punch, a girl's story, and nothing else.

"Don't move while I read. Don't lift a goddamn finger. Put everything in your hands down. Tico, if you squeeze that can I'm going to kill you. Nick, put your feet down and sit up. Drop your pencils, shut your traps, and listen."

Emma had found the vein, her own sunken, protected treasure. And what could have been a vacant, walking corpse strode into our room on her pulsing blocks of words, forty-two pages, margins justified, telling us she wanted to live. I could only amplify her words, trying to make her words live through my mouth.

Her story was harrowing, vague, and dark. It crossed back through

doors that others might have said leave closed, doors posted DO NOT
ENTER.

Dark is lonely, she wrote. *Pain even worse. Falling down a deep dark
hole, nothing sharp enough for what I need—maybe I'll stay a while.*

Did she mean stay in the deep dark, barely alive in that hellish hole?
Or did she mean to say, *I will return, I will emerge?* What *here?* Stay
where? I knew the answer, I knew the story, I knew the ending. But I
could feel her terror of not knowing, and I could feel the edge at which
the class listened, hearing without blinking, watching without breathing, not knowing how she would resolve it.

He did *this* to our classmate, to Emma? He did this to *her?* This
girl, barely twelve, who came here pale and scared, who had been
among us every day—she had carried this gash, this violation? And
she sat now before the class, having written it all for us, giving it back
as an offering.

*Light and dark, so different, yet so close. They say there isn't one
without the other. I don't know. Maybe it's true. They are so separate,
light and dark. I don't know if I am making any sense at all.*

*Maybe you just have to touch my shoulder and jolt me awake and
away from what is beneath my eye-lids; Force me to see it as it is and not
the war within my head.*

This was tragedy wrought to its uttermost. All tragedy, all wounds,
all blackout. Would it be light or dark? And who, or what, would quell
the war? Yeats said even if "all the drop-scenes drop at once / Upon a
hundred thousand stages, / It cannot grow by an inch or ounce." The
only cure for tragedy and disintegration was to make something out of
it. The story was the cure, because it took the war out of her head. The
story—her art—externalized, excised, exorcised. The story made it past,
let her pass, let her put it away, returned her to the power she still possessed. The story gave her control to end it because she decided she
would end it—her terms, her words.

It will never end, this roller coaster life. Just as long as I'm safe I think I'll be okay. Because I know I can always drift off and be safe in the power of my dreams, glaze over and never utter another word. I can go wherever I want just in my dreams and if it's good, everything will be picture perfect and never fail in the power of my dreams, my dreams.

Four times, the words *my dreams*. What was the story but a dream, a dream to obliterate the nightmare? In the dream, silence was filled, nothing was left unsaid. The story was a dream ride, a portal to the deep-buried volumes. In the dream she was master, shaping a glazed image of what she dreamed for herself beyond all words: picture-perfect, drifting, safe, unfailing, free.

I wish I could fly away like in my dreams. I wish I could forget and never remember. I wish I wasn't afraid of anything anymore. I wish people would open their eyes. See the world as it is. I wish I knew myself, not this person you're looking at.

Emma wished to see how her story would end, so the tragedy could not ever grow by inch or ounce. But she would grow, she would *become*. In a story she could climb from the dark deep hole. *Succisa virescit*: when cut down, it grows back stronger. She would rage, she would shake, but in her story she could see heaven blazing in her head, and heaven for Emma was the power to say that what was done to her was *done*, finished forever. Just keep flying and never go back.

When I finished reading, there was silence. I turned over the last page and looked at my students ringed around me. They all looked up, then to Emma, who looked down through her light brown bangs at her hands under the table.

Then they exploded, unlike any twelve voices I had ever heard, shouting, clapping, calling her name. They wouldn't stop. I looked at her while she looked down while they shouted, "Hell yeah, Emma."

"Okay, you cretins, okay. Comments? Feelings? Reactions? Glimmerings? Epiphanies? Revelations?"

They could shout, but they couldn't speak. I thumbed the pages of the story, waiting for them to begin.

"I didn't know," said Annie. "I mean, I don't really understand. I mean, I do, I think I do, but . . ."

"Annie, you feel like you know what she felt?"

"Yeah, I do."

"But?"

"But it's also what she experienced. So I can't know it. But I felt it."

"She made you feel?"

"Yeah."

"What'd she make you feel?"

"She made me feel her strength. It made me feel hope."

"Nick?"

"Um, God, I just, I mean, Emma, you're really brave to write that."

"It made me cry, and it made me want to kill him," said Zoe, "and it made me proud of you."

"It's like she used the story to kill him," said Doug. "She used her life as a weapon against him, or it. To make the evil go away."

"How does that happen?" I asked. "I mean, how does telling the bad thing make it go away?"

"I don't know," said Tico, "but he is a worthless piece of shit and I think Emma is the strongest person I have ever known."

"Right on, brother."

"I can't believe she wrote that," said Mira.

"It's amazing, isn't it?"

"The world is a sick place," said Mira, looking across the table.

"And look at how she responded," I said. "She made it beautiful with what she wrote. She didn't make what happened go away. But she has herself, and no one else does."

"Emma is whatever the opposite of sick is," said Mira.

"Emma could be the thing that would heal the world," I said.

"Is he going to go to jail?" asked Janine.

"I don't know, I hope so," answered Emma. "He's being prosecuted."

"Goddamn son of a bitch," said Tico.

"So there will be a trial?" asked Janine.

"Yeah."

Nick offered his hand. "Emma, uh, if you want we will come to the trial and kick his ass."

"We will fuck people up if they mess with us," said Tico.

"If he doesn't go to jail we'll go find him and fuck him up," said Steve.

"Right on, brother."

"We'll come after him with our mob."

"What does it mean that she wrote this?" I asked. "Why would she take the chance to write this? What's gained by this kind of disclosure? Does it do any good? Is it right? Some people would say she shouldn't write a story like this. That this has nothing to do with learning."

"What else could she write? Nothing else would matter," said Nick.

"If she doesn't write her own story, then he has her life," said Annie. "Then he has written it for her. But if she writes her story, her life is her own."

"I don't think it's the truth that's wrong," said Zoe. "What's wrong is someone who would say we can't write the truth."

"We will fuck those people up who say we can't write the truth," said Tico. Everyone laughed, Emma too.

"If someone says we can't write the truth, then we will be writing lies that avoid the truth," said Steve.

"How do we know this is the truth?"

"I think it was the truth because I could feel it," said Sophie.

"Because we all felt it," said Tico. "All at once."

"I love Emma," said Najat.

"Love her? What do you mean? How?"

"Because, like, she is one of us. I sort of felt like it was me. I didn't want that to happen to her. Or us. Or anybody."

"Love. Us. You felt love. She made you feel love from that horrible thing that happened to her. What kind of power is that?"

"That's some real power," said Doug.

"That's some ass-kicking power," said Tico.

"Goddamn, that's unbelievable, Emma," I said. "That's just amazing. It's a beautiful story."

"Emma, when his trial comes, we'll come and have a cheering section," said Tico, "and when he tries to talk, we will kick him in the jimmies."

"I agree, Tico," I said. "I permit you all to stand behind Emma in court and kick the son of a bitch in the jimmies." She smiled again.

Emma had more work to do, more words to write. For now she had come as far as she could. She had brought us to a place we had never been. Beautiful survival. Did I make her story beautiful? No. Did I teach her to write? No. But she and they and I had made the place where her words could be written, read, heard, and felt. The story was inside her. She found a key, and she let us in, and we all walked out together.

Only the word *I*, lovely and terrifying, would take us to the place we needed to go. That was true, and I wouldn't forget it.

Holding up her story again, I asked, "What's it all about?"

The answer echoed through our schoolhouse and out the open front door, perhaps even to the river and woods and mountains beyond.

I remembered the first day of the school, when I had nothing but a handful of seeds—my ideas and an almost-dozen kids.

"Everybody, come up here," I said, as I pushed the book to the middle of the table so everyone could huddle around, with our heads nearly touching. I wanted them close.

"See, the circle is the key," I explained. "It's a perfect whole. Not hole-in-the-ground. Whole as in what?"

"Complete," came the answer.

"Yes, complete, whole. Look. Here's a snake, in a circle, eating its tail, symbolizing rebirth and regeneration. And this is the rose window at Chartres Cathedral in France."

"Oh, I've seen that," said Nick.

I remembered back to October when the leaves were stripped from the trees by gray rains. On the day snow was first visible on the ridge we hiked to Skylight Pond, the whole class running the last mile through the woods. In such moments, between the shouts of adolescent glee, feet pounding over the wet mossy stones, little fragments of poems echoed through me, in the woods, along the wet trail. Fleetingly, before I loaded the Golden Chariot of Knowledge with six wet and cold red-cheeked teenagers, I thought of Shakespeare's sonnet. "That time of year thou mayest in me behold / When yellow leaves, or none, or few, do hang / Upon those boughs which shake against the cold, Bare ruined choirs, where late the sweet birds sang."

I was lucky to be a teacher in such a place.

Our landlord had asked that we not stick things into the walls, but we could never resist. We hung posters of M. C. Escher, Yeats, River Phoenix, drawings of goosefoot maple leaves and photocollages of our hands. Mira posted a poem she had written called "Little Brown Girl" and Janine hung a small plastic American flag. Zoe posted Eleanor Roosevelt's quote above my desk. "No one can make you feel inferior without your consent." We tacked up a postcard of Langston Hughes, pictures of Johnny Depp and Vishnu, tiny origami cranes made out of Wrigley's chewing gum wrappers, and a small color photocopy of *The Calling of St. Matthew*. Sophie hung a poster of French soccer star Thierry Henry. I nailed a Jesus Action Figure (with movable arms) to the window casing. Doug hung a picture of the Milky Way. Najat colored a photocopy of Abe Lincoln in Warholian fluorescent green and tacked it to the ceiling. We hung our environmental ethics agreement and an unsigned copy of an Independent Declaration of Principles and Ideals. We hung lists of topics we had talked about: Greek Revival architecture, Bo Diddley, screw tourniquets, John Brown, Senegalese metalsmiths. We hung paper airplanes from strings, a poster for a production of *Macbeth,* and the words of Dante. I hung a "Celebrate King Day" poster. In the science room we hung a wall-sized painting on butcher paper of the Green Mountain National Forest—painted in twelve distinct styles with dripping, cracked tempera—rising from the forest floor through maples and poplars to the leafy canopy. I pinned a Butterfinger wrapper next to a Polaroid of myself on which was written, "Wicked cool teacher." Nailed to the front door was a rubber frog with its back legs torn, now repaired with tape, with a sign announcing: "North Branch School: We Put Things Back Together." I hung a note Nick had written to me that said, "Think, don't feel" and then asked, "But *why?*" On the dark beams overhead we stapled vocabulary definitions, the words we had used in a year of talking: *cretin, deciduous, rill, burnish, understory, euphony, incandescent.* On the science room wall were our names and our quotes we had painted in September.

We had begun the school year by making mandalas. I had wanted my students to know that all the various strains of their adolescent beings were fully welcomed. As the year progressed we made other mandalas, each one more complex, more colorful, more fully realized. Doug's last one placed a fencer at the center, lunging forward with a crudely drawn épée—an image of himself as classically heroic. Mira's featured an image of a girl gazing into a mirror, which captured perfectly the point at which my students were poised—somewhere between vanity and compassion, anxiety and self-love, soul-searching and childish joy.

The school took the shape of us. We had not formed to fit curricular demands, state standards, administrative directives, or anyone else's idea of what we should be. Like Coltrane's "Spiritual," we were swinging along and gaining depth, dipping into the subterranean alone and together, ascending in a golden light. The school, the year, the seasons, the calendar, the fact that we gathered together every morning—that was the rhythmic pulse, the structure that held and supported us. None of it could have been planned, predicted, drawn up, or mapped on a syllabus. That was what my students loved: They had made it, it was theirs, and they knew it.

In the delicate and volatile place between self and others, between the "I" and our "we," the school approached its own harmony. Solitary horns assembled in a dark house, seeking a measure of the divine— some wild honking, sinuous and broken, or flailing sheets of sound, bending and rapid bursts, squealing, and sometimes, fleetingly, so exquisitely lyrical as to make us know what rapture was.

If I had a prayer to say into a school, to any school, every year and every day and every hour, it would be shoveling coal onto the fire that said, *Make meaning move.* That is what adolescents had to do. They came wanting to make sense of where they had been and wanting to claim something about where they aimed to go. Dynamism, movement, and transformation were the essence of their beings. They craved to be trusted, for their teachers, parents, and mentors to believe they possessed the power of gods to weave themselves cloaks of light, earth, sea, fishes, fowl, and their own experiences. They wanted to make meaning, and in making meaning they moved; then they could say, *I am.*

The power to act, to create and build—that distinguished our being here. Perhaps it was lofty to think so, but that was the glory of which we were capable.

Octavio Paz's poem "Hymn Among the Ruins" speaks of days in which "words which are flowers become fruits which are deeds." Paz writes of an illimitable beauty in which all hostility melted and Earth overspilled with unending golden light. In my most idealistic moments I imagined a school of such radiance, where the traditional barriers that diminished students—separated, deflated, or disheartened them, or caused them to withhold their best selves—would vanish and the flowing fountain of images would multiply. Our school was not going to be a holding pen or a knowledge depository; it would be a fountain, a flower, a mirror, a seed, a fruit-bearing tree. The fruit was in the deed, in the school growing out of the mind, out of *my* mind, beyond dreams and into real life.

If our students were to believe that their voices had value, then most surely they needed to be free to create from the wellspring of self-understanding, from a clear vision of the lives they were living. What mattered most was what would be found inside, in the wiring of their minds and the architecture of their hearts. I only had to stand before them and call out, as Theodore Roethke did, "We think by feeling. What is there to know?"

We only had to ask what acreage of the heart and mind was allotted to perceptions of beauty. What was the delicate and rugged topography of a child's self-comprehension? What square footage was devoted to kindness and love? Where, beyond all resource rooms, required assemblies, cinder-block halls, and neatly bordered bulletin boards, would we find in our schools courage, tenderness, and devotion to each other?

How could we, parents and teachers, help children assemble and make manifest the infinite, diverse dimensions of their hearts and minds? And how to overlay these individual projections onto a collective blueprint that would at once be our mirror, our work of art, and our map into the future?

It was through ourselves, as full of the world as each of us were, as idiosyncratic as our diverse histories implied, come together in a place in the woods on a mountain to do a natural thing, to make meaning, to make a home for our thoughts which, I knew, was proper to grow wise in.

Once I had walked into school on a cold morning, asking each student to tell me what smell was.

"What I mean, you dingbats, is when you smell something, are you smelling air loaded with some smell flavor? Are there little smell *things*? What the hell is it exactly? I wanna know."

"How should we know?" Tico responded. "You're the teacher."

"Yeah, Tico, I'm the teacher, and I want to teach you how to want to know something. I want to know what smell *is*. When you smell bacon, what are the little things you're smelling? Does a particle of air get loaded with the luggage of bacon flavor?"

"I love the smell of bacon," said Steve.

"Christ, I love bacon too, but that's not the point. I want answers. I want to know what smell *is*."

They were exasperated. "Go look it up, Tal."

"That's what my dad always says," said Mira. "It's so annoying."

"Okay, you annoying little fart knockers. I'll remain curious and searching on my quest for knowledge. You can live in pathetic darkness."

"Whatever, Tal."

On the last day of school, after the last story and before our final ceremony, I told them that they had to write something to keep with them.

"A little note to yourself, a poem, whatever. Instructions for life. The truth you now know. Something you don't want to forget. Attach it to yourself. Let it be the luggage you take with you. Shove it in your pocket, sock, stick it in your ear, under your hat, in your jock, I don't care. But it has to be on your person somehow when you leave. Write something that matters. We'll read 'em out loud to see how they sound."

They scrambled, looking for pencils and paper, put their heads down, and wrote. If we had a final exam, this was it.

As they finished, they looked up.

"Let's hear what you got. Debbie?"

"It's called "The Escape,"" she said meekly.
"A title and everything. Nice. Okay. Let her rip."
She read:

*"We were trying to fly away, trying to escape.
We were almost there, almost to freedom,
Then, all of a sudden, we were jerked back down,
Back down to earth, to reality,
Back to where being the same is being normal.
We watched and waited, for our next chance,
Then, it came, and we started over,
Again, we were trying, reaching to get there.
So many times we have started over,
We were almost afraid to make it.
Now we are here, we are as free as birds,
We have what we wanted,
We are in a place where being different is being normal,
We are free to fly in a sky that is our thoughts,
We are free to wonder why."*

We sat in silence. Where did such words come from? How far had we reached? Perhaps I could have made a ten-page research paper and a final exam be our coup de grâce. A poem like this was something else altogether.

"Debbie," I asked, "do you mean to say that in your poem the *we* is—"

"Yes, Tal, the *we* is *us*."

"Um. Okay. Beautiful. All righty then. Go, Steve."

He read the following poem:

"And for whatever it's worth, what is smell?

People say you can smell rain before it falls,
But where does it fall from?
It is from where it falls that we can get these answers.
So when I go to sleep,
It's as though I'm falling,
Falling up into the sky.
The dreams of men, women, and children drift out into space.
I see a dream of Love.
It's unbearably beautiful."

His words, read quickly, now hovered in the room. I gazed at him in amazement. He held his paper and looked up. Mira stared at him. Nick looked at me with raised eyebrows. Tico looked at Emma, who looked up at me. If there had been lines drawn in the air, we could have seen a taut imperfect net holding all that we had caught.

"Holy shit, Steve. That *is* beautiful."

I did not know how long this dream—this knowledge of the place from which answers fell—would live in Steve. How long could he sustain a belief in such fleeting, evanescent beauty? They would all leave, they would all eventually go to other schools, other towns, to jobs, other lives, some hard or full of misfortune. I could not imagine what would stay with them embedded in their memories or hearts before they walked away from this table, this room, out of the dimming light of whatever we had tried to get across.

But a dream of love was living in Steve now—an unbearably beautiful dream, humming in the room and through us just before we stepped over the threshold into the world.

I invited the parents to our closing ceremony on the final afternoon to see the results, such as they were, of our year on the mountain. Each student read a speech about something important or memorable. Tico spoke about finding a place in the school and the feeling of knowing he was integral. Doug spoke about the joy in his newfound freedom to be a nerd and the fact that North Branch seemed to draw out and celebrate the inner nerd in everyone. Nick wrote a character sketch of me, his remembrance of the time I discussed with him the magical importance of hammers and the size of my huge muscles. Emma spoke about having a safe place to express her feelings. Janine wrote that the North Branch School was the first school she had ever loved. Annie wrote about the joy of having a teacher, me, whose idea of a good field trip was to go to the town dump and collect materials for art projects—in a brilliant turn, she connected those remarks to overcoming her fear of dirty things. Mira spoke about being able to create our own school: "Hearing what you guys wrote, hearing what I wrote. Wondering why the words are different, wondering why they're just the same. Figuring out that I wrote those words. Figuring out that you guys heard those words. Seeing what we did, seeing what we made together."

I read speeches describing each student, thanking them for what they gave.

Then I asked, "Now, are you ready for the final exam?"

I looked at them in our little room, dim as ever, the afternoon sun bright outside the door.

"Since the North Branch School believes that standardized testing is very important, I believe that it is only right for us to end the year with a high-stakes test."

There was nervous laughter from the parents.

Our high-stakes test—the only one like it in any school I had ever heard of.

"So here it is. Please answer in full volume. The question: What's it all about?"

"LOVE!"

We crowded onto the deck. The pink chairs were completely rotted, ferns spilled from the edge of the woods, bee balm and lamb's ears sprouted up around the stepping-stones Tico had placed in the garden in September. On the table were huge bouquets of early summer flowers, irises, lupines, and wild daisies, ice cream and cake. The parents and my twelve students laughed and smiled with each other in the warm June afternoon.

I walked to the Golden Chariot of Knowledge. Mia came behind me.

"We did it," she said.

"We did it."

She hugged me. I looked over her shoulder at our little gray clapboard schoolhouse in the woods.

"We'll do it again next year."

"We'll do it again."

I opened the door, but before I could get in Janine came running toward me. She was crying and she reached out to hug me.

"Thank you for making this school."

"You're welcome, my little friend."

I climbed into the van and backed out of the narrow, rutted driveway, heading down the mountain to home.

For more information about the North Branch School, please go to

www.northbranchschool.org

afterword

In the fall of our second year, Mia received a phone call from our landlord. We had to be out of the house at the end of the year. With eight new students—twenty all together—the septic system couldn't handle us. In addition, the house, our little schoolhouse that had endured so much with us, was suffering from the relentless wear and tear of a herd of adolescents. The North Branch School would have to find a new home.

What I didn't tell our students and parents was that we had little time, almost no money, no alumni from whom to draw support, no foundations begging to endow us, and no experience in building an actual school building. And there was virtually no property for sale in the town of Ripton suitable for a school.

The board and I visited potential locations for a new school. Falling-down houses with subsiding foundations. Hunting camps with no septic systems. An old house off the grid, deep in the woods up a rutted logging road. A leaning farmhouse with a vast population of garter snakes writhing in the well. Despairing, I began making a list of local churches and empty barns.

Then, like a gift, a piece of land was offered to us, right down the hill from the old schoolhouse. The property was flat, wooded, next to a small pasture, at a crossroads, a stone's throw from Ripton Elementary School, on a paved road, and close to downtown Ripton. A little re-search in the town records yielded a miracle: Sometime in the 1940s, the property had been zoned for ski clubs, beauty salons, and public *and* private schools. We accepted the offer and purchased the property with borrowed money. *We're going forward,* I told everyone. *We're going to do it. The North Branch School will have a real home.*

By mid-August before the third year, we had a frame up, a sturdy skeleton of historic timbers scavenged from a local farmhouse. The corner posts, standing in what a century before had been a sheep pas-ture, were as straight and strong as when they had been milled in 1850. The beams, which had been saplings before settlers even entered Ver-mont, stretched across what would be our classrooms. Dark tamarack pole rafters reached toward the open sky above us.

In November, we prepared to move in. We backed the trailer to the cellar door. Out of the dank darkness and into the rain and down the cel-lar stairs came our beakers and rulers, our brooms and mud boots, our chairs and shelves and tables and markers and files. We carried our col-lection of books down the stairs in dozens of soggy boxes filled with dust. And then, like blood circulating through the building, we brought the books up into the warm empty rooms, our damp volumes of poetry, ency-clopedias, and field guides, stacks of books growing on the tables like teetering, pulp stalagmites. Others we laid facedown on the warm, radi-ant floors to draw out the dampness. Dry books were shelved, three thou-sand at least, in newly labeled sections, as rain pattered down on the roof.

The next morning, we moved into our new school building—our new home—and we began again.

At our open house that fall, we read poetry to a com-munity audience. In December, we held the school's first dance. In January, we built a Model Utopia with a toy train chugging down Paradise Road. In February, we studied astronomy. In March, we wrote a play. In April, we created a woodland pond and built a model wetlands ecosystem. In May, we won the Great Vermont Debate. And then in June, we joyously graduated nine students, all of whom had been with us since the beginning.

At the end of the ceremony, I read Langston Hughes's "In Time of Silver Rain." I imagined my students like the boys and girls of the poem, passing down the roadway in the silver rain, where flowers lifted their heads, with wonder spreading and singing too. Clichéd? Probably. But I was a teacher. I had to believe it could be true.

In 2008, we built an addition to the school. The school now has twenty-seven students by design, nine students for each of grades seven, eight, and nine. We are still essentially a one-room schoolhouse. A school with sunlight, plants, junky sculptures made out of recycled machines, and dogs sleeping under the table. The curriculum is designed around three themes, one for each year: Freedom and Revolution, Utopia and Dystopia, and Religion and Belief. Correspondingly, in science for each of those years we study life sciences, earth science, and physical science. All of the students study these topics together, as a collective and independently. Creative writing, conferences, emotional intelligence, poetry, literature seminars, playwriting, running around in the woods, building cars out of pasta and toothpicks, drawing, ceramics, snowball fighting—everything we did in the first year remains part of what the school does today.

In the meantime, Doug headed to Swarthmore. Sophie and Emma ended up together at St. Lawrence University. Annie is working toward the completion of her major in anthropology at the University of Vermont. Tico worked as a bike mechanic—putting his ever busy hands to use. Nick worked on and off with his father as a carpenter and did his part assisting in the addition of the current school building. Najat recently published her first photographs. And Zoe had her first art show and organizes any and all alums for gatherings.

I asked Annie what she keeps from her time at North Branch.

The school taught me what community should be! When I think of my community, I think of the NBS and the people there. Even though I don't keep in touch like I should, the people there helped shape me and I know they will accept me. I felt at home at the NBS, I felt free, and I keep that feeling with me and search for it in other places and try to create it where I live. I learned more in those two years at the NBS than in any two years before or since. The NBS nourished my integrity, and while sometimes that curiosity and wonder fade in the face of deadlines and woe, I still lie in bed at night thinking about the grandeur of the universe, the inside of the veins of a leaf, my daily contribution to humanity; I still ask insolent questions after class and listen to pebbles. Whatever I was when I came into the NBS, whatever parts of me that are simply my nature, those would have been squashed or dulled or lost or ruined or quite possibly have driven me mad without being channeled and enhanced by the school. I'm holding you personally responsible, at least in part, for creating what I am becoming. Everything I learned from the NBS is still busily shaping who I am. Last week, I found myself in a writing class about to tell somebody to "feel the feeling."

It seems like utter lunacy is the only plan that ever really worked. I have come up with a few "benchmark criteria" for the NBS to maintain its efficacy and preserve the integrity of its mission. If you ever build a locker-filled hallway with no windows or eliminate recess, the school is utterly lost. If, however, the students continue to attempt to trim your nose hairs with hedge clippers, if your science teacher still wears those horrid bicycle shorts, if you have to tell the kids that yes, it's all right that they wrote eighty pages extra and their project presentation will be three hours long, if you've got a dog or a mouse or a squirrel tearing through the building, if the kids call you at indecent hours because you are the one they know will listen and help: then you've got a school, and a good one.

And last, Steve, our poet of the North Branch and Ripton woods, now works in Middlebury, Vermont, as the foreman on a loading dock. He came to a performance of the school play last spring, and he told me, "I write a poem every night."

acknowledgments

I owe thanks to many individuals who have supported me in the writing of this book. First, deep appreciation to all of the pioneer families who joined us in our venture to start the North Branch School and who have stayed close as the school has grown. Thanks also to the families who followed, who have helped the school grow, and who have supported the school and my work with the students in so many ways.

Thanks especially to those who were involved at the beginning: Anza Armstrong, Marcia Croll, Mia Allen, and Cindy Seligmann. Many meetings with those four, and their faith in what we were doing, kept me moving forward; thanks to the other members of the school's board: Michael Seligmann, Mike Hussey, and Sue Halpern, who helped me navigate the process of pulling this book together and supported me when the path forward seemed obscured; and a heartfelt thanks to Donna Rutherford, who was in the background every step of the way.

I am indebted to several readers: Hector Vila of Middlebury College; Blair Kloman, who helped with early editing; Felix Kloman, a dedicated reader of all things North Branch; and to Robert Coles and Pat Conroy, who gave generously of their time; and, with gratitude to

Bill McKibben, who urged me to start writing and read one draft after another, always offering encouragement and wise suggestions.

Many thanks to the great teachers at the Paideia School, who taught and inspired me along the way, especially Martha Schein, Thrower Starr, Paul Bianchi, Joseph Cullen, Bob Souvorin, Paul Hayward, Robert Falk, Jane Harmon, and Steve Sigur. A special thanks to Bernie Schein, a mentor and teacher whose artful and uncompromising example I keep close to heart; to Ron Miller and David Mallery, enthusiastic supporters; to Paul Cubeta, who long ago preordained my decision to become the head of a school; to my teaching colleagues at NBS: Eric Warren, Chris Lacey, and Rose Messner, each of whom gave me inspiration and feedback on my teaching and who have mastered the art in their own ways; to early teaching collaborators "on loan" from Middlebury College: Susie Strife, Molly May, and Lauren Markham; and thanks to the members of the Bristol/Lincoln literary study group, Tom Verner, Max Yost, and Richard Wyatt, whose insights as readers and teachers filtered into these pages; and to former students Harper Alexander and Anna Waldron.

Thanks to all the good people at St. Martin's Press and especially to Vicki Lame, who gave me steady editorial guidance; my copy editor, Cynthia Merman, who cleaned up my act, and to James Meader, of Picador Books, who gave early advice and helped move this book in the right direction.

Thanks also to Jim Sanford and Gary Rutherford for giving me a place to practice my teaching; to my parents, Ginger and Ralph Birdsey and brother Peter Birdsey, all of them teachers; to all the generous supporters of the North Branch School, both near and far; to Dina Rae Wolkoff, who supported, encouraged, and counseled me throughout, and without whom this book would not exist; and, always, my great debt to all of my students, past and present, who taught me most of what I needed to know.